MESSERSCHMITT
Bf 109

MESSERSCHMITT BF 109

THE DESIGN AND OPERATIONAL HISTORY

JAN FORSGREN

FONTHILL

Fonthill Media Language Policy

Fonthill Media publishes in the international English language market. One language edition is published worldwide. As there are minor differences in spelling and presentation, especially with regard to American English and British English, a policy is necessary to define which form of English to use. The Fonthill Policy is to use the form of English native to, or familiar to, the author. Jan Forsgren was born and educated in Umeå, Sweden; therefore British English has been adopted in this publication.

Fonthill Media Limited
Fonthill Media LLC
www.fonthillmedia.com
office@fonthillmedia.com

First published in the United Kingdom and the United States of America 2017

British Library Cataloguing in Publication Data:
A catalogue record for this book is available from the British Library

ISBN 978-1-78155-586-6

Typeset in 10pt on 12pt Bembo Std
Printed and bound in England

The process of writing a book consists of long, lonely hours by the computer. However, no book such as this one could have been completed without the kind assistance of several individuals. In particular, I wish to thank Gregory Alegi, Boris Ciglic, Mikael Olrog, and Carl-Fredrik Geust for providing information and many photographs of Bf 109s evaluated by Russian pilots; Bengt Hermansson, Ulrich Hild, and Wolfgang Mühlbauer of the DEHLA Archives for locating many rare photographs; Aleksandar Ognjevic, Mikael Olrog, and my good friend Miro Patocka for the loan of books and many interesting discussions about the Bf 109 in general; and in particular the Avia S-199 and Brett Stolle (NMUSAF) for providing information and, in particular, photographs.

Last but not least, I wish to thank my editor at Fonthill, Jay Slater, for having faith in my writing abilities.

Apologies to anyone I've forgotten!

Preface

Since the 1930s, countless books and articles have been written about the Messerschmitt Bf 109. Several books are general histories, while others cover specific variants or operators, the latter including detailed day-to-day accounts of individual *Jägdgeschwader* (fighter wings) of the Luftwaffe. For the plastic modeller, information on the Bf 109 colour schemes abound, particularly regarding the latter 'G' and 'K' variants. Several autobiographies and biographies detailing the combat career of many Luftwaffe Bf 109 pilots, including Adolf Galland, Erich Hartmann, Hans-Joachim Marseille, and Werner Mölders are available.

This book is an attempt to provide a concise, general history of the Messerschmitt Bf 109. The first three chapters include details on Willy Messerschmitt and his career in aviation, the genesis and development of the Bf 109, and a technical description along with a brief history of the BFW and Messerschmitt companies. The competitors to the Bf 109 in the contest in selecting the Luftwaffe's first monoplane fighter—the Arado Ar 80, the Focke-Wulf Fw 159, and the Heinkel He 112—are mentioned.

The successive Bf 109 variants are briefly described, including the numerous *Rustsätze* (factory modification kits) and *Umbau* (field modification kits). Details on prototypes and projected developments of the basic Bf 109, such as the Me 209 and Me 309, have been included.

From its entry into service in February 1937, the Bf 109 served as the Luftwaffe's sole single-engine monoplane fighter until the introduction of the Fw 190A in the summer of 1941. Even then, the majority of the Luftwaffe's *Jägdgeschwader* continued to fly Bf 109s until the end of the war, as did a number of short-range reconnaissance units.

The Spanish Civil War saw the Bf 109 committed to combat operations for the first time, which meant that new tactics suitable for the new fighter had to be developed. The operational use of the Bf 109 in different campaigns, from the *Anschluss* (Annexation) of Austria in March 1938 until the final days of the crumbling Third Reich and the unconditional surrender on 8 May 1945 forms the main section of this book. Apart from day fighter operations, details on Bf 109 operational use by fighter bomber (*Jabo*), reconnaissance, and advanced flight training units are also discussed.

A Bf 109E seen on a pre-delivery test flight. (*NMUSAF*)

With the Bf 109 being used by all of Germany's allies, as well as some neutral countries, detailed information about these operators have been included. In fact, Bf 109s continued in use with several air arms until the early 1950s. Re-engined variants of the basic Bf 109 entered production in Czechoslovakia and Spain, with the former country selling a number of S-199s to Israel in 1948.

Further information includes Luftwaffe ranks, a description of the estimation of damage (combat-related or otherwise) to Luftwaffe aircraft, pre-war Luftwaffe Bf 109 fighter units, details on Bf 109 production between 1935 and 1945, as well as Allied evaluation and assessment of the Messerschmitt fighter.

Regarding the eternal and ever-lasting debate on the proper designation of this, the most famous of all German fighter aircraft, I have elected to use Bf 109 throughout. This is due to the fact that it was conceived and built by the Bayerische Flugzeugwerke GmbH (Bavarian Aircraft Manufacturing Ltd, BFW) company. Even when built by other German aircraft manufacturers, the Bf 109 designation was retained. However, when quoting contemporary post-action and evaluation reports, the designation Me 109 will appear in most instances.

Contents

Abbreviations and Glossary

AdlA: *Armee de l'Air* (French Air Force).
ANR: *Aeronautica Nazionale Repubblicana.*
ARR: *Aeronautica Regalâ Românâ* (Royal Romanian Aeronautics).
BFW: *Bayerische Flugzeugwerke.*
CEMA: *Centre d'Essais du Matériel Aériennes Militaires* (Test Centre of Military Aviation Material).
Dipl. Ing.: *Diplom Ingeneur* (Master of Science)
DLV: *Deutsche Luftsportverband* (German Aviation Sports Union).
EdA: *Ejercito del Aire* (Spanish Air Force).
Experten: Luftwaffe terminology for Ace.
Jägdwaffe: Fighter element of the Luftwaffe.
JRV: *Jugoslovensko Ratno Vazduhoplovstvo* (Yugoslav Air Force, 1945–1959).
Kette: Three-aircraft formation.
MAVAG: *Magyar Allami Vagon Es Gepgyar* (Hungarian State Waggon and Engineering Factory).
MKHL: *Magyar Királyi Honvéd Légierö* (Royal Hungarian Air Force).
NIIVVS: *Nauchno-Ispytatel'nyi Institut Voenno-Vozdushnye Sily* (Scientific Research Aero Institute Military Air Forces).
NOVJ: *Partizanska Eskadril NOVJ* (Partisan Air Force—Yugoslav People's Liberation Army).
Orlyak: Group.
Polk: Wing (Royal Bulgarian Air Force).
RA: *Regia Aeronautica* (Royal Italian Air Force).
RAE: Royal Aircraft Establishment.
RAF: Royal Air Force.
RHAF: *Magyar Királyi Honvéd Légierö* (Royal Hungarian Air Force).
Rotte: Two-aircraft formation.
SAAF: South African Air Force.
SC: *Sprengbombe Cylindrisch* (Cylindrical High Explosive bomb. SC 50 etc. indicates a 50-kg bomb).

Schwarm: Four-aircraft formation.
SD 2: *Sprengbombe Dickwandig* (2-kg anti-personnel Butterfly bomb).
SVZ: *Slovenské Vzdušne Zbraně* (Slovakian Air Force).
USAAF: United States Army Air Force.
VVKJ: *Vazduhoplovstvo Vojske Kraljeve Jugoslavije* (Royal Yugoslav Air Force).
VVNV: *Vazdushni na Negovo Velichestvo Voyski* (His Majesty's Air Force, Bulgaria).
V-VS: *Voyenno-Vosdushnye Sily* (Soviet Military Air Force).
W Nr: *Werk Nummer* (construction number).
W/o: Written-off.
Yato: Squadron (Bulgarian Air Force).

Comparative Luftwaffe and RAF ranks

Luftwaffe	**Abbreviation**	**RAF**	**Abbreviation**
Generalfeldmarschall	Gen FM	Marshal of the RAF	MRAF
Generaloberst	Gen Ob	Air Chief Marshal	ACM
General der Flieger	GdF	Air Marshal	AM
Generalleutnant	Gen Lt	Air Vice-Marshal	AVM
Generalmajor	Gen Maj	Air Commodore	Air Cdre
Oberst	Ob	Group Captain	Grp Capt.
Oberstleutnant	Oblt	Wing Commander	Wg Cdr
Major	Maj	Squadron Leader	Sqn Ldr
Hauptmann	Hptm	Flight Lieutenant	Flt Lt
Oberleutnant	Oblt	Flying Officer	Fg Off.
Leutnant	Lt	Pilot Officer	Plt Off.
Unteroffizier	Uffz	Non-Commissioned Officer	NCO
Fahnenjunker	Fhj	–	–
Oberfeldwebel	Obfw	Flight Sergeant	FS
Feldwebel	Fw	Corporal	Cpl
Obergefreiter	Obgfr	Leading Aircraftsman	LAC
Gefreiter	Gfr	Aircraftsman 1st Class	AC 1
Flieger	Fl	Aircraftsman 2nd Class	AC 2

Luftwaffe Aircraft Damage Table

During the war, any Luftwaffe aircraft damaged or destroyed in combat was surveyed, following which the extent of damage by a rising percentages scale was established. This system also applied to aircraft damaged (or destroyed) in accidents.

Damage by per cent	Remarks
0–9	Minor damage, which can be partly repaired by the unit's Head Mechanic
10–24	Minor damage, repairable at unit level
25–39	Major damage, requiring rebuild or repair at unit level
40–44	Damage to engine or aircraft systems (e.g. electrical), requiring replacement at unit level
45–59	Heavily damaged, but repairable by exchanging major components
60–80	Written off, with minor components reusable
81–99	Total loss, over own territory
100	Total loss, either over sea or enemy territory

Notes on Luftwaffe Fighter Units

Compared with the RAF, the Luftwaffe employed a different organisation for its aerial units. Beginning in April 1936, the Luftwaffe was divided into thirty-six *Luftgau* (literally Air Districts), each responsible for administration, maintenance, supply, and training. Handling the practical side of Luftwaffe operations was the responsibility of the *Luftflotte* (Air Corps). There were a total of eight *Luftflotten*, numbered 1 to 6, 10, and *Luftflotte Reich*. Each *Luftflotte* covered a specific geographical area, e.g. *Luftflotte* 5 covered operations in Finland and Norway. Each *Luftflotte* had fighter (*Jägd*), bomber (*Kampf*), and reconnaissance (*Aufklärung*) units at its disposal according to operational requirements.

The biggest tactical fighter unit was the *Jägdgeschwader* (the closest RAF equivalent being Wing), which consisted of up to four *Gruppen* (Groups), each of which normally had three *Staffeln* (squadrons). Each *Staffel* had a nominal strength of between twelve and sixteen aircraft, including reserves. Each *Jägdgeschwader* also had a *Stab* (HQ Flight), which normally had three or four Bf 109s. Until early 1942, each *Jägdgeschwader* also had an *Ergänzung* (Training and replacement) *Staffel*. These were abolished, being deemed 'ineffective', with aircraft and staff being used to form IV./JG 1.

Somewhat simplified, the various *Gruppen* or even *Staffeln* of a *Jägdgeschwader* could during their existence be attached to different *Luftflotten* according to operational requirements, initially flying over the Western Front before being transferred to North Africa or the Eastern Front. Thus, a *Jägdgeschwader Staffel* or **Gruppe** often operated independently, away from other units of a particular *Jägdgeschwader*. With the arrival of the Fw 190 in mid-1941, a number of Bf 109 *Gruppen* converted to the former fighter. Although the Fw 190 was easier to fly for relatively inexperienced pilots, many of the more seasoned pilots preferred the Bf 109. Apparently, some pilots declared themselves willing to desert if they were ordered to convert from the trusted Bf 109 to the more modern Fw 190.

The smallest tactical formations employed by the Luftwaffe were *Schwarm* and *Rotten*, which had been developed during the Spanish Civil War. Until then, the *Kette* formation had been the norm. Latin numerals were used to indicate a *Gruppe*, with Roman numerals indicating each *Staffel*, e.g. II./JG 51 (indicating the second Gruppe of *Jägdgeschwader* 51 and 9./JG 5 (indicating the ninth *Staffel* of *Jägdgeschwader* 5). Bf 109s were also used by a number of *Nahaufklärungsgruppen* (close-range reconnaissance groups, NAGr), as well as flight training schools and a large number of secondline units.

Jägdgeschwader Identification Markings and Insignia

With the introduction into service of the Bf 109, a new type of identification markings were introduced in December 1937. This saw two fighter units, JG 132 and JG 134, having their aircraft adorned with sequential numerals, with the *II Gruppe* adding a horizontal bar above the numerals. Identification in the air of individual aircraft proved difficult, resulting in a directive that the numerals were to be located in front of the *Balkenkreuz*, and the horizontal bar to the rear. Bf 109s belonging to the *III Gruppe* were to be identified with a vertical bar, although aircraft of JG 2, JG 52, and JG 77 continued to be marked with a wavy line similar to those of earlier Luftwaffe fighters. The identification numerals and bars of the various *Staffeln* were painted in different colours: white (1, 4, and 7 *Staffeln*) with no outline; red (2, 5, and 8 *Staffeln*) outlined in white; and yellow (3, 6, and 9 *Staffeln*) outlined in black. The three aircraft belonging to the *Stab* (HQ) Flight had a chevron containing a triangle within its angles in front of the *Balkenkreuz* and a vertical bar behind (lead aircraft only), with the other being marked with a chevron (no triangle), and two horizontal bars in front of and behind the *Balkenkreuz*.

When completed, each Bf 109 was assigned a four-letter *Stammkennzeichen* (factory identification letters), which was used as a radio call-sign. As opposed to bomber units, which used a four-letter alphanumeric unit identification code known as *Verbandkennzeichen* (unit identification letters), the *Jägdgeschwader* units used the aforementioned system of identification numerals, bars, and chevrons. There were numerous examples of specific markings indicating a particular *Jägdgeschwader* or its various *Gruppen* and *Staffeln*. For instance, Bf 109s of JG 53 were adorned with an Ace of Spades (*Pik As*). There were, of course, numerous exceptions, particularly during the latter stages of the war. For those interested in delving into Luftwaffe Bf 109 markings and insignia, a wide range of articles and books exist. John Weal's three-part series 'Luftwaffe Markings', which appeared in *Wings of Fame*, Volumes 16 to 18, is a good starting point on this extensive subject.

A rather uninterested-looking Willy Messerschmitt, cigarette in hand, at a display during the visit of Charles Lindbergh to the Messerschmitt Works Augsburg, 1938.

Introduction

The Messerschmitt Bf 109 remains one of the most famous fighter aircraft of the world. To a large extent, the name Messerschmitt is synonymous with the German Luftwaffe of the Second World War, and, in particular, its single-seat fighters. From 1 September 1939 until 8 May 1945, the Bf 109 was the most numerous Luftwaffe fighter aircraft. More than 33,000 Bf 109s were built, which makes it the second most produced combat aircraft of all time, only beaten by the Russian Ilyushin Il-2 Shturmovik ground-attack aircraft. Even today, the Bf 109 retains third place regarding aircraft production numbers. The most produced aircraft of all time is the Cessna 172 light plane.

The Messerschmitt Bf 109 is also the most successful fighter ever produced, with its pilots scoring thousands of aerial victories against Allied air arms. The elite fighter unit of the Luftwaffe, *Jägdgeschwader 52*, only flew successive variants of the Bf 109s throughout its existence and its pilots claimed more than 10,000 aircraft shot down—the majority on the Eastern Front. Although the flight and handling characteristics of the Bf 109 made it difficult to master, a pilot who had become accustomed to its idiosyncrasies had a lethal weapon in his hands.

Taking to the air for the first time in May 1935, the Bf 109 was initially regarded with some suspicion, both by fighter pilots and the RLM. The monoplane fighter featured several innovations, including an enclosed cockpit and retractable undercarriage, which took some time in getting used to by the German fighter pilots, used as they were to fly open-cockpit biplanes. Indeed, the Bf 109 proved difficult to fly, particularly during take-off and landing. However, the Bf 109 was a supreme air superiority fighter, effectively ruling the skies of Europe between 1939 and 1942. Following the introduction of more modern Allied fighters, the Spitfire Mk. IX and the US P-51 Mustang in particular, the Bf 109 became outclassed. Nevertheless, the Bf 109 remained in production until the end of the war. Most of the highest-scoring Luftwaffe aces would fly the Bf 109. The famous British test pilot Eric 'Winkle' Brown would later refer to the Bf 109 as '... sinister ... to me it looked lethal from any angle, on the ground or in the air; once I had climbed into its claustrophobic cockpit it felt lethal!'

In late 1936, three Bf 109 prototypes were rushed to Spain for operational evaluation by the *Legion Condor*. In the event, the sojourn in the war-torn skies of Spain was both brief and inconclusive. Nevertheless, the initial production variant, the Bf 109B-1, was supplied to the *Legion Condor* during the spring of 1937. It first saw action during the Battle of Brunete. It was soon realised that the Bf 109 was superior in most respects to the various fighters fielded by the Spanish Republican Air Force, including the Polikarpov I-16 monoplane. New air combat tactics were soon developed to establish the best use of the new fighter. By the end of the Spanish Civil War, more than 130 Bf 109s had been supplied to the *Legion Condor*, with most of the surviving aircraft being handed over to the Spanish Air Force in April 1939.

The exploits of the Bf 109 in Spain were veiled in secrecy, with the first detailed scrutiny of the new fighter's capabilities by foreign powers occurring during the 1937 Fourth International Air Meet at Zurich, Switzerland. The appearance of the Bf 109 heralded a new era in fighter design and aerial tactics; the biplane fighter, which had reigned supreme since the Great War, was now fast becoming obsolescent. Nevertheless, even if the biplane fighters could not match the Bf 109's speed, the former enjoyed superior manoeuvrability and a better turning radius than the Bf 109, which made them so well-suited to the old dogfight tactics. Indeed, biplane fighters would remain in front-line service until 1939–1940 with most major air arms, with some new designs—including the Gloster Gladiator, Fiat CR.42, and Polikarpov I-153—actually entering large-scale service in 1938 and 1939.

Between 1939 and 1945, the Bf 109 and its subsequent variants served as the most numerous single-engine fighter of the Luftwaffe. The Bf 109 served on every front and was flown by many of the Luftwaffe's highest scoring aces. Apart from the pure fighter role, many Bf 109s were used as fighter-bombers and in ground-attack duties, while others served as dedicated aerial reconnaissance aircraft. Late in the war, many Bf 109Gs were converted as two-seat conversion trainers to speed up pilot training. The Bf 109 could also be used as an *ad hoc* transport, carrying a mechanic squeezed into the rear fuselage. This was actually an important aspect and there were obvious advantages to having a mechanic crammed into the rear fuselage during transfers to a new airfield. However, the mechanic was required not to have claustrophobic tendencies as the available space was strictly limited.

With the German *Kriegsmarine* intending to bring aircraft carriers into service, a carrier variant of the Bf 109 was produced. This was the Bf 109T ('T' for *Träger*, or carrier), which was developed from the Bf 109E. Although no aircraft carriers were completed, the Bf 109T subsequently entered service with regular Luftwaffe units.

Like its contemporary, the Supermarine Spitfire, the basic Bf 109 design was successively developed throughout its production life. Apart from large-scale production in Germany itself, Bf 109 production lines were established in Hungary and Romania as well. With the defeat and surrender of Germany in May 1945, Bf 109s continued to fly in several countries, including Bulgaria, Finland, Romania, Spain, and Switzerland. Post-war, the basic Bf 109 was developed and put into production in Czechoslovakia and Spain as the Avia S-199 and Hispano HA-1112 respectively. Incredibly, the Avia S-199 was the first fighter to serve with the Israeli Air Force.

By the early 1950s, most Bf 109s had been retired, with the last of the Avia S-199s being withdrawn from use in 1955. However, the HA-1112 continued in Spanish service until the mid-1960s. Several HA-1112s were subsequently used in films, usually finished in generic Luftwaffe colours and markings. Some HA-1112s are still flying today, having recently been joined by a few restored Bf 109s. To many fighter pilots and aviation enthusiasts alike, the Bf 109 remains one of the best known fighter aircraft in the history of air combat.

1

Genesis of the Bf 109

Wilhelm Emil 'Willy' Messerschmitt

Born in Frankfurt am Main on 26 June 1898, Wilhelm Emil 'Willy' Messerschmitt developed an interest in aviation from an early age—particularly Zeppelin airships. A visit to an aviation exhibition held at Frankfurt in 1909 influenced Messerschmitt to begin building model aeroplanes. In early 1914, Willy began to work for glider pilot and designer Friedrich Harth at Bamberg. When war broke out, Harth was called up for military service.

Messerschmitt finished the construction of a Harth-designed glider, which was eventually air tested in 1915. The following year, Harth and Messerschmitt built a jointly-designed glider. At the age of nineteen, Messerschmitt joined the Imperial German Army. With the signing of the Versailles Treaty, Germany was forbidden to

Wilhelm Emil 'Willy' Messerschmitt in later life. (*Wolfgang Mühlbauer/DEHLA Archives*)

A BFW M 18. (*ETH Archives*)

develop and build heavier-than-air aeroplanes. This ban was gradually lifted, with German manufacturers developing a wide array of gliders and light aircraft. Harth and Messerschmitt again joined forces and continued to build gliders, with one of the first post-war designs being the S9 ('S' indicated *Segelflugzeug*—sailplane).

In 1921, Harth was seriously injured in a sailplane crash. However, Messerschmitt was considering designing motorised aircraft, something which eventually led to an end of his working relationship with Harth. In 1922, Messerschmitt formed Flugzeugbau Messerschmitt. The first aircraft design for which Messerschmitt was solely responsible was the S 16 two-seat light aeroplane powered by a 21-hp Douglas Sprite engine. The first aircraft to be identified by the M (Motorised) prefix was the M 17 Ello. Powered by a 32-hp Bristol Cherub III engine, the M 17 was used on a long-distance flight from Bamberg to Rome.

The following year, Flugzeugbau Messerschmitt was re-organised as Messerschmitt Flugzeugbau GmbH. The subsequent M 18 light transport established Messerschmitt as a force to be reckoned with. However, the harsh economic realities of the Weimar Republic meant that Messerschmitt was put under intense pressure from the Bavarian State Government to merge his company with the recently-established *Bayerische Flugzeug Werke* (BFW) at Augsburg. Another company that would eventually merge with BFW was Udet Flugzeugbau GmbH, which had been formed in 1922 by First World War ace Ernst Udet. In the event, an agreement was signed on 8 September 1927 in which Messerschmitt would concentrate on design and development work, and BFW on aircraft manufacture. Messerschmitt was also to retain patent rights for his designs. As a result, Messerschmitt and BFW were two separate entities working, for all practical purposes, as one company.

The first aircraft built following the agreement was the M 20, a ten-seat airliner. The national airline, *Deutsche Lufthansa* (DLH), placed an order for two M 20s. However, the M 20 prototype crashed on its maiden flight, with the pilot bailing

A BFW M 20 airliner. (*ETH Archives*)

out at too low an altitude and being killed on impact. The pilot was a close friend of Erhard Milch, the Managing Director of DLH, which resulted in the cancellation of the M 20 order. The crash badly affected the future relationship between Messerschmitt and Milch. The order was eventually re-instated after a second, modified M 20b prototype was successfully test-flown on 2 August 1928.

Simultaneously, the *Reichsverkehrsministerium* (German Air Ministry) decided sell off its BFW ownership to private investors. Messerschmitt himself acquired a 12.5 per cent share. Another notable design was the M 23 two-seat light aircraft. Several M 23s were flown to great success during the 1929 and 1930 European air races, as well as being used for flights to Greenland and Africa. It was also used in aerobatic competitions. Interestingly, Rudolf Hess (second only to Hitler in the Nazi hierarchy until his defection to Britain in May 1941) bought an M 23.

Incidentally, when Messerschmitt finally gained his pilot's licence in 1929, the company sales director, Fritz Hille, publicly complained that this was an, '… irresponsible distraction from his [Messerschmitt's] duties as developmental head.' Apparently, Messerschmitt's aircraft design skills were superior to his piloting proficiency as a company test pilot usually accompanied him on business flights across Germany. On one occasion, Messerschmitt forgot to retract the undercarriage when taking off in the company Bf 108, with the slightly embarrassed right seat 'safety' pilot remaining silent during the entire flight.

The Stock Market Crash of 1929 deeply affected Europe, particularly Germany. With several types of aircraft under development, including the M 22 twin-engine bomber and the M 23 two-seat monoplane, the company's finances worsened rapidly. To make matters worse, DLH cancelled its order for M 20bs and demanded repayment of deposits. This was a major blow, with BFW filing for bankruptcy on 1 June 1931.

The fact that Messerschmitt owned the design and patent rights eventually resulted in the re-emergence of the Bayerische Flugzeugwerke A.G. in May 1933. With active support from the BFW receiver, DLH were eventually forced to accept the M 20bs, as well as one M 29 air mail aircraft.[1]

However, Erhard Milch, by now the newly-appointed State Secretary for Aviation and the head of the RLM, did his utmost to restrict the activities of BFW, which was co-managed by Messerschmitt and Rakan Kokothaki. According to Milch, BFW should not receive any orders for any of its own designs, instead being confined to building aircraft designed by other companies. Initially, thirty Dornier Do 11 twin-engine bombers and twenty-four He 45 single-engine army co-operation aircraft were ordered from BFW. This placed BFW on a firm footing, with the number of employees rising from eighty-seven to 524 by the end of 1933.

In June 1933, BFW obtained an order from Romania for a light transport aircraft. The resulting M 36 was delivered to the Romanian airline LARES, along with an agreement to build further aircraft in Romania. However, this led to strong criticism from RLM officials; Messerschmitt was to concentrate on building aircraft for Germany and not other countries. However, trying to keep BFW afloat meant seeking foreign contracts in lieu of RLM orders.

The next design, the M 37, was to change the fortunes of BFW. Before taking to the air in March 1934, the M 37 had been redesignated as the Bf 108.

The highly advanced Bf 108 was a four-seat tourer designed specifically for participation in the 1934 *Challenge de Tourism Internationale* air race. The Bf 108 was of all-metal stressed-skin construction, having an enclosed canopy and a retractable undercarriage. Slots were fitted to the forward leading edge of the wings, with spoilers initially fitted that were eventually replaced by conventional ailerons. Apart from Messerschmitt himself, Dipl. Ing. Robert Lusser (who had joined BFW on 1 November 1933), Dipl. Ing. (*Diplom Ingeneur*, the German equivalent to Master of Science) Walter Rethel (both former employees of Heinkel) and Hubert Bauer were heavily involved in the design of the Bf 108.

Initially, the German team and the RLM were not particularly enamoured with the Bf 108. When one of the aircraft crashed, there were strong demands for the Bf 108 to be withdrawn from the contest. In the event, the three Bf 108s ended up in fifth, sixth, and tenth places, and were victorious in the overall racing section of the *Challenge de Tourism Internationale*. The Bf 108 went on to become a great success for BFW. It was eventually named *Taifun* ('Typhoon') on account of its high speed. Before 1939, Bf 108s were used on many long-distance flights, with the Luftwaffe and many other air arms placing large orders.[2]

However, the RLM—and Erhard Milch in particular—persevered in having a low opinion of Messerschmitt. Indeed, he was told that the design and development of a new single-seat fighter for the recently reformed Luftwaffe was way out of his league. Messerschmitt tested the waters by spreading the news that he was considering accepting a Professorship at the Danzig Technical University. Upon learning this, the RLM bluntly told Messerschmitt to accept the post, and that his current work 'was of no importance'.

A Bf 108 Taifun. The Bf 109 lineage is clearly visible. (*Swedish Aviation Historical Society*)

However, the eventual acceptance of the Bf 109 as the Luftwaffe's standard single-seat fighter resulted in Messerschmitt's status as an aircraft designer rising sharply, with lucrative production contracts being placed by the RLM, as well as paving the way for other types of combat aircraft, including the Bf 110, Me 210 and Me 410 twin-engine heavy fighters, the Me 163 rocket fighter, and the revolutionary Me 262 jet fighter.[3] The Me 209 was developed as a high-speed racer and managed to secure the world speed record in 1939. Other notable Messerschmitt aircraft were the Me 321 assault glider, the Me 323 six-engine transport, and the Me 264 heavy bomber. The latter was intended to reach targets in North America, but did not enter series production. By 1945, some 45,000 aircraft bearing Messerschmitt's name had been built.

Following the end of the war, Messerschmitt was imprisoned at Heilbronn. During the Nuremburg Trials, Messerschmitt was sentenced to two years in prison; the Messerschmitt factory at Regensburg had used slave labour, including Russian prisoners of war. One irreversible fact was that Willy Messerschmitt had been a member of the Nazi Party, having held membership number 342354.

Following his release, Messerschmitt reregistered the company name Messerschmitt AG. With Germany forbidden to produce aeroplanes, Messerschmitt developed pre-fabricated houses (a much-needed commodity in post-war Germany), built by the Neue Technik GmbH at Augsburg, as well as the KR 175 and KR 200 tri-cycle light two-seat cars. Messerschmitt then offered his services (unsuccessfully) to South Africa, eventually moving to Spain in 1951, where he assisted the company Hispano in redesigning the basic Bf 109G. During his Spanish sojourn, Messerschmitt also designed a tri-cycle undercarriage advanced trainer, the Hispano HA-100 Triana (similar in appearance to the contemporary North American T-28 Trojan), which, in the event, did not enter production. However, the HA-200 Saeta (Arrow) two-seat jet trainer was used by both the Spanish and Egyptian air arms, with some still operated today by Warbird enthusiasts, particularly in the USA. The last design in which Messerschmitt was actively involved was the HA-300 light-weight supersonic fighter. Two HA-300s were built in Egypt, the first of which was flown in 1964. For various reasons, series production did not happen.

With the re-establishment of the Luftwaffe in 1955, Messerschmitt AG returned to aircraft, receiving contracts to overhaul North American T-6 and Lockheed T-33A trainers. Large-scale production of the CM-170 jet trainer, Fiat G.91 light strike aircraft, and the Lockheed F-104 supersonic fighter followed in conjunction with other German aircraft manufacturers. In 1965, Messerschmitt purchased all assets of the former Junkers company, which led to the formation of Messerschmitt Bölkow Blohm GmbH (MBB) four years later. On 19 May 1989, MBB became part of the Deutsche Aerospace AB (DASA), which continues to produce high-performance helicopters alongside being an important part of the Airbus consortium.

Willy Messerschmitt died on 15 September 1978, aged eighty. He was unquestionably one of the most prominent and best known of all German aircraft designers.

Birth of the Bf 109

When, in late 1933, the *Technisches Amt* (Technical Department) of the recently formed *Reichsluftfahrtministerium* (Air Ministry, RLM) concluded a series of investigations regarding the requirements for future combat aircraft of the still-secret Luftwaffe; this included a single-engine fighter. It was intended that the new fighter would replace the biplane fighters, including the Arado Ar 65, then entering service. The most important features for the new fighter were high level speed, high rate of climb, as well as retaining the manoeuvrability of the biplane fighter. According to the requirements outlined in the *Rüstungsflugzeug* IV specification, such a fighter was to have an armament consisting of two fixed machine guns or one 20-mm cannon, an endurance of ninety minutes at full throttle at an altitude of 6,000 metres (19,690 feet). It was to have a maximum speed of 400 kph (250 mph) at an altitude of 6,000 metres (19,690 feet) and a service ceiling of 10,000 metres. Being able to operate at such altitudes of course meant fitting oxygen breathing apparatus for the pilot. The wing loading was to remain below 100 kg/m^2, which would make it possible to operate from airfields measuring 400 × 400 metres.

In February 1934, three companies were awarded a contract to develop prototypes, Arado, Heinkel and the BFW. A fourth company, Focke-Wulf, was awarded a contract more than six months later in September 1934.

It has been claimed that the success of the four-seat Bf 108 tourer influenced the RLM decision to include BFW in the fighter competition. This is inaccurate, as the contract to build a Bf 109 prototype was awarded four months before the first flight of the Bf 108. Additionally, the Bf 108 was initially seen as a disaster, with one of the aircraft participating in the *Challenge de Tourisme Internationale* being written off in a crash. Nevertheless, the Bf 108 and the Bf 109 shared a number of design features, such as forward leading edge slats, a narrow-width retractable undercarriage, and an enclosed canopy.

With the ongoing conflict between Milch and Messerschmitt, the Technical Office (C-Amt) of the RLM firmly believed that BFW stood little or no chance against Arado and Heinkel in particular, with both of the latter companies having a fair amount of previous experience in fighter aircraft design. Apart from the Bf 109, three rival fighter designs were included in the competition: the Arado Ar 80, the Focke-Wulf Fw 159, and the Heinkel He 112.

Design work of the Bf 109, which initially carried the designation P.1034, began at Augsburg-Haunstetten in March 1934. A wooden full-scale mock-up, constructed to ease equipment fitting tests as well as assisting in the final configuration, was demonstrated to RLM officials on 11 May 1934, with discussions being centred upon the choice of engine and the proposed armament. The latter was to consist of two rifle-calibre MG 17s mounted in the upper fuselage decking. Additional punch would come from a 20-mm MG/C30 cannon centrally mounted between the engine blocks and firing through the propeller spinner.

By late 1934, the first Bf 109 prototype (W Nr 758) was essentially complete and assigned the designation Bf 109a. Soon afterwards, it was redesignated the Bf 109 V1 ('V' standing for *Versuch*, i.e. 'trials'). The configuration of the new fighter was finalised in mid-January 1935. A trial installation of a BMW 116 mock-up engine had earlier been made, but as development of this engine had been cancelled in late 1934, the Junkers Jumo 210 was chosen, with the Daimler Benz DB 600 also being seen as a possibility for installation in later models. In the event, a Rolls-Royce Kestrel V inline engine was fitted to the Bf 109 prototype. Four Kestrels had been acquired by the RLM from Rolls-Royce, which in early 1935 purchased a Heinkel He 70 for use as an engine test bed.[4]

In the event, BFW received two of the Kestrel engines, with Arado and Heinkel getting one each. Developing a suitable liquid-cooled 1,000-hp engine had already been addressed in late 1930 by the German aero engine industry, but such an engine would not be available until several years later in the shape of the Daimler-Benz DB 601 engine.

First Impressions

Prior to the first flight, the former Great War ace Ernst Udet paid a visit to the BFW factory. Udet was given the grand tour, which included the Bf 109. Eyeing the new fighter, Udet exclaimed: 'This machine will never make a fighter.' History was to prove him wrong. It was recognised that the undercarriage fitted to the Bf 109 was not particularly strong and, as a safety precaution, a horizontal metal bar was fitted between the undercarriage legs in anticipation of taxing trials. The undercarriage legs were fitted to the fuselage, retracting outwards into the wings. (Having the main undercarriage fitted in this way did have one advantage. Whatever the reason, a wingless Bf 109 fuselage could easily be towed on the ground, something which was not possible with the competing fighters. Undercarriage retraction trials initially caused some problems, as the undercarriage did not retract properly; the wheels got stuck against the outer skin of the wing. This was easily rectified, and ground trials were completed with few additional problems.

Above: The Bf 109 V1. A Heinkel He 45 can be seen in the background. (*Wolfgang Mühlbauer/ DEHLA Archives*)

Left: A close-up of the Bf 109 V1. (*Wolfgang Mühlbauer/DEHLA Archives*)

The Bf 109a prototype (registered as D-IABI) was flown, ahead of the Arado 80, Focke-Wulf 159 and Heinkel 112 fighters, for the first time on 29 May 1935 by twenty-seven-year-old Hans-Dietrich 'Bubi' Knoetzsch. Knoetzsch's first flight in the Bf 109 lasted twenty minutes, following which he landed safely to the relief of all present.

Initial Bf 109 flight trials showed considerable promise. On 15 October, the Bf 109 was flown to Rechlin by Knoetzsch, with a planned intermediate stop at Jüterbog to refuel. While at Jüterbog, Knoetsch took time to unload some personal effects. The new fighter was eyed curiously by the pilots, including future ace Adolf Galland, and the mechanics of JG 132. Compared with the Heinkel He 51, the Bf 109 appeared somewhat frail and futuristic.

Upon arrival over Rechlin, Knoetzsch engaged in aerobatic manoeuvring that greatly impressed the assembled crowd. However, D-IABI was damaged upon landing when the undercarriage collapsed. The Bf 109 ended up in the somewhat embarrassing pose of being perched tail-high on the nose, the intact undercarriage leg, and a wing tip. Apparently, the pilots that had gathered considered this to be a 'perfect three-pointer (landing)'.[5]

Possibly at the request of Heinkel, a detailed report on the mishap was compiled, which stated in part:

> The aircraft was flown at Rechlin by a factory test pilot. The accident sequence began with a very hard touchdown, followed by a bounce and a subsequent drop from about 1 to 1.5 metres. The left main landing gear and the tail wheel contacted the ground first. Upon impact the tail wheel separated and the fuselage cracked in three places. The left main landing gear strut was bent inwards, moment(s) later the left wingtip hit the ground, which was followed by a quick swing to the right. The aircraft came to rest in an inverted position [NB: this suggests that it overturned and did not merely end up in a tail-high position]. After the accident the aircraft was taken apart, which gave me an opportunity to take a close look at various subassemblies.[6]

Knoetzsch was blamed for the poor landing, resulting in his immediate dismissal. He was also accused of exposing the secret fighter to curious JG 132 personnel at Jüterbog. Knoetzsch would eventually find new work in the Netherlands, testing the Fokker D.XXI fighter. The accident, along with the novel features of the Bf 109V 1, made it a target for severe criticism, both from the *Reichsluftfahrtministerium* (RLM) and Luftwaffe test pilots. Most fighter pilots still believed in the open-cockpit biplane fighter and the enclosed cockpit, high wing loading and automatic leading-edge slots of the Bf 109 V1 seemed a bit too much of a radical departure. Also, the pilot had a very poor forward view—blocked by the engine and propeller—when taxiing on the ground, resulting from the very steep angle of the aircraft. In order to have at least some forward view, the pilots had to resort to performing a weaving pattern when taxiing prior to take-off. Incidentally, during operations from primitive, dusty, and unprepared airfields—particularly in North Africa and Russia—it was common practice to have a mechanic sit on the wing prior to take-off, assisting the pilot in obtaining a clear view of the runway.

Along with the He 112 V1, the Bf 109 V1 underwent a thorough evaluation at Travemünde in late 1935. In February 1936, the He 112 V1 and the Bf 109 V2 were flown to Rechlin for the final comparative tests. It was clear to all concerned that the competition now stood between the Bf 109 and the He 112. The second Bf 109 prototype, registered as D-IUDE (W Nr 809) joined the test programme in early 1936. During three days, 26–27 February and 2 March, the Bf 109 V2 was shown off in spectacular fashion by the BFW test pilot Hermann Wurster. Although Wurster was a relatively inexperienced pilot, he performed a power dive from an altitude of 7,000 metres, as well as demonstrating the spin characteristics of the Bf 109. During the trials, the He 112 V2 pilot, Gerhard Nitschke, was forced to bale out when he failed to recover from a flat spin.

Subsequent trials with different pilots indicated that the He 112 was more pleasant to fly and also had far better landing characteristics. The Bf 109 did, in fact, have superior speed and climb rate, while other flight characteristics were far from benevolent. Rechlin test pilot Gerhard Geike later wrote that he found the spin and landing characteristics of the Bf 109 to be less than perfect. Geike stated that, 'it took great skill to land the aircraft on both wheels simultaneously. As the airflow separation did not occur simultaneously at both wingtips, the aircraft always stalled on one side before touch-down, and the wheel on that side touched the ground first.' Geike and his colleagues were surprised when the Bf 109 was selected over the He 112. 'In spite of its faults, (the Bf 109) had been given preference because of its better performance, lower weight, and cheaper construction.'[7]

Another very important aspect was the time required to construct a Bf 109. Messerschmitt claimed that a mere 6,000 hours were needed to complete a Bf 109 from start to finish, as opposed to 15,000 hours for one series He 112. According to Ernst Heinkel, the first He 112 took no less than 40,000 hours to complete. The licensee AGO, which had no previous experience in building all-metal aircraft stated that they needed an average of 7,500 hours to build one Bf 109. Another aircraft manufacturer, Arado, stated similar figures for the first fifty aircraft, after which the number of work hours per airframe would be reduced to 6,500. During the latter stages of the war, the work hours necessary for completing one Bf 109 reached as low as 4,000.

Another view of the Bf 109 versus He 112 competition was later offered by one of the BFW test pilots, Herman Wurster:

> As I was getting ready to climb into the He 112 cockpit, the chief of flight test department, Dipl. Ing. Francke came up to me and said: 'Herr Wurster, just remember that you cannot do the same crazy things in the He 112 that you had shown us in your Me 109' … The Bf 109's superior manoeuvring characteristics were confirmed by other military and civilian test pilots. Among them was General Udet, one of the leading aces of the Great War, as well as an accomplished aerobatic pilot. If anyone was qualified to express opinion about flight characteristics of a fighter aircraft, it was certainly General Udet. The same

> can be said about General Robert Ritter von Greim, who was also impressed with the Bf 109's performance. Both Udet and von Greim performed a number of flights not just for fun and because of their seniority, but because they wanted to test the new designs in conditions closely simulating actual combat. I could attest to the Bf 109's superiority having flown numerous mock dogfights against the other two competing fighters.[8]

According to Wurster, the Bf 109 won because it was 'quite simply a better aircraft'. Additionally, the construction of the Bf 109 airframe was far better suited for mass production, being both cheaper and requiring less specialised jigs and tools than the He 112. In the event, having lost the fighter contest the He 112 was released for export by the RLM. On the other hand, the performance characteristics of the Bf 109 remained a closely guarded secret.

Attempts were subsequently made to rectify the aerodynamic problems encountered with the Bf 109, with the forward leading edge automatic slats improving things slightly. Continued spin trials were documented by having a film camera installed behind the pilot's seat.

A milestone occurred in March 1936 when the RLM placed an order for Bf 109s. This marked the first time that BFW had received an order for military aircraft. It was also, incidentally, the month when the Supermarine Spitfire first took to the air. In a document dated 12 March 1936, it is stated that production of the Bf 109 with the Jumo 210 engine, two-blade propeller, and an armament consisting of two MG 17s was to proceed, with the Bf 109 V3 being modified to this standard as soon as possible for flight trials at Travemünde. Production of the Bf 109 was to be limited to the Jumo 210 variant, with the possibility of fitting the fuel-injection Jumo 210 at a later stage considered. It was also expected that a BMW 116 engine would be experimentally fitted in a Bf 109 by August 1936. This never happened, though.

Following its accident, the Bf 109 V1 was rebuilt and flown to Travemünde in early 1936 for continued trials. The aircraft was returned to Augsburg on 17 July. Shortened leading edge slots were tested, with the final flight of the Bf 109 V1 taking place on 11 February 1938. It was then consigned to storage before being unceremoniously scrapped, having outlived its usefulness. Interestingly, no thought appears to have been made of putting the first Bf 109 prototype on display at the huge *Deutschen Luftfahrt Sammlung* (German Aircraft Collection) in Berlin, alongside other prominent German aircraft of the interwar period.

Having initially exhibited a low regard of the Bf 109, Udet became convinced of its qualities. However, the Luftwaffe was at this juncture—like virtually all of the world's air arms—influenced by the theories of the Italian Giulio Douhet, who foresaw that any future war would be won primarily through strategic air power. Douhet believed that large fleets of heavy strategic bombers could bomb the enemy into submission and final surrender without the need for the bloody trench warfare that had characterised the Great War of 1914–1918. The role of the fighter aircraft was still seen as limited to that of traditional dogfighting and bomber escort, something, which had essentially remained unchanged since 1918.

An air-to-air image of Bf 109 V3, D-IOQY. (*Wolfgang Mühlbauer/DEHLA Archives*)

During an aerial demonstration held at Rechlin on 3 July 1936, Udet, flying a Bf 109, performed mock attacks against a number of bombers and their He 51 fighter escorts. Such was the superiority of the Bf 109, and Udet's flying skills, that he 'shot down' all of the attacking aircraft. Still, the Luftwaffe High Command was not ready to abandon the 'bomber-will-always-get-through' tactics. During the summer of 1936, the formal Luftwaffe flight evaluation of the Bf 109 began in earnest, and was led by Dipl.Ing. Karl Francke.

One major propaganda coup for the Bf 109 (and BFW) occurred in August 1936 when the second Bf 109 prototype was flown by Dipl. Ing. Karl Francke over Berlin, where the XI Olympic Games had just been inaugurated, introducing the fighter to the large German audience present at the Berlin Olympic Stadium.

Meanwhile, the production facilities at Augsburg-Haunstetten were rapidly expanding. In 1935, BFW received orders for thirty-two Bf 108s, as well as ninety Arado Ar 66s, 115 Gotha Go 145 basic trainers, seventy Heinkel He 45s reconnaissance aircraft, and thirty-five Heinkel He 50 dive bombers. By late 1936, preparations for series production of the Bf 109 at Augsburg was proceeding rapidly. The first production aircraft would be delivered to the Luftwaffe in December 1936. In order to increase the Bf 109 production volume, it was eventually decided to transfer the Bf 108 production line to Regensburg by 1938, soon to be followed by the Bf 109. Augsburg would retain design and development, with aircraft production concentrated to Regensburg. The Bf 109 was also built under licence by other German aircraft manufacturers, including AGO, Arado, Erla, Fieseler, and Focke-Wulf.

Messerschmitt Bf 109 V1 Technical Data and Performance Characteristics
Engine: 1 × 695-hp, Rolls-Royce Kestrel V
Wingspan: 10.00 metres
Length: 8.6 metres
Height: 3.4 metres
Track width: N/A
Wing area: 16.3 m^2
Weight, empty: 1,502 kg
Weight, maximum: 1,904 kg
Maximum speed: 470 kph
Range: N/A
Service ceiling: 8,000 m
Armament: N/A

Further Bf 109 Prototypes

A further thirteen prototypes, designated Bf 109V 2 to V 14, were constructed in 1936 and 1937. Before the end of the war, some fifty Bf 109 prototypes, including some modified from production aircraft, had flown. The Bf 109 V2 joined the flight test programme at Travemünde in early 1936. Compared with the first prototype, the V2 was powered by a 610-hp Jumo 210 A driving a fixed-pitch two-blade wooden Schwarz propeller. No armament was fitted. In the event, it was the superior overall performance of the Bf 109 V2 exhibited in the comparative trials against the Ar 80, Fw 159, and He 112 that paved the way for Messerschmitt's fighter.

The Bf 109 V3, D-IOQY, was the first to feature armament, consisting of two MG 17s (500 rounds each) fitted in the upper fuselage decking. A 20-mm MG C/30L cannon was to be fitted between the engine cylinder blocks, firing through the propeller spinner. This never took place because this (for its time) heavy aerial weapon was still under development. It was also intended for the V3 to carry five SC 10 bombs on Elvemag 5 C X bomb ejectors fitted inside the centre fuselage. These were apparently not tested during flight trials due to problems with the electrical fuses. The Bf 109 V3 was extensively tested at Travemünde during the summer and autumn of 1936, before being shipped to Spain in early December.

Powered by a 640-hp Jumo 210 B, the Bf 109 V4, D-IALY, became the Bf 109B prototype. Flown for the first time on 23 September 1936, the Bf 109 V4 had an armament consisting of two MG 17s. Following a brief evaluation at E-Stelle Travemünde, the Bf 109 V4 was returned to Augsburg, and was subsequently shipped to Spain.

The fifth prototype, Bf 109 V5, D-IIGO, was armed with three MG 17s. It was used to test the EPAD 17 pneumatic, electric gun firing system at Travemünde, Rechlin and Tarnevitz. It remained in use until 1938 at least.

The Bf 109 V6, D-IHHB, was the third Bf 109B-series prototype. Armed with three MG 17s, it was shipped to Spain for operational trials in December 1936. However, it became the first Bf 109 to be lost in a fatal crash. This occurred on 11 February 1937 in the vicinity of Cáreces, Spain, with the death of Lt Paul Rehahn.

The Bf 109 V7, D-IJHA, was powered by a 730-hp Jumo 210 G which was fitted with direct fuel injection. In contrast to most other Bf 109 prototypes, the V7 was unarmed. It was demonstrated at Zurich International Air Meet. Upon the aircraft's return to Germany it was used in a variety of test programmes at the BFW Augsburg factory.

Bf 109 V8, D-IPLU, had one MG 17 mounted in each wing. However, these mechanically operated machine guns proved troublesome due to the severe vibrations experienced during firing. Apart from armament trials, the Bf 109 V8 also saw use in endurance trials. At an unknown juncture, its Jumo 210 D engine was exchanged for a DB 600 engine. This was reportedly the only Bf 109 to be fitted with the latter type of engine. A direct development of the DB 600, the DB 601, would eventually power thousands of Bf 109Es and Fs. The Bf 109 V9 D-IPLU made its public debut during the Zurich International Air Meeting. It was then transferred to Rechlin for extended trials.

The tenth Bf 109 prototype, D-IAKO, powered by a Jumo 210 D, joined the test programme in late 1937. Amazingly, its buried remains were found in 1993 at Oberpfaffenhofen. The Bf 109 V11 *Waffenflügel* (gun wing) featured a redesigned wing, with shortened forward leading edge slats and aileron mass balances. These modifications were due to a pair of MG 17s mounted in the wings. Armament tests were carried out at Travemünde, with the aircraft eventually being returned to the manufacturer in late 1937. The four-gun *Waffenflügel* armament would eventually become standard for Bf 109E.

The Bf 109 V12 was also used for *Waffenflügel* armament trials. One MG FF cannon was mounted in the right wing, with the left wing having provision for either one MG FF or one MG 17. Initial firing trials at Travemünde had to be aborted when the rivets for the mounting fixtures of the MG FF came loose due

The Bf 109 V7 was one of the Bf 109s despatched to the International Air Meeting in Zurich. (*Wolfgang Mühlbauer/DEHLA Archives*)

to the heavy recoil of the cannon. The problem was quickly solved by replacing the rivets with bolts. Continued trials showed little problem when firing the guns in level flight, but in the end, the cannon mounting had to be redesigned. Subsequently, the MG 17 became the standard armament for the Bf 109B and C, with a few of the latter being modified to carry two wing-mounted MG FF cannons.

The Bf 109 V13 was specially modified for an attempt at capturing the world speed record, which at the time was held by US billionaire Howard Hughes. Hughes had obtained an average speed of 567.115 kph over a 3-km course in his Hughes H-1 racer. The Bf 109 V13 was similar in most respects to the Bf 109B, albeit lacking armament and being powered by a specially modified DB 601 A engine designated as the DB 601/III 'Renmotor' ('racing engine'). Following its appearance at the International Air Meeting in Zurich, preparations began in earnest at capturing the world speed record. In order to obtain the optimal aerodynamic performance and achieve maximum speed, all joints were smoothed.

On 11 November 1937, Dipl. Ing. Hermann Wurster performed the four flights required by the Federation Aviation Internationale (FAI) between Augsburg and Buchloe. Wurster averaged a speed of 610.950 kph, beating Hughes by a substantial margin. German authorities claimed that Wurster had been flying a B.F. 113R, powered by a 950-hp DB 600. Wurster went on to make a further eight (unsuccessful) attempts in December 1937 and January 1938 at breaking his own record. The Bf 109 V13 was used in coolant system trials for the Me 209 racer. On 30 November 1938, the aircraft was handed over to an Aviation Technical College at Munich.

Similarly to the Bf 109 V13, the Bf 109 V14 began life as a standard Bf 109B airframe. However, as it was selected to appear in Zurich to participate in the short circuit speed competition, it was fitted with the 1,565-hp DB 601 Renmotor II. At the event, the Bf 109 was flown by Ernst Udet, although he had to force-land due to engine problems.

The record-breaking Bf 109 V13. (*Wolfgang Mühlbauer/DEHLA Archives*)

Several more Bf 109s were eventually used, both before and during the war, for test and development of successive variants, as well as armament, engine, propeller, pressure cabin, and various ancillary equipment trials.

Early Bf 109 Prototypes					
	W Nr	Registration	Date of First Flight	Engine	Remarks
Bf 109 V1	758	D-IABI	29 May 1935	Rolls-Royce Kestrel V	Scrapped
Bf 109 V2	809	D-IILU	12 Dec. 1935	Jumo 210 A	Written off at Travemünde 1 Apr. 1936
Bf 109 V3	810	D-IOQY	8 Apr. 1936	Jumo 210 C	Bf 109A prototype. Armed with two MG 17s. To Spain
Bf 109 V4	878	D-IALY	23 Sep. 1936	Jumo 210 B	Bf 109B prototype. Armed with two MG 17s. To Spain
Bf 109 V5	879	D-IIGO	5 Nov. 1936	Jumo 210 B	
Bf 109 V6	880	D-IHHB	11 Nov. 1936	Jumo 210 D	To Spain. Written off 11 Feb. 1937
Bf 109 V7	881	D-IJHA	5 Nov. 1936	Jumo 210 G	Participated in International Air Meeting at Zurich
Bf 109 V8	882	D-IMQE	29 Dec. 1936	Jumo 210 D/ DB 600	Armed with two MG 17s
Bf 109 V9	1056	D-IPLU	23 Jul. 1937	Jumo 210 G	Participated in International Air Meeting at Zurich
Bf 109 V10	1010	D-IAKO	Oct. 1937 (unconfirmed date)	Jumo 210 D	
Bf 109 V11	1012	D-IFMO	1 Mar. 1937	Jumo 210 D	Armed with four MG 17s

Bf 109 V12	1016	D-IVRU	13 Mar. 1937	Jumo 210 D	Armed with three MG 17s and one MG FF
Bf 109 V13	1050	D-IPKY	10 July 1937	DB 601/III	Participated in International Air Meeting at Zurich
Bf 109 V14	1029	D-ISLU	28 Apr. 1937	DB 601/III	Participated in International Air Meeting at Zurich

In December 1936, three prototypes—the V3, V4, and V6—were sent to Spain for operational evaluation. Initially this proved problematic, with the Bf 109V3 suffering damage during its first post-assembly flight. On 14 January 1937, Hannes Trautloft flew the first operational sortie. By the end of the month, the Bf 109V3 and V4 were returned to Germany.

Public Demonstrations

At the time, the deployment of Bf 109s to Spain remained largely unknown. As mentioned previously, the first occasion that foreigners, and indeed the German general public, had a brief opportunity to view the Bf 109 was during the 1936 Berlin Olympics. This public demonstration, however, consisted of an overflight.

For the inauguration of Budapest-Budaörs airport on 20 June 1937, a hastily assembled nine-aircraft Bf 109 display team was assembled. Led by Maj. von Janson of the RLM, the pilots had had virtually no time to rehearse prior to the display. During take-off, the canopy of one of the Bf 109s was torn off, leaving eight aircraft to attempt a formation looping. This failed miserably, with the German fighters being barely visible to the assembled crowd. The following day, all nine Bf 109s were flown back to Bad Aibling.

The fourth International Air Meeting, held at Zurich-Dübendorf in Switzerland between 23 July and 1 August 1937, finally gave the world its first up-close view of the Messerschmitt fighter. A total of five Bf 109s were sent to Dübendorf, including the V7, V8, and V9 prototypes, all powered by the Jumo 210Ga; and the Bf 109V 13 (D-IPKY) and V 14 (D-ISLU), both powered by specially modified racing engines. After the latter was written off on 27 July, a Bf 109B-1 was sent to Switzerland as replacement.

Compared with the British Hawker Fury, the Czech Avia B.534, and the Italian Fiat CR.32, the Bf 109 appeared both frail and futuristic. In the end, the overall performance of the various German aircraft, and the Bf 109 in particular, participating

Bf 109 V14 D-ISLU seen at Dübendorf. (*Wolfgang Mühlbauer/DEHLA Archives*)

in the International Air Meeting showed a clear edge over aircraft from all other nations. The Germans publicly boasted that the Bf 109 was already in large-scale operational service with the Luftwaffe—an outright propaganda lie that remained unchallenged by gullible journalists. Although Bf 109s were serving in Spain, only three Luftwaffe units, I./JG 132, II./JG 132, and I./JG 234, had taken delivery of Bf 109s. None of these units had, however, attained full operational strength.

Interestingly, the Bf 109 was challenged in the short circuit speed competition by a British aircraft, the Percival Mew Gull racer, flown by Charles Gardner. Apart from the short circuit speed competition, Gardner was to participate in the dive competition as well. However, due to the Bf 109s being more powerful, Gardner opted out of the latter. The race took place on 23 July. The pair of Bf 109's were flown by Ernst Udet in D-ISLU (Bf 109 V14) and Karl Francke in D-IJNA (Bf 109 V7), with the latter being added to the race at the last minute. Flight International reported:

> The speed race was something of a flop. At the last minute, there being only two entrants—Gardner with his Mew, and Col. Udet in his 950-hp BFW Me 109—the Germans had asked that a second BFW should be entered, this time with a 640-hp Junkers Diesel. Gardner could hardly refuse such a request, so we had two up-to-the-minute fighters matched against one 200-hp civil racer. As it happened Col. Udet (in Bf 109 V14) dropped out with throttle trouble and the last-minute entry, flown by Karl Francke (in Bf 109 V7), came in to win over a 125-mile course of four local circuits at an average speed of 255 mph—probably well throttled back.[9]

The climb and dive competition section took place on 27 July and involved climbing to an altitude of 3,000 metres and then diving rapidly before flying across the finishing line at an altitude of between 100 and 400 metres. Flying the

The wreck of D-ISLU. Amazingly, Ernst Udet walked away only with bruises. (*Wolfgang Mühlbauer/DEHLA Archives*)

Bf 109 V13, Carl Francke reached 3,200 metres in 105 seconds before a power dive. Francke's total time was two minutes and 5.7 seconds, which secured first place.

Bf 109s were also flown to victory in an Alpine 367 km circuit race on 27 July, with Maj. Hans Seidemann flying the Bf 109 V9 to first place in the 'A' Category (single-seat aircraft) of the race, with his winning time being fifty-six minutes and 47.1 seconds. During the race, Ernst Udet had to force-land near Thun due to a broken oil line. The Bf 109 V14 was wrecked, but Udet only suffered a bruised shoulder. The 'C' Category (three-aircraft formation flight), held two days later on 29 July, saw Hptm Restemeier (Bf 109 V7), Oblt Trautloft (Bf 109 V9), and Oblt Schleif (Bf 109B) secure a victory over the Czech Air Force team's Avia B.534s by a narrow margin. During the race, one of the German pilots experienced engine problems, forcing the other two to throttle back in order to retain formation.

When the International Air Meeting ended on 1 August, the new Bf 109 had emerged as the clear winner, beating the fighters of all other nations. It was obvious that the Luftwaffe had begun re-equipping with the world's best single-seat fighter.

The following year, two US pilots were allowed to fly the Bf 109. On 15 July 1938, the US pilot Al Williams visited Kassel, where Fieseler was churning out Bf 109s. Williams, a former US Marine Corps and air-racing pilot, was touring Europe promoting the petrol company Gulf flying a Grumman Gulfhawk. Being on friendly terms with Ernst Udet, Williams was given the opportunity to fly a Bf 109D. Williams later wrote a detailed account on his impressions of the German fighter:

> For the first take-off, I had set the flaps at about 15 degrees to facilitate the take-off. On the way in for a landing I found that 20 degrees on the flaps was a more suitable angle of attack. The controls, sensitive ailerons, and tail group were fully effective to the time the wheels touched. So much for that. This, after all, was supposed to be an outstanding single-seat fighter, and in the half hour allowed me, I was determined to find out if the Messerschmitt was or was not what it was cracked up to be.
>
> The most delightful features of the Messerschmitt were, first, in spite of its remarkably sensitive reaction to the controls, the ship showed no disposition to wander or 'yaw' as we call it; neither was there any tendencies to 'hunt'. It was a ship where the touch of a pianist could be in keeping with the finesse of the response. And, likewise, I am sure that any ham-handed pilot who handled the controls in brutal fashion would soon be made to feel ashamed of himself. Seldom do we find a single-seater that does not stiffen up on the controls as the ship is pushed to and beyond its top speed.
>
> The longer one is at the flying business, the more firmly convinced he becomes that he knows very little about it. I must say, however, the Messerschmitt Me 109 is the finest airplane I have ever flown.[10]

Williams also mentioned that he considered the Bf 109 superior to all other single-seat fighters, also noting its ease of maintenance. He was told that an engine could be changed in twelve minutes—an incredible achievement when considering that changing the engine of a US combat aircraft would require between twenty-four and thirty-six hours.

During a visit to Germany in October 1938, the world famous pilot Charles Lindbergh was given the Grand Tour of the BFW factory at Augsburg. Accompanied by a French test pilot, Détroyat, Lindbergh was only allowed to fly the Bf 108. The problem was, apparently, that the Germans would not grant Détroyat an air test of the Bf 109 and thus had to decline Lindbergh the opportunity as well. However, on 21 October, Lindbergh finally got his hands on a Bf 109 at Rechlin (with Détroyat not present) later commenting:

> The plane handled beautifully. I spent a quarter of an hour familiarizing myself with the instruments and controls, then spent fifteen minutes more doing manoeuvres of various types—rolls, dives, Immelmanns, etc. After half an hour I landed, took off again, circled the field, and landed a second time. Then I taxied back to the line. The Bf 109 takes off and lands as easily as it flies.[11]

By the time Williams and Lindbergh flew the Bf 109, the fighter was already in large-scale service with the Luftwaffe. Within a few months, the first Bf 109Es would roll off the assembly line.

Technical Description

This technical description is based on the Bf 109G, although most of the features apply for all major production variants.

The Messerschmitt Bf 109 was a single-seat fighter, featuring an enclosed cockpit and retractable undercarriage. It was of all-metal stressed-skin construction and could be built within 4,000 to 6,000 man hours, which thus suited the aircraft for mass production. The high wing loading was offset by means of slats fitted to the forward leading edge of each wing.

Fuselage

The fuselage consisted of three sections—front fuselage, rear fuselage, and tail section—all held together by flush 120° rivets. The engine bearers, firewall, and support for the machine gun mountings were fitted to the front and upper section of the front fuselage. A centre spar bearer was fitted to the lower end of the engine firewall, onto which, by means of two tubular struts, the main undercarriage legs were fitted. An air intake was fitted to the left-hand side of the front fuselage (on variants operating in desert climates, a sand filter was fitted onto the air intake).

The cockpit area contained the pilot's seat, instrument panel, windscreen, and canopy, which opened to the right. The cockpit was unpressurised. In case of an emergency, the canopy could be jettisoned. The cockpit floor, upon which the pilot's seat was fitted, was mounted onto the spar centre section and connected to the fuselage by means of riveted brackets. The rear fuselage consisted of two halves each made up of seven sections, which were joined together at the upper and lower joints by longerons.

The front section of the rear fuselage contained the fuel tank, radio, oxygen, and compressed air bottles, as well as a small luggage compartment containing a tool kit, engine starting handle, and emergency rations. The rear fuselage was covered by an outer 0.8-mm aluminium metal skin. The even-numbered fuselage skin panels were flanged in front and to the rear onto which the odd-numbered panels were riveted. Remarkably, the rear fuselage section remained essentially similar throughout the production life of the Bf 109.

The tail section was bolted onto the rear fuselage, supporting the stabiliser, elevators, fin, and rudder. Due to the need to counteract engine torque during take-offs and landings, the fin had an asymmetric aerodynamic profile. The tail section also housed the tailwheel and its supporting components.

Wings

The wings had solid main and auxiliary spars onto which the ribs were riveted. The wing main spar consisted of two beams that were riveted to a duraluminium plate, forming a section. The outer dural sheet skin was flush riveted to the spars. The wing-fuselage attachment points were constructed out of steel and flush riveted to the lower and upper spar flanges. The wings contained recesses for the main undercarriage wheels, as well as undercarriage strut channels, which allowed the undercarriage to be completely retracted following take-off.

Ailerons and flaps were fitted to the trailing edge of the wings, with slats being mounted on the forward leading edges. The wings also contain radiators, machine guns, and ammunition compartments. Ease of access was achieved with a number of removable hatches.

Undercarriage

The main undercarriage consisted of a pair of cantilever oleo all-metal struts, which were fitted to the lower section of the centre fuselage, retracting outwardly into the wings. Undercarriage fairings were mounted to the inner side of each oleo strut. When retracted, the undercarriage was held in place by means of an uplock system, which, when retraction was complete, engaged a catch within the wheel bay.

In case of hydraulic failure, the undercarriage could be lowered by means of an emergency handle. When pulling the handle, the catches were released by means of a cable, and the undercarriage would lower and lock into position under its own weight. The rear fixed wheel undercarriage was fitted in the rear fuselage—on some variants, the rear wheel was retractable.

Propeller

A three-blade all-metal variable pitch propeller, built by VDM, was fitted, onto which a spinner was mounted. The pitch of the propeller could be controlled by the pilot by means of an electrical switch mounted on the engine throttle.

Electrical and Hydraulic Systems

A 24-volt electrical system, powered by means of a battery, was fitted in the rear fuselage. Electrically operated systems included the propeller pitch, armament, fuel pump, engine monitoring, flight monitoring, and navigational gear. The hydraulic system was used to operate the undercarriage, brakes, radiator flaps, and oil-cooler flap by means of a hydraulic pump fitted inside the rear fuselage.

Competitors

Apart from the Bf 109, three more fighter aircraft prototypes were built: the Arado Ar 80, the Focke-Wulf Fw 159, and the Heinkel He 112.

Ar 80

At the time, Arado was one of the few aircraft manufacturers in Germany experienced in fighter aircraft design. The Ar 65 was the first fighter of the reformed Luftwaffe, while the Ar 68 would remain in service until the early stages of the Second World War. Both the Ar 65 and Ar 68 were single-seat open-cockpit biplanes armed with a pair of rifle-calibre machine guns—essentially similar to the biplanes that had seen service during the Great War.

Designed by Dipl. Ing. Walter Blume, the Ar 80 was an open cockpit, fixed undercarriage inverted gull-wing monoplane of all-metal monocoque construction.

The intended power plant for the production Ar 80 was a 600-hp Junkers Jumo 210C. An inspection full-scale wooden mock-up of the Ar 80 took place in July 1934. However, the Ar 80 V1 (registered as D-IRLI) was powered by a Rolls-Royce Kestrel VI engine—the same engine that had powered the Ar 67a fighter prototype. It had been intended to fit a retractable undercarriage, but instead a conventional fixed, spatted undercarriage was fitted due to various issues. The Ar 80 V1 was flown in March 1935 and destroyed in a crash soon afterwards. During its few flights, it was discovered that the aircraft was underpowered as well as suffering from excessive drag. Additionally, the airframe structure was heavier than expected.

Arado Ar 80 D-ILOH. (*Arlanda Civil Aviation Collection*)

A second prototype, the Ar 80 V2 (D-ILOH), was powered by a 695-hp Rolls-Royce Kestrel V inline engine. The Ar 80 V2 had been modified with an enclosed cockpit. Although flight tests proved disappointing, the Ar 80 V2 achieved a maximum speed of 410 kph at an altitude of 4,000 metres. It was clear that the Ar 80 stood no chance against the Bf 109 and He 112. Although the Ar 80 V2 was unarmed, it was proposed that a future production variant would be armed with two 7.92 mm MG 17s.

When a Jumo 210 C engine finally became available, this was immediately fitted to the Ar 80 V2. The more powerful Jumo 210 C gave the Ar 80 a higher service ceiling, although at a cost of lower performance characteristics at low altitude and an inferior rate of climb when compared to the Kestrel-powered aircraft. The Ar 80 V2 was thoroughly evaluated, but it was clear that it was out of the fighter competition.

Nevertheless, three additional Ar 80 prototypes were completed. The Ar 80 V3 (D-IPBN) featured a modified straight wing with dihedral. Powered by a Jumo 210 C, the Ar 80 V3 was eventually converted into a two-seat test bed. These tests included firing a 20-mm cannon through the propeller spinner. It was also used for Fowler flaps trials, which were intended for the Ar 240. The final two Ar 80s were the V4 (D-INEI, later reregistered as D-ILNI) and the V5 (D-IROK).

Arado Ar 80 V3 Technical Data and Performance Characteristics
Engine: 1 × 620-hp Junkers Jumo 210 C
Wingspan: 11.80 metres
Length: 10.10 metres
Height: 2.95 metres
Track width: N/A
Wing area: 21.0 m^2
Weight, empty: 1,645 kg
Weight, maximum: 2,100 kg
Maximum speed: 425 kph
Range: 600 km
Service ceiling: 10,000 m
Armament: N/A

Fw 159

The worst of the lot was the Focke-Wulf Fw 159. A parasol-wing monoplane, the Fw 159 featured an enclosed canopy and a retractable undercarriage; it seemed both fragile and anachronistic. Designed by Robert Blaser, the Fw 159 was similar to the company's earlier Fw 56 Stösser (Falcon) single-engine lightweight fighter.[12]

Focke-Wulf Fw 159 D-IUPY. (*Arlanda Civil Aviation Collection*)

Focke-Wulf had only received an order to develop a new fighter in September 1934, which made it difficult to achieve the ready-to-inspect date of June 1935. Nevertheless, the first Fw 159 prototype flew in November 1935. Problems arose immediately when one of the undercarriage legs refused to extend. The pilot, *Flugkapitän* Wolfgang Stein, managed to get the Fw 159 down in one piece, but was slightly injured in the crash. The second prototype, the Fw 159V2 (D-INGA), featured a strengthened undercarriage. Nevertheless, the undercarriage continued to cause severe problems. The delicate and complicated undercarriage of the Fw 159 would, incidentally, have caused severe difficulties under field conditions. A third prototype, the Fw 159V3 (D-IUPY), was built, being powered by a 600-hp Jumo 210 B engine. However, it was apparent that the Fw 159 was a non-starter.

Interestingly, a developed variant, designated the Fw 259, was announced. The Fw 259 was to be powered by a DB 601 engine. Unsurprisingly, no Fw 259s were built.

Focke-Wulf Fw 159V2 Technical Data and Performance Characteristics
Engine: 1 × 680-hp Junkers Jumo 210Da engine
Wingspan: 12.40 metres
Length: 9.77 metres
Height: 3.75 metres
Track width: N/A
Wing area: 20.2 m²
Weight, empty: 1,875 kg
Weight, maximum: 2,250 kg
Maximum speed: 405 kph at 4,500 metres
Range: 650 km
Service ceiling: 7,200 metres
Armament: 2 × 7.92-mm MG 17s

He 112

Designed by Dipl. Ing. Heinrich Hertel, the Heinkel He 112 was initially seen to have the best chance of securing the RLM contract for a new Luftwaffe fighter. Of an all-metal monocoque construction, the He 112 had a retractable undercarriage but did not feature an enclosed cockpit. The He 112 retained the trademark elliptical wing shape of the He 70 and He 111.

A wooden full-scale mock-up of the He 112 was inspected by RLM officials in October 1934. Powered by a 695-hp Rolls-Royce Kestrel V engine, the He 112 V1 (D-IADO) was first flown in September 1935. The He 112 had excellent flight characteristics, although drag was higher than anticipated.

A second prototype, the He 112 V2 (D-IHGE), had a reduced wingspan, and was followed by the third prototype (D-IDMO) which was the first to be fitted with armament, consisting of two 7.92-mm MG 17s. A further five He 112 prototypes were built, with the He 112 V4 (D-IZMY) being considered as the production prototype for the proposed He 112A series. In all, eight prototypes were built.

In the event, and to almost everyone's surprise, the Bf 109 was selected as the Luftwaffe's new fighter. Having lost the competition, Heinkel received permission to produce He 112s for export.

Despite the fact that the He 112 had lost against the Bf 109, the He 112 V4 was despatched to Spain for operational evaluation. Its twin 20-mm cannon armament earned the He 112 V4 the nickname *Kanonenvogel* (literally, 'cannon bird'). Attached to 2./J88, the Heinkel fighter was written off in an accident in July 1937. Following the selection of the Bf 109 as the Luftwaffe's new fighter, the basic He 112A was completely redesigned. Powered by a 680-hp Jumo 210Ea engine, the He 112 V9 was the prototype for the He 112B, which proved to be faster than the Bf 109B-1 then entering Luftwaffe service. An order for thirty He 112Bs was subsequently placed by the Imperial Japanese Naval Air Force, with the initial twelve shipped to Japan in early 1938.

However, the second batch of twelve was pressed into Luftwaffe service due to the Sudeten Crisis. Briefly serving with III./JG 132, the Heinkel fighters were highly regarded by the Luftwaffe pilots. Both I. and II./JG 132 were operating Bf 109Cs, which were considered inferior in most respects. In the event, the He 112s were returned to Heinkel for resale soon after the signing of the Munich Peace Agreement. Meanwhile, the Japanese had chosen to cancel the contract for the remaining He 112s. Compared with indigenous fighters such as the Mitsubishi A5M, the He 112B was markedly less manoeuvrable. Seventeen of the He 112s were eventually sold to Spain, where they remained in service until after the end of the Second World War. Two other countries ordered the He 112B, Hungary and Romania, with the latter committing its twenty-four aircraft into combat on the Eastern Front.

A total of ninety-eight He 112s, including prototypes, were built. None exist today, although a full-scale wooden replica can be seen at a US aviation museum.

Heinkel He 112 V4 Technical Data and Performance Characteristics
Engine: 1 × 690-hp Jumo 210Da
Wingspan: 11.50 metres
Length: 9.00 metres
Height: 3.70 metres
Track width: N/A
Wing area: 23.20 m^2
Weight, empty: 1,680 kg
Weight, maximum: 2,230 kg
Maximum speed: 488 kph at 3,500 metres
Range: N/A
Service ceiling: 8,000 metres
Armament: N/A

2

Variations on a Theme

Nine Bf 109 basic variants entered production—the Bf 109A, B, C, D, E, F, G, K, and T respectively—with more than 100 sub-variants of the Bf 109G alone appearing through factory or field modification kits. The following is a brief run-through of the different Bf 109 variants.

Bf 109A (*Anton*)

The initial production variant was the Bf 109A. As related earlier, the Bf 109 V3 served as the series prototype for the Bf 109A. A total of 19 Bf 109As were delivered in January and March 1937. All aircraft were issued with civilian registrations; D-IIBA (W Nr 808), D-IUDE (809), D-IHNY (810), D-ITGE (883), D-IXZA (884), D-IMRY (994), D-IPLA (995), D-IVSE (996), D-IZQE (997), D-IMTY (1000), D-IPSA (1001), D-IMQU (1002), D-IVTO (1003), D-ILZY (1004), D-IJFY (1005), D-IBLE (1006), D-IHDU (1007), D-IYTY (1008) and D-IOMY (1009). The Bf 109As were armed with a pair of MG 17s and also offered provision for five SC 10 bombs. Fifteen Bf 109As were supplied to Spain during the spring of 1937.

Bf 109B (*Berta*)

The Bf 109B was the first variant to enter large-scale production. Many books and articles claim that two sub-variants, the B-1 and B-2, were produced, with one source stating that a small number of Bf 109B-0 pre-production aircraft powered by the Jumo 210 B were built. One Bf 109B-0 (W Nr 1114) was written off at Müritz on 17 July 1937, killing its pilot, Dr Kurt Jodlbauer.

An early Bf 109B, clearly identifiable by the huge, wooden two-blade propeller. (*NMUSAF*)

Contemporary German sources do not differentiate between a Bf 109B-1 and B-2, referring instead to it as the Bf 109B, although numerous publications refer to two different sub-variants of the basic Bf 109B.

Entering production in February 1937, with initial deliveries to JG 132 and *Legion Condor* in Spain, the Bf 109B was at the time the most modern fighter in the world. Powered by a Jumo 210 D, the initial Bf 109B production batch featured a two-blade wooden propeller built by Schwarz, later replaced by a two-blade VDM constant-speed metal propeller. Other distinguishing features of early and late-production aircraft was that the former had engine exhaust stubs that were flush with the cowling, while the underwing oil coolant intake was moved slightly outboard on late-production aircraft.

The armament of the Bf 109B consisted of a pair of MG 17s, each with 500 rounds, mounted in the upper forward fuselage, with aiming performed through a reflector gun sight. A third MG 17, firing through the propeller spinner, was often removed in service as this machine gun suffered from both overheating and jamming. An additional problem was the excessive vibration caused when firing the gun. One novelty was a FuG 7 radio.

The Bf 109B was the first monoplane fighter in large-scale service with the Luftwaffe. A total of 341 Bf 109Bs were built by BFW, Erla and Fieseler, with production ending in early 1938. Apart serving with Luftwaffe fighter units, a few Bf 109Bs were transferred to the *Kriegsmarine* in 1938 for evaluation as carrier-based fighters. With the end of the Spanish Civil War, the remaining *Legion Condor* Bf 109B's were transferred to the *Ejercito del Aire.* A single Bf 109B was also delivered to Slovakia for training purposes. By September 1939, the Bf 109B had been completely withdrawn from front-line service, although many continued in use as advanced trainers. On 1 May 1940, there were 214 Bf 109Bs in Luftwaffe service, with another fifty-seven undergoing repairs.

Messerschmitt Bf 109B Technical Data and Performance Characteristics
Engine: 1 × 680-hp Junkers Jumo 210 D
Wingspan: 9.90 metres
Length: 8.70 metres
Height: 2.45 metres
Track width: 2.00 metres
Wing area: 16.40 m^2
Weight, empty: 1,432 kg
Weight, maximum: 1,955 metres
Maximum speed: 460 kph
Range: 530 km
Service ceiling: 8,750 metres
Armament: 2 or 3 × 7.92-mm MG 17s

Bf 109C (*Clara*)

The Bf 109C-1 can best be described as an interim variant. The Bf 109V8 served as the pre-series prototype for the Bf 109C. Powered by a Jumo 210 Ga, the first Bf 109Cs rolled off the BFW factory at Augsburg. Only fifty-eight Bf 109C-1s were built, with twenty-seven delivered by 31 March 1938. A few received strengthened armament and were designated Bf 109C-3s. Five Bf 109Cs were sent to Spain and used by the *Legion Condor*. By 1939, most of the Bf 109Cs had been transferred to second-line units, with some aircraft being relegated for use as decoys. On 1 May 1940, thirty-seven Bf 109Cs remained in Luftwaffe service, with an additional eight undergoing repair.

A Bf 109C seen during pre-war manoeuvres. The Luftwaffe mechanics were commonly known as '*Schwartze Männer*'. ('black men') due to the colour of their uniforms. (*NMUSAF*)

Bf 109C variants

The Bf 109C-1 was a sole production variant, armed with four 7.92-mm MG 17s.

The Bf 109C-2 was a proposed variant with an additional centrally-mounted MG 17.

A few Bf 109C-1s were upgraded to Bf 109C-3 status (one being W Nr 1722), with the wing-mounted MG 17s being replaced by two 20-mm MG FFs (sixty rounds each).

The Bf 109C-4 was a proposed variant with a centrally-mounted 20-mm MG FF cannon.

Messerschmitt Bf 109C-1 Technical Data and Performance Characteristics
Engine: 1 × 730-hp Jumo 210 Ga
Wingspan: 9.87 metres
Length: 8.55 metres
Height: 2.45 metres
Track width: N/a
Wing area: 16.17 m^2
Weight, empty: 1,597 kg
Weight, maximum: 2,296 kg
Maximum speed: 470 kph at 4,500 metres
Range: 625 km
Service ceiling: 9,500 metres
Armament: 4 × 7.92-mm MG 17s

Bf 109D (*Dora*)

Entering production at the same time as the Bf 109C, the Bf 109D was essentially similar to the earlier variant. One difference was that the tail wheel assembly was redesigned, with the Bf 109D also having provision for a flare gun on the right hand side of the canopy that could be fired and reloaded by the pilot. It had originally been intended that the Bf 109D would be powered by the DB 601, however, due to development problems, the Bf 109D had to revert to using the Jumo 210 Da. There was only one Bf 109D production model: the Bf 109D-1.

Five Bf 109D-1s were sent to Spain in 1938 for combat evaluation. A large number of Bf 109Ds were still in service with front-line fighter squadrons in September 1939 and saw service during the Polish campaign and the 'Phoney War' on the Western Front. However, by May 1940 only a few Bf 109D-1s remained in front-line service. Many were eventually transferred to second-line units and used as advanced trainers by various A/B *Schulen* (flight training schools). Most of the Bf 109D-1s still in service had the Jumo 210 Da engine exhaust collectors replaced by units identical to those fitted to the DB 601 engine.

An excellent pre-war photo of a Bf 109D-1. (*ETH Archives*)

A Bf 109D-1. (or possibly a Bf 109C) seen following a belly landing. (*NMUSAF*)

An air-to-air view of a Bf 109D-1. Note the large, pre-war swastika. (*NMUSAF*)

A total of 647 Bf 109D-1s were built by AGO, Arado BFW, Erla, and Focke-Wulf. Some 139 had been built until 31 March 1938, with production ending in late 1938. A few Bf 109D-1s were delivered to Hungary and Switzerland. On 1 May 1940, 440 Bf 109D-1s remained on charge with the Luftwaffe, with another 115 being unserviceable.

Messerschmitt Bf 109D-1 Technical Data and Performance Characteristics
Engine: 1 × 680-hp Jumo 210 Da
Wingspan: 9.90 metres
Length: 8.70 metres
Height: 2.50 metres
Track width: 2.00 metres
Wing area: 16.40 m²
Weight, empty: 1,760 kg
Weight, maximum: 2,424 kg
Maximum speed: 450 kph at 3,000 metres
Range: N/a
Service ceiling: 10,000 metres
Armament: 4 × 7.92-mm MG 17s

Bf 109E (*Emil*)

The Bf 109E can be described as the first mature Bf 109 variant. In 1938 and 1939, the Bf 109E was arguably the best single-seat fighter in the world. It was also the first production variant to be powered by the DB 601 engine.

The DB 601 was a liquid-cooled twelve-cylinder inverted Vee engine, which had a mechanical direct fuel injection that negated the need for a carburettor, which meant that fuel continued to be supplied to the engine even during negative *g*-forces, unlike the Rolls-Royce Merlin. The DB 601 also had other distinct advantages, including better fuel economy, and the ability to run on inferior fuel. During take-off, the DB 601 A was rated at 1,050 hp and at 1,100 hp at an altitude of 2,700 metres. Apart from the Bf 109E and F series, variants of the DB 601 engine also powered early variants of the Bf 110 twin-engine heavy fighter. In all, some 19,000 DB 601 engines were built between 1937 and 1943, with it also being produced under licence in Italy and Japan.

The first series Bf 109E-1s rolled off the assembly line in November 1938 having been preceded by an initial batch of ten pre-series Bf 109E-0s. Many of the early production aircraft were supplied to Spain, with others being sold to Switzerland and Yugoslavia. Apart from production by BFW and Messerschmitt, the Bf 109E was built by AGO, Arado, Focke-Wulf, Erla, and WNF, with production totals slightly more than 3,500.

In 1940, the Bf 109E effectively ruled the skies over Europe, only being rivalled by the Supermarine Spitfire and, to a lesser extent, the Hawker Hurricane.

Bf 109s undergoing maintenance. (*NMUSAF*)

An early production Bf 109E seen early in the war. The jumping ferret insignia indicates that the aircraft belongs to 8./JG 51. (*NMUSAF*)

Operational experience over France and Britain in 1940 had made it clear that the Bf 109E was seriously lacking in range, as well as suffering from inadequate armour protection for the pilot. As a result, provision for an external drop tank was introduced in late 1940.

Specific fighter-bomber and reconnaissance variants were built. The Bf 109E remained in production until early 1941, with many aircraft being modified through factory or field modification kits. These included variants powered by the DB 601 N engine and fitted with the GM-1 engine boost system while others were modified for tropical (desert) operations. By the following year, the Bf 109E had virtually disappeared from Luftwaffe front-line service. Many Bf 109E's were supplied to Germany's allies. Following the end of the war, a small batch of Bf 109E's were built in Switzerland.

Bf 109E Production Variants

The pre-series batch of Bf 109E-0s numbered ten aircraft. The ten Bf 109E-0s, and the first four Bf 109E-1s, featured an elongated air intake cover, with the engine nozzles being similar to those fitted to the Jumo 210 engine.

The Bf 109E-1 initial production variant was armed with four MG 17s

The Bf 109E-3 was armed with two MG 17s and three MG FFs, with one firing through the propeller spinner

The Bf 109E-3a was the export designation for the Bf 109E-3 (Switzerland and Yugoslavia).

The Bf 109E-4 featured a strengthened canopy framing and armoured head rest.

The Bf 109E-5 reconnaissance aircraft was based on the Bf 109E-1 and powered by the DB 601 A. Provision was made for one Rb21/18 camera.

The Bf 109E-6 reconnaissance aircraft was based on the Bf 109E-1. Powered by the DB 601 N, it included provision for two HK 12.5/7 × 9 motorised hand cameras.

The Bf 109E-7 fighter-bomber (*Jabo*) had the provision for a 300-litre drop tank or ETC 500 bomb rack.

The Bf 109E-8 fighter was based on the Bf 109E-1. It had increased range and armour protection and was powered by the DB 601 E.

The Bf 109E-9 reconnaissance aircraft was similar to the Bf 109E-6 in that it offered provision for one Rb50/30 high-altitude camera and was powered by the DB 601 E.

Factory Modification Designations

The Bf 109E/B fighter-bomber (*Jabo*) had the ability to carry one SC 250 bomb on a centreline bomb rack.

The Bf 109E/BN fighter-bomber (*Jabo*) was similar to the Bf 109E/B, albeit being powered by a DB 601 N.

The Bf 109E/N was powered by a DB 601 N.

The Bf 109E/Z was fitted with a GM-1 boost system. The aircraft were either modified at their respective factories or at the Dortmund modification depot.

The Bf 109E/NZ was similar to the Bf 109E/Z but powered by a DB 601 N.

The Bf 109E trop was fitted with a sand filter for desert operations. Apparently, no such modifications of different Bf 109E sub-variants were made at the respective factories but at various depots instead.

The Bf 109E-7 trop was fitted with tropical equipment for desert operations.

Field Modification Designations

The Bf 109E/U1 featured armoured protection for the radiator.

The Bf 109E/U2 had strengthened armour protection for *Jabo* duties, along with provision for an SG-container.

The Bf 109E/U3 reconnaissance aircraft offered provision for two Rb 12.5/7 x 9 cameras and was also fitted with a FuG 17 radio.

Messerschmitt Bf 109E-3 Technical Data and Performance Characteristics
Engine: 1 × 1,100-hp DB 601 A
Wingspan: 9.85 metres
Length: 8.63 metres
Height: 3.4 metres
Track width: N/a
Wing area: 16.17 m^2
Weight, empty: 2,005 kg
Weight, maximum: 2,505 kg
Maximum speed: 570 kph at 3,800 metres
Range: 663 km
Service ceiling: 11,000 metres
Armament: 2 × 7.92-mm MG 17s, 2 × 20-mm MG FF cannons

Bf 109F (*Friedrich*)

According to some Luftwaffe pilots, the Bf 109F represented the ultimate Bf 109 variant. With a more powerful engine and reduced armament, the performance of the Bf 109F matched that of the Supermarine Spitfire Mk V, and also had the edge over the most modern Russian LAGG-3, MiG-3, and Yak-1 fighters.

Design work on the Bf 109F had already begun in January 1939, with several early-model Bf 109Es assigned for specific equipment tests. The true Bf 109F prototypes were the Bf 109 V24 and Bf 109 V25.

The engine destined for the Bf 109F was the 1,350-hp DB 601 E. In the end, continuous development problems with the DB 601 E meant that the DB 601 N became the standard engine for the initial production batches. The DB 601 N had an output of 1,175 hp, which was essentially similar to the DB 601 A. The main difference lay in the use of higher octane C3 fuel, which allowed for higher compression and resulted in better engine performance for the DB 601 N.

Compared with the earlier Bf 109E, the Bf 109F airframe was aerodynamically refined, including the engine cowling, tail section, and wings. The wingspan of the Bf 109F was slightly larger than on earlier variants due to the rounded wingtips. The tail wheel was semi-retractable, with the lower part of the wheel being visible. To allow cooling of the centrally-mounted cannon, it was originally planned to fit

The Bf 109V23 was used in the Bf 109F development. (*NMUSAF*)

a specially designed ducted propeller spinner. However, in its place, the propeller spinner of the Me 210 was adopted. The armament, initially consisting of MG 17s and one 15-mm MG 151 cannon, was concentrated to the forward fuselage, with the wing guns removed altogether. The MG 151 did, in fact, provide a better punch, rate of fire, and higher muzzle velocity than the higher calibre 20-mm MG FF cannon. All Bf 109F variants had mountings for a 300-litre drop tank to increase range.

A small Bf 109F-0 pre-production batch was built at Regensburg and used for service trials, with at least five being converted from Bf 109Es (W Nr 5601 to 5605). Interestingly, with Hitler deciding to curtail development of all combat aircraft having already convinced himself that the war was won, there followed a delay of several months in the development of the Bf 109F.

Bf 109F Prototypes	**W Nr**	***Stammkennzeichen* (registration)**	**Remarks**
Bf 109 V22	1800	D-IRRQ	Supercharger air intake scoop tests. Powered by a DB 601 A engine
Bf 109 V23	1801	D-ISHN/CE+BP	Powered by a DB 601 E engine. Modified with tri-cycle undercarriage and used in Me 309 tests
Bf 109 V24	1929		Also reported as W Nr 5604
Bf 109 V25	1930	D-IVKC	Engine coolant and oil/fuel systems
Bf 109 V26	5605	VK+AC	Engine coolant and oil/fuel systems

An air-to-air view of two early model Bf 109Fs. (*NMUSAF*)

The initial production variant was the Bf 109F-1, with slightly more than 200 delivered between August 1940 and February 1941. The first Bf 109Fs reached JG 51 during the first days of October 1940. Having a lighter armament than the earlier Bf 109E, many Luftwaffe pilots initially held a low opinion of the new Bf 109 variant. Several early-production Bf 109Fs were lost in what seemed like unexplainable accidents. It was eventually determined that the deletion of the stabiliser struts resulted in the tailplane being weakened to such an extent that it was literally ripped off during high *g* manoeuvres. The solution was to fit two horizontal metal strips being fitted on each side of the tail section.

The Luftwaffe fighter pilots were soon unanimous in their praise of the Bf 109F, although the reduced armament caused Ob Adolf Galland to replace the pair of MG 17s with two MG 131s. Nevertheless, the Bf 109F was the major Luftwaffe single-seat fighter between 1941 and early 1943, seeing service on all fronts. Apart from its main role as a fighter, the Bf 109F was also used as a fighter bomber, reconnaissance aircraft and, during the latter stages of the war, as an advanced trainer. A few Bf 109Fs were delivered to Hungary, Italy, and Spain.

Bf 109F-1

As recorded earlier, the Bf 109F-1 entered limited production in late 1940. As far as is known, there were no Bf 109F-1 sub-variants. Power was provided by a DB 601 N, with the armament consisting of one MG FF/M and two MG 17s.

An early production Bf 109F-1 W Nr 5627. (*NMUSAF*)

Bf 109F-2

The Bf 109F-2 entered production in early 1941 with approximately 1,360 Bf 109F-2s being built. Powered by a DB 601 N, the armament was amended to consist of one MG 151/15 cannon firing through the propeller spinner, and a pair of MG 17s.

Factory Modification Designations

The Bf 109F-2/Z was intended to have the GM-1 boost system installed, but none were built or modified.

Field Modification Designations

The Bf 109F-2/B was able to carry one SC 250 bomb or four SC 50 bombs.

A few Bf 109F-2 trop were retrofitted with supercharger air-intake sand filters for desert operations.

The Bf 109F-2/U1 featured heavier armament consisting of two 13-mm MG 131s and one MG 151/15 cannon. One (W Nr 6750) was used by Oblt Adolf Galland in late 1941.

One Bf 109F-2, coded VD+AJ (W Nr 8195), was experimentally fitted with a ski undercarriage, but it was not adopted for service.

Performance dropped considerably when fitted with skis, which remained an experiment. (*NMUSAF*)

Bf 109F-3

There exists some uncertainty if any Bf 109F-3s were actually built. The C-Amt plan of October 1940 called for fifteen aircraft to be produced by WNF, although it would appear that these were built by BFW at Regensburg instead. Powered by the improved DB 601 E, the armament of the Bf 109F-3 consisted of one MG FF/M and two MG 17s. Some aircraft were delivered to JG 51, which recorded the loss of two Bf 109F-3s in mid-1941. No sub-variants of the Bf 109F-3 are known.

Bf 109F-4

The major production variant of the 'F' series was the Bf 109F-4, with 1,841 being built by Erla and WNF. Apart from the improved DB 601 E engine, there was initially little to differentiate the Bf 109F-4 from the earlier Bf 109F-2. The new engine required a redesign of the supercharger air intake. The MG 151/15 cannon was replaced by a higher calibre MG 151/20 cannon.

Factory Modification Designations

The Bf 109F-4/B was a fighter-bomber variant. One SC 250 bomb or four SC 50 bombs could be carried.

The Bf 109F-4/R1 carried two additional MG 151/15s in underwing pods.

Only five Bf 109F-4/R2 reconnaissance variants were produced, each carrying one Rb 20/30 camera with their radios removed.

Thirty-six Bf 109F-4/R3 reconnaissance variants were built or converted, each carrying carried one Rb 50/30 camera with their radios removed.

Only one Bf 109F-4/R4 reconnaissance variant, carrying one Rb 75/30 camera with the radio removed, was built or converted.

Only one Bf 109F-4/R8 reconnaissance variant, carrying one Rb 75/30 camera with the radio retained, was built or converted.

The Bf 109F-4 trop had a supercharger air-intake sand filter installed for desert operations.

The Bf 109F-4/Z was fitted with a GM-1 boost system.

Field Modification Designations

The Bf 109F-4/U1 was intended to carry two MG 131s instead of two MG 17s.

Only one Bf 109F-5 reconnaissance variant was built.

Additionally, it had been intended that AGO, Arado, BFW, Erla, and WNF would build a total of 1,281 Bf 109F-6s. These plans were cancelled, as was production of the Bf 109F-8, with a total of 1,112 to be manufactured by BFW, Erla, and WNF. By May 1942, production of the Bf 109F came to an end, with deliveries of the first Bf 109G-2s beginning the same month.

Messerschmitt Bf 109F-4 Technical Data and Performance Characteristics
Engine: 1 × 1,350-hp DB 601 E
Wingspan: 9.924 metres
Length: 9.020 metres
Height: 3.2 metres (tail elevated)
Track width: 1.975 metres
Wing area: 16.05 m^2
Weight, empty: 2,020 kg
Weight, maximum: 2,890 kg
Maximum speed: 606 kph
Range: 706 km
Service ceiling: 11,600 metres
Armament: 1 × 20-mm MG 151/20 cannon and 2 × 7.92-mm MG 17s. Additional capability to carry either one SC 250 bomb, four SC 50 bombs, or 96 SD 2 bombs

Bf 109G (*Gustav*)

More than two-thirds of all Bf 109s built were 'G' models, with major production in several sub-variants resulting in more than 22,000 being produced.

Colloquially named *Gustav* by the Luftwaffe fighter pilots, the Bf 109G was the most numerically significant single-seat fighter in Luftwaffe service from early 1943 until the end of the war. It was used on every front, from the Arctic to North Africa, serving with—at one time or another—the majority of the day-fighter units, as well as some night-fighter units. Among the various production variants of the basic Bf 109G were high-altitude fighters (which featured a pressurised cockpit), fighter-bombers, fighter-reconnaissance, and night-fighters.

Throughout its production life, the basic Bf 109G airframe was continuously modified and upgraded, with a wide range of weaponry and specialised gear being fitted to different sub-variants. Compared with the earlier Bf 109F, the Bf 109G was heavier, which reduced overall performance. Nevertheless, the Bf 109G was the aircraft of choice for many of the seasoned Luftwaffe pilots. The even-numbered sub-variants (G-2, G-4, G-6, G-8, G-10, and G-14) were all non-pressurised, while the odd-numbered (G-1, G-3, and G-5) featured a pressurised cockpit—the latter being the only such production aircraft of the entire Bf 109 series. A two-seat advanced training variant was also developed, with some being converted from early Bf 109G variants.

The most numerous of all Bf 109Gs was the Bf 109G-6, which began to reach Luftwaffe fighter units in early 1943. By 1944, the Bf 109G-6 was becoming obsolete and outclassed by most Allied fighters. During the summer of 1944, the Bf 109G-6 began to be replaced by the Bf 109G-14, which was an attempt to introduce a standard production Bf 109G variant incorporating all of the modifications and improvements of the earlier variants. The Bf 109G-10 was introduced during October 1944, being essentially similar to the Bf 109K-4. What follows is a brief overview of the various sub-variants of the Bf 109G.

The most-produced Bf 109 variant, the Bf 109G-6. This particular aeroplane landed landed in error at RAF Manston on 21 July 1944. (*NMUSAF*)

The V-tail as fitted to a Bf 109G-0. (*NMUSAF*)

Bf 109G-0

The trio of prototypes (W Nr 14001 to 14003, coded VJ+WA to VJ+WC) were built at Regensburg in October 1941, with service trials beginning at Rechlin in early 1942 with the *Erprobungsstaffel* Bf 109G. Following completion of the flight trials in July 1942, *Erprobungsstaffel* Bf 109G was disbanded.

With the DB 605 not yet available, the Bf 109G-0s were initially powered by the DB 601E. However, the basic DB 605 would become the standard engine of the Bf 109G and 'K' series, with more than 42,000 DB 605s being produced during the war. One distinguishing feature of the Bf 109G from the G-2 series and onwards was the *Beulen* (literally, 'bumps' or 'boils') fitted on both sides of the upper forward fuselage, covering the MG 151/20 cannon breeches.

One of the Bf 109G prototypes (W Nr 14003) was experimentally fitted with a V-shaped tail section (similar to the post-war Beech Bonanza and the Fouga CM-170 Magister), and subjected to air tests between March and April 1943. The flight characteristics apparently showed a marked inferiority over the standard Bf 109, with the modified aircraft showing a tendency to yaw on take-off. One improvement was a slight increase of speed, although this was insufficient to introduce this modification to production aircraft.

Bf 109G-1

The Bf 109G-1 was produced in limited numbers only, with deliveries beginning in February 1942. Six early-production aircraft were delivered to *Erprobungsstaffel Bf 109G*, with personnel from both Daimler-Benz and I./JG 1 taking part in the evaluation of the new fighter. Operational evaluation was conducted by *ErgänzungJägdguppe* West (EJGr. West). Most Bf 109G-1s were issued to units on the Western Front, including specialised high-altitude *Staffeln*, such as 11./JG 2 and 11./JG 26 for operations against Allied bombers. Some Bf 109G-1s remained in service until early 1943.

Factory Modification Designations

The Bf 109G-1/R2 featured a pressurised cockpit. The armour of the pilot's seat was removed, along with ability to fit an external drop tank. A GM-1 boost system fitted.

Bf 109G-2

The Bf 109G-2 was the first major production variant to see operational service on every front. The Bf 109G-2 lacked cockpit pressurisation, as well as the GM-1 engine boost fittings. A small air intake for cockpit ventilation was fitted on each side of the front fuselage. It was also the first variant to be fitted with the *Beulen* on the fuselage. Entering service in the summer of 1942, the Bf 109G-2 had been largely supplanted by early 1944. One unit, JG 5, operated Bf 109G-2s as late as November 1944.

Factory Modification Designations

The Bf 109G-2/R1 fighter-bomber had the provision for two 300-litre drop tanks carried underneath the wings. Provision was also made for an ETC 500 IXb bomb rack carrying one SC 250 bomb beneath the centre fuselage.

The Bf 109G-2/R2 reconnaissance aircraft was fitted with a GM-1 boost system. One of four different cameras could be carried: the Rb 75 cm × 30 cm, Rb cm 50 × 30 cm, 20 cm × 30 cm, or 12.5/7 cm × 9 cm

The Bf 109G-2/R3 had increased range.

The Bf 109G-2/R6 had increased armament, consisting of two underwing MG 151/20 machine gun pods.

The Bf 109G-2 trop was equipped with a supercharger air-intake sand filter on the left-hand side of the engine cowling for desert operations. Each Bf 109G-2 trop also had a so-called *Sonderwerkzeug* ('special tool') consisting of two small fittings that could be attached to the left side of the cockpit, onto which an umbrella was fitted. The umbrella was an absolutely necessity to give the pilot some shade from the hot desert sun.

Field Modification Designations

The Bf 109G-2/U1 was to have been fitted with the Me P6 reversible-pitch propeller, but this was not proceeded with. Mention must also be made of the single Bf 109Ga-2 built in Hungary.

Bf 109G-3

Only fifty Bf 109G-3s were built in early 1943. Essentially similar to the earlier Bf 109G-1, the Bf 109G-3 featured cockpit pressurisation, and delivered to specialised high altitude *Staffeln* within JG 1, JG 11, and JG 54 were made.

Field Modification Designations

The Bf 109G-3/U2 was fitted with a GM-1 boost system. It was intended to fit a cut-down Me 210 propeller after 1 August 1944, but it is uncertain if this occurred.

Bf 109G-4

The Bf 109G-4 had an unpressurised cockpit, with a FuG 16Z radio fitted as standard. The increased weight of the Bf 109G-4 saw the introduction of larger-sized main wheels (660 × 160 mm) and tail wheel (350 ×135 mm). Due to the larger tail wheel, it was usually locked in the down position, with the retraction mechanism having been removed. In some instances, the retraction mechanism remained fitted, although deactivated. A few Bf 109G-4s were supplied to Germany's allies.

Factory Modification Designations

The Bf 109G-4/R1 offered provision for an ETC 500 IXb bomb rack.

The Bf 109G-4/R2 offered provision for an ETC 50 VIId bomb rack.

The Bf 109G-4/R3 offered provision for two 300-litre capacity drop tanks as well as one Rb 75/30 or Rb 50/30 camera. Armament consisted of two MG 151/20 cannons.

The Bf 109G-4/R6 offered provision for two MG 151/20 cannons underneath the wings.

The Bf 109G-4 trop was fitted with a sand filter on the left-hand side of the engine cowling for desert operations.

Field Modification Designations

The Bf 109G-4/U3 offered provision for a MW-50 engine-boost injection. Most served with reconnaissance units.

Bf 109G-5

The Bf 109G-5 was the final variant to feature cockpit pressurisation. Basically similar to the Bf 109G-6, the first Bf 109G-5s reached operational units during the autumn of 1943; the majority of Bf 109G-5s were issued to units serving on the Western Front. Production output was relatively small, with the final Bf 109G-5s being delivered in mid-1944. Production also included the Bf 109G-5/AS, which was powered by a DB 605 D engine fitted with a MW-50 boost injection. The fin and rudder was also increased in size. Some Bf 109G-5s were subsequently modified by Erla at its Antwerp factory by the retrofitting of DB 605 D engines.

Factory Modification Designations

The Bf 109G-5/R2/AS was retrofitted with a DB 605 AS engine.

Field Modification Designations

The Bf 109G-5/U2 GM-1 had a boost system fitted.

The Bf 109G-5Y was fitted with a FuG 16zy radio.

Bf 109G-6

The Bf 109G-6 was the major production variant, with some 12,000 being built between early 1943 and December 1944. The Bf 109G-6 was operated by fighter, fighter-bomber, and fighter-reconnaissance units on every front—an ever-changing delivery schedule and RLM directives make exact production numbers difficult to establish.

Early and late-model Bf 109G-6s differed considerably in external appearance. The armament of the initial production Bf 109G-6s included a pair of MG

131s mounted in the upper forward fuselage instead of the MG 17s fitted to earlier variants.

In mid-1944, a larger-size fin and rudder were fitted. With the Bf 109G-6, wooden airframe components were introduced. It is interesting to note that the Bf 109E airframe included 9 kg of wooden components, which was reduced to a mere 6 kg in the Bf 109F. However, with the worsening situation and increasing lack of high-grade metals, it was decided to increase the number of wooden components. One aspect of this was to introduce additional manufacturers in the Bf 109 production programme, with the actual cost of each wooden tail section being 20 per cent less than its metal counterpart. Interestingly, wooden Bf 109G wings were built in mid-1943 by Wolf Hirth GmbH. Although tested, these wings remained an experiment.

Among the wooden manufacturers was the Deutsche Edelmöbel AG, located in what is today the Czech Republic. When a Regensburg-built Bf 109G-6 shed its wooden tail in July 1944, the post-crash investigation showed that many of the wooden tail units built by Deutsche Edelmöbel were deficient. The wood used was often of sub-standard quality and had not been properly glued together. Additionally, screws were found to have been hammered into the wooden parts by disgruntled Czech workers. Nevertheless, wooden tail units became standard on late-model Bf 109Gs and K-4s. Interestingly, the Luftwaffe did not issue a manual regarding the maintenance of the wooden tailplanes until December 1944.

On later Bf 109G-6 variants, the so-called Erla *Haube* (Erla 'hood') became standard and was retrofitted to many aircraft. The Erla *Haube* increased pilot visibility considerably compared with the earlier heavily-framed canopy. A lengthened tail wheel fork was fitted to some Bf 109G-6s. Overall, the modifications improved the pilot's forward vision and the handling characteristics during take-offs and landings. The lengthened tailwheel would become standard on most Bf 109G-10s and Bf 109G-14s. Apart from the Luftwaffe, the Bf 109G-6 was used by other air arms, also being built in Hungary and Romania.

The Bf 109G-6/AS appeared in early 1944, powered by a DB 605 AS engine in order to increase high-altitude performance. The DB 605 AS engine was basically a DB 605 A fitted with the supercharger of the DB 603. As a result, the engine mount and engine cowling had to be redesigned, with the new more powerful DB 605 AS also requiring a new, larger tail section.

Factory modification designations

The Bf 109G-6/R1 fighter-bomber, fitted with an ETC 500/IXb bomb shackle, had the ability to carry one SC (or SD) 250 bomb.

The Bf 109G-6/R2 bomber-destroyer was fitted with four ETC 50/VIIId bomb shackles and had the ability to carry four SC 50 bombs. It was also armed with two 210-mm WGr Dodel rockets.

The Bf 109G-6/R3 could carry a 300-litre drop tank.

A close-up of a DB 605 AS engine. (*Bengt Hermansson/Forced Landing Collection*)

The Bf 109G-6/R4 was a fighter-reconnaissance variant. Armament was reduced to a single MG 151/20, and it could carry either one Rb 75 × 30 or one Rb 50 × 30 camera.

The Bf 109G-6/R6 was fitted with two additional pod-mounted MG 151/20s beneath the wings.

The Bf 109G-6/R7 was fitted with additional radio navigation gear, including the circular *Peilrufanlage* antenna. Apparently, it was not used operationally.

The Bf 109G-6 trop was fitted with tropical gear for desert operations.

Field Modification Designations

The Bf 109G-6/U2 was fitted with a GM-1 boost system.

The Bf 109G-6/U4 was armed with two 30-mm MK 108 cannons.

The Bf 109G-6/U4N night-fighter was fitted with exhaust flame dampeners and anti-glare shields, as well as a FuG 350 Naxos radar. Armament was increased to one MK 108 cannon firing through the spinner, a pair of MG 131s in the upper forward fuselage, and two pod-mounted MG 151/20s beneath the wings. Only a few were converted.

The Bf 109G-6/U5 had armament consisting of one MG 151/20, and two pod-mounted MK 108 cannons beneath the wings.

The Bf 109G-6/U6 had armament consisting of three MK 108s, including two mounted in pods beneath the wings. Possibly, this design modification did not reach operational status.

Bf 109G-8

The Bf 109G-8 was a dedicated photo-reconnaissance variant. Production of the G-8 began at WNF in August 1943, and 167 Bf 109G-8s were built, with 739 G-8/R5s built by the end of 1944. Apart from the camera installation, the Bf 109G-8 was essentially similar to the Bf 109G-6. The rear fuselage between frames 5 and 6 was strengthened, and two obliquely-mounted Rb 12.5/7 x 9 cm cameras were normally carried. Alternately, a single Rb 32/7 x 9 could be carried. Initially, an Rb II camera was mounted in the forward leading edge of the left wing. In the event, this camera was omitted from late-production aircraft. The first Bf 109G-8s reached the reconnaissance units in November 1943. A few Bf 109G-8s were transferred to Germany's allies.

Factory Modification Designations

The Bf 109G-8/R1 had the ability to carry a ETC 500 IX b bomb. A few were converted.

The Bf 109G-8/R5 was the major production variant. The FuG 17 radios were replaced with FuG 16 ZS.

The Bf 109G-8/R6 had the ability to carry two underwing MG 151/20s. A few were converted.

Field Modification Designations

Bf 109G-8/U2 GM-1 had an engine boost fitted.
Bf 109G-8/U3 MW-50 had an engine boost fitted.

Bf 109G-10

Appearing after the Bf 109G-14, the Bf 109G-10 was powered by a DB 605 D engine fitted with a MW-50 boost, being essentially similar to the Bf 109K-4. The Bf 109G-10 entered production during the autumn of 1944, with deliveries beginning in October. Earlier Bf 109G variants were modified to Bf 109G-10 standard. Aircraft powered by the DB 605 AS were designated Bf 109G-10/AS and were similar in appearance to the Bf 109G-14.

Factory Modification Designations

The Bf 109G-10/R1 had the ability to fit an ETC IXb bomb rack.

The Bf 109G-10/R5 had two underwing MG 151/20 machine gun gondolas.

The Bf 109G-10/R6 Had PKS-12 semi-auto pilot, providing automatic control for the rudder only, with the pilot retaining control of the ailerons and elevators.

The Bf 109G-10/R7 Had two underwing 210-mm rocket tubes fitted.

Field Modification Designations

Bf 109G-10/U4 Had 30-mm BK 108 cannons fitted in the engine

Bf 109G-12

The Bf 109G-12 was a two-seat conversion trainer. Due to the high attrition rate and the urgency to train new pilots, a two-seat conversion training variant of the Bf 109G, known as the Bf 109G-12, was developed in early 1944.

It was planned to convert 500 Bf 109s from existing war weary G-2s, G-3s, G-4s, and G-6s. A field conversion kit was developed by AGO, with actual conversion performed by Blohm & Voss at Hamburg, and Land und See Leichtbau GmbH, Neumunster. To make room for a second, rear cockpit, internal fuel capacity was reduced to 240 litres. However, a 300-litre external drop tank was usually fitted. The fuel filler cap was moved further back, with the battery being moved from the centre fuselage to the gun compartment. In order to provide the instructor in the rear seat some forward vision, the panels on both sides of the rear canopy

The Bf 109G-12 prototype. This particular Bf 109G-12 was last heard of in Italy in July 1944a. (*NMUSAF*)

were slanted outwards. Additionally, a periscope was fitted in the rear cockpit. For instrument flight training, a blind flying canopy could be fitted in the rear cockpit.

Most Bf 109G-12s retained at least part of the armament. It is unclear how many were actually converted, with 170 delivered by June 1944. Most of the Bf 109G-12s were assigned to fighter training schools. A few were also committed to combat during the final weeks of the war.

Bf 109G-14

In an attempt to produce a standard production variant, the Bf 109G-14 was to supersede all earlier variants. The initial Bf 109G-14 production batches were essentially similar in appearance to the earlier Bf 109G-6, being powered by the DB 605 A engine fitted with a MW-50 boost. However, the Erla *Haube* and *Peilrufanlage* (radio transmitter antenna) soon became standard on the Bf 109G-14, so too the wooden tail section. The Bf 109G-14/AS was fitted with larger-size (660 x 190 mm) main wheels and the Fo 987 oil cooler. The majority of Bf 109G-14s were fitted with FuG 16ZY radios, with the designation being changed to Bf 109G-14 y or Bf 109G-14/AS y. Plans included the fitting of an autopilot, although this apparently did not reach operational units.

A Bf 109G-14 seen during the final months of the war. Note the Erla *Haube*, tall wooden fin and rudder, and the short tail-wheel fork. (*NMUSAF*)

Factory Modification Designations

The Bf 109G-14/R3 had the ability to carry a 300-litre drop tank.

The Bf 109G-14/R6 was fitted with two underwing MG 151/20 machine gun pods.

Field Modification Designations

The Bf 109G-14/U4 MK 108 had cannons fitted in the upper forward fuselage instead of the standard MG 151/20s.

Finally, although two 'Bf 109G-16s' were listed as being destroyed in combat between 1944 and 1945, this designation did not officially apply to any known Bf 109G variant. In all likelihood, the Bf 109G-16 designation was a clerical error.

Messerschmitt Bf 109G-6/R6 Technical Data and Performance Characteristics
Engine: 1 × 1,475-hp DB 605 A
Wingspan: 9.92 metres
Length: 9.03 metres
Height: 2.50 metres
Track width: N/a
Wing area: 16.10 m^2

Weight, empty: 2,673 kg
Weight, maximum: 3,400 kg
Maximum speed: 621 kph at 6,900 metres
Range: 998 km (with external drop tank)
Service ceiling: 11,735 metres
Armament: 2 × 13-mm MG 131s (300 rounds each), 1 × 20-mm MG 151/20 cannon (150 rounds), and 2 × 20-mm MG 151/20 cannons (120 rounds each) in underwing pods

Bf 109K: The Final Production Variants

According to the German phonetic alphabet, the Bf 109K became known as *Kürfurst*, not Karl, as is often stated. With the many different late-model Bf 109G variants in service providing a constant source of problems during maintenance and actual operations, an attempt was made to introduce a standardised, upgraded variant. This would become known as the Bf 109K, with the Bf 109G-10 being essentially similar. Initially, six different sub-types, the Bf 109K-2, Bf 109K-4, Bf 109K-6, Bf 109K-8, Bf 109K-10, and the Bf 109K-14 were planned. All of these were to have unpressurised cockpits. No pressurised variants were deemed necessary, hence why there were no K-1, K-3 and so on. The Bf 109K-2 was to have been virtually identical to the Bf 109G-10, but remained a project.

Powered by a 1,800-hp DB 605 D engine, the Bf 109K-4 entered production in late 1944. A total of 221 K-4s were built at Regensburg in November 1944, and another 325 in December 1944. The exact number of Bf 109K-4s built is unknown, but production probably exceeded 1,700. Initial deliveries were made to III./JG 27 in October 1944. Interestingly, one contemporary US aviation magazine referred to the Bf 109K-4 as the 'Me 109M', describing it as, 'a meaner Messerschmitt.'

Compared with the Bf 109G series, the wingspan of the K-4 was reduced by 4 mm. It had been intended to include as much wood as possible in the wings, rudders and stabiliser. In the end, only the tail surfaces were constructed out of wood. The use of wood (a non-strategic commodity) was due to the increasing lack of aluminium. As it turned out, the wooden tailplanes were heavier than their metal counterparts, also lacking in flexibility. The main undercarriage wheels were covered by separate covers, although these were usually not fitted. The Bf 109K-4 remained in Luftwaffe service until the end of the war, with a few being supplied to Italy.

Factory Modification Designations

The Bf 109K-4/R1 could carry an ETC 500/IXb or Schloss 503 centreline bomb rack fitted beneath the fuselage.

The Bf 109K-4/R2 could be fitted with Rb 50/30 camera behind the cockpit.

The Bf 109K-4/R3 could carry a 300-litre external drop tank.

The Bf 109K-4/R5 offered provision for two Rb 12.5/7 x 9 or two Rb 32/7 x 9 cameras mounted in the fuselage

The Bf 109K-4/R6 had a BSK 16 gun camera mounted in the forward leading edge of the left wing.

Bf 109K-6

The Bf 109K-6 was powered by a DB 605 DCM engine and entered production in early 1945. Two additional 30-mm MK 108 cannons were mounted in the wings, increasing the 'punch' of the aircraft. Due to the weight increase and subsequent reduction in performance (and most likely the terrifying recoil when firing all three MK 108s simultaneously), these pair of MK 108s were usually removed by front-line squadrons. A BSK 16 gun camera was mounted in the forward leading edge of the left wing.

Bf 109K-8

The Bf 109K-8 was a fighter-reconnaissance variant, with provision for one Rb 50/30 or two Rb 32/7 × 9 cameras mounted in the rear fuselage. Armament consisted of one 30-mm MK 103 mounted in the engine, and two wing-mounted 30-mm MK 108 cannons, with a BSK 16 gun camera located in the forward leading edge of the left wing. It seems unlikely that any Bf 109K-8s actually entered service.

Bf 109K-10

The Bf 109K-10 had one 30-mm MK 103 cannon mounted in the engine and was similar to the earlier K-4 in other respects. Few, if any, Bf 109K-10s were delivered.

Bf 109K-14

The Bf 109K-14 was powered by a 1,700-hp DB 605 L engine featuring a two-stage mechanical compressor driving a four-bladed propeller. Two Bf 109K-14s were allegedly delivered to II./JG 52 a few days before the war ended, although this remains highly unlikely.

Messerschmitt Bf 109K-4 Technical Data and Performance Characteristics
Engine: 1 × DB 605 D rated at 1,550 hp (take-off), and 1,800 hp with MW 50
Wingspan: 9.92 metres

Length: 9.02 metres
Height: 3.37 metres
Track width: 2.10 metres
Wing area: 16.05 m^2
Weight, empty: 2,346 kg
Weight, maximum: 3362 kg
Maximum speed: 680 kph at 9,000 metres, 710 kph at 7,500 metres with GM 1
Range: 650 km
Service ceiling: 13,500 metres
Armament: 2 × 13-mm MG 131s (300 rounds each) and 1 × 30-mm MK 108 cannon (65 rounds). Ability to carry 250 kg of bombs/rockets

Bf 109T (*Toni*)

Possibly the most fascinating of all Bf 109 variants, the Bf 109T was intended for naval operations. By the early 1930s, the aircraft carrier was used by Great Britain, Japan, and the USA. In April 1934, the *Kriegsmarine* initiated a study for a 15,000-ton carrier based on the British Hermes class. This was recognised as being too small, with the 25,000-ton Courageous class becoming the standard template aircraft carrier by mid-1934. In the event, the Naval Treaty with Britain, signed on 18 June 1935 permitted the construction of two aircraft carriers. The first of these, named *Graf Zeppelin*, was launched at Kiel on 8 December 1938. The second carrier, also to be built at Kiel, was never completed, and its unfinished hull was scrapped in 1940.

In early 1937, a small number of Bf 109Bs were transferred to the *Kriegsmarine*. The Bf 109s were attached to *Küstenjägergruppe 136* to evaluate its merits as a possible

The Bf 109V17 undergoing catapult trials in 1938. (*Wolfgang Mühlbauer/DEHLA Archives*)

carrier-based naval fighter. In 1939, it was planned that *Graf Zeppelin* would have a complement of thirty-three aircraft, including twenty Fi 167s, thirteen Ju 87Cs, and ten Bf 109Ts. Initial plans called for the conversion of sixty Bf 109E-3s, eventually amended to seventy new-build aircraft under the designation Bf 109T, with the prefix letter 'T' standing for *Träger* ('carrier'). The number of Bf 109Ts to be built changed constantly over the following year, from 155 to seventy.

By mid-1940, *Graf Zeppelin* was 95 per cent complete. However, due to changing requirements, an order to stop further work on the carrier was issued on 12 July. With Kiel being within range of RAF Bomber Command, the unfinished carrier was towed to Gotenhafen (present-day Gdynia). Considering the large-scale British efforts to hunt down and sink the battleships *Bismarck* and *Tirpitz*, it may be safe to say that the RAF and Royal Navy would have spared no effort in sending *Graf Zeppelin* to the bottom of the sea. By the end of the war, *Graf Zeppelin* was taken over by the Russians. It was never completed and eventually sunk off the Polish coast in 1947. Remarkably, a plan to convert three Norddeutscher Lloyd passenger liners to auxiliary carriers was proposed in 1942. Although work was initiated, this was soon abandoned.

As a result of the changing requirements, it was decided that only the first seven *Tonis* were to be completed as Bf 109T-1s fitted with arrester hooks and catapult gears; the remaining sixty-three became T-2s, with the latter having most of the carrier gear removed. The first Bf 109T was not delivered until February 1941, with production being completed four months later.

Instead of operating from carrier decks, most of the Bf 109T's were assigned to Luftwaffe units in Norway and the Netherlands. The increased wingspan made it suitable to operate from short, unprepared runways. Amazingly, the final Bf 109Ts remained in service until the spring of 1944.

Bf 109T carrying the factory code RB+OP. Note the longer wingspan of this variant. (*Wolfgang Mühlbauer/DEHLA Archives*)

A close-up of a Bf 109T cockpit. Note the life raft stored behind the pilot seat. (*Wolfgang Mühlbauer/DEHLA Archives*)

Messerschmitt Bf 109T-2 Technical Data and Performance Characteristics
Engine: 1 × 1,175-hp DB 601 N
Wingspan: 11.08 metres
Length: 8.76 metres
Height: 2.60 metres
Track width: N/A
Wing area: 17.50 m^2
Weight, empty: 2,000 kg
Weight, maximum: 3,078 kg
Maximum speed: 575 kph at 6,000 metres
Range: 915 km (with auxiliary drop tank)
Service ceiling: N/A
Armament: 2 x 7.92-mm MG 17s and 2 x 20-mm MG FF

Prototypes and Projects

Bf 109H

With increasing numbers of USAAF heavy bombers flying at high altitude and making their presence known over German-occupied Europe, development of a specialised high-altitude fighter began in early 1943. Two parallel development programmes saw Messerschmitt working on the Me 209H ('H' signifying *Höhe*, meaning 'altitude') and the modification of a standard production Bf 109F-4. The former programme was eventually cancelled, with a modified Bf 109F known as the Bf 109H.

The wingspan was extended to 11.92 metres, with the main undercarriage legs moved outwards. Although an uprated DB 601 engine was fitted initially, this was soon replaced by a two-stage supercharger DB 628A. This engine, as well as other Bf 109H features, was tested in the Bf 109V 50. The first Bf 109H took to the air in July 1943, with a small batch of pre-series Bf 109H-0s being built. The Bf 109H-0 was based on the Bf 109F-4/Z powered by the DB 601E fitted with GM-1 boosting. The Bf 109H-0s did not see action but were used instead for high-altitude tests, during which severe wing flutter was encountered. Limited series production followed nevertheless, with the Bf 109H-1 being based on the Bf 109G-5.

Service evaluation took place in early 1944 at Guyancourt, France. One Bf 109H was used to fly reconnaissance sorties over the Allied fleet in the western Mediterranean in June 1944. The Bf 109H-1 had good flight and handling characteristics, although one aircraft was lost when the left wing was ripped off during a high-speed dive. In the event, the Focke-Wulf Ta 152 was chosen for production as the Luftwaffe's standard high-altitude fighter. However, only slightly more than fifty Ta 152s had been delivered before the war ended in May 1945.

As related elsewhere, three sub-variants of the Bf 109G—the Bf 109G-1, G-3, and G-5 respectively—featured pressurised cabins as they were dedicated high-altitude fighters.

Bf 109L

The Bf 109L was a modification of the basic Bf 109G series. The width of the fuselage was enlarged, with increased wing span and wing area for high-altitude operations. It was intended to fit a Jumo 213E engine to the Bf 109L. Maximum speed at 10,700 metres was estimated at 760 kph, but no Bf 109L flew.

Bf 109S

In 1940, a two-seat advanced training variant of the Bf 109 was planned, which was to be designated the Bf 109S—with 'S' signifying *Schulflugzeug*, meaning 'training aircraft'. However, it was deemed that the Luftwaffe did not require such an aircraft and the Bf 109S subsequently remained on the drawing board. The idea was revived in 1944, with a small number of Bf 109G-12s reaching Luftwaffe training units.

During the war, the Bf 109 V24 was sent to France for wind-tunnel testing by Caudron-Renault at Chalais-Meudon. In an attempt to improve the low-speed handling characteristics, a particular system of air discharge over the upper surfaces of the wings were tested. By the summer of 1944, work on the Bf 109S was abandoned.

Bf 109TL

At the request of the RLM in early 1943, Messerschmitt investigated the possibility of converting the basic Bf 109G with a jet engine. Ultimately deemed impractical, the idea was then put forward of modifying the Me 155A fighter for jet propulsion. (See Me 155 for further details.) In the end, the Me 262 jet fighter had already flown in 1942, entering service in the summer of 1944, thus making sure that the jet-powered Bf 109 would remain unbuilt.

Bf 109W

Early in the war, a float-equipped Bf 109 was briefly considered. With a pair of floats taken from an Arado Ar 196, the Bf 109W would have operated in the narrow confines of Norwegian fjords. However, no evidence of any Bf 109s actually being converted to floatplane fighters appears to exist. Performance would have been marginal. Nevertheless, Allied attempts at creating a floatplane fighter included trials with Supermarine Spitfires and Grumman Wildcats.

Bf 109X

The Bf 109 V21 (W Nr 1770) was experimentally fitted with a 1,200-hp Pratt & Whitney SCG Twin Wasp radial engine. Registered as D-IFKQ, the Bf 109X also featured a cut-down rear upper fuselage and a bubble canopy, which made it rather similar in appearance to the Fw 190. It was evaluated at E-Stelle Rechlin in 1940. This was not the only radial-engine powered Bf 109, with one Bf 109F (reportedly W Nr 5608) being fitted with a BMW 801—the engine that powered the Fw 190A.

Bf 109Z

Similar in concept to the later North American F-82 Twin Mustang, the Bf 109Z ('Z' denoting *Zwilling*, meaning 'twin') consisted of a pair of Bf 109F airframes mated together through a central wing and tail section; the sole pilot was to fly from the left-hand fuselage. The Bf 109Z was designed for *Zerstörer* and long-range escort missions. One prototype was completed in 1942, but damaged beyond repair in an Allied air raid before taking to the air, leading to the project's eventual cancellation. Production variants were to have been based on the Bf 109G.

The armament of the projected Bf 109Z-1 *Zerstörer* would have consisted of no less than five 30-mm MK 108 cannons. Other variants planned included the Bf 109Z-2, which would have had a reduced cannon armament but the ability to carry 1,000 kg of bombs, with the Z-3 and Z-4 variants being modifications of the earlier Z-1 and Z-2. The Bf 109Z-3 and Z-4 were to be powered by two Jumo 213 engines. The *Zwilling* concept reached fruition with the He 111Z, a few of which were built for use as tow planes for assault gliders.

Fieseler-Skoda FiSk 199

An attempt at increasing the Bf 109Gs poor range was made in early 1942 by Skoda-Kauba Flugzeugbau, Prague. A Bf 109G-2/R1 was modified as a fighter-bomber (*Jabo*) with greatly extended range by fitting two 300-litre drop tanks, one beneath each wing, and the capability of carrying one SC 500 bomb beneath the fuselage. In order to provide sufficient ground clearance, a third undercarriage leg was mounted under the centre fuselage. The first flight, performed by Heinrich Beauvais, was made on 30 June 1942. In the event, this modification was not

The FiSk 199 was an unsuccessful attempt to increase the range of the Bf 109. (*NMUSAF*) .

adopted for service. This particular undercarriage configuration of the FiSk 199 was revived for the post-war Orličan L-40 Meta Sokol light plane.

Messerschmitt Me 155

The Me 155 began life in late 1942 as a carrier-capable fighter based on the Bf 109G. However, although the aircraft carrier *Graf Zeppelin* was never completed, the Me 155 did eventually proceed to flight status as the Blohm und Voss Bv 155 high-altitude fighter that, ultimately, in the event, bore little resemblance to the Bf 109.

The Me 155A of November 1942 was to be a fighter-bomber capable of carrying one SC 1000 bomb. The Me 155 was not proceeded with, although a standard Bf 109G was subsequently modified with increased wing span and a redesigned fin as the Me 155B high-altitude fighter. It was proposed to modify the basic Me 155B with two Jumo 004 B turbo jet engines. The jet-powered Me 155 was to utilise the wing of the Me 409, with a redesigned tail section and a nose wheel undercarriage.

However, in August 1943 the RLM ordered the transfer of the Me 155 programme to Blohm und Voss. The Bv 155 prototypes were eventually built, with the Bv 155 V1 taking to the air on 8 February 1945. In the event, the Bv 155 did reach beyond-prototype testing. One uncompleted Bv 155 is held by the US National Air & Space Museum.

Messerschmitt Me 209

The Me 209 began life in 1937 as the P.1059. The intention was to capture the world speed record. Construction of three prototypes was started, with the new aircraft being officially known as the Me 209. The Nazi propaganda machinery referred to the new aircraft as the Me 109R, thus suggesting that it was a straight development of the basic Bf 109. In reality, the Me 209 was not designed as a fighter but as a high-speed racer. Compared with the Bf 109, the Me 209 was considerably smaller, also having an inwardly retracting undercarriage. The first prototype, registered as D-INJR, first flew on 1 August 1938 by Dr J. H. Wurster, chief test pilot and engineer at Augsburg. Power was provided by the tenth DB 601 engine built. This particular engine was provided with a methanol boost, giving a one-minute rating of 2,300 hp at 3,500 rpm.

The second prototype, D-IWAH, flew on 8 February 1939 but did not last long—it was written off on 4 April when flown by Fritz Wendel. Wendel later described the flight and handling characteristics of Me 209.

> With its tiny wing and, for those days, horrifying wing loading, the 209 was a brute. It had a dangerous tendency to nose down without any reason or warning, and it touched down on the runway like a ton of bricks. Even on the ground its

characteristics were no more ladylike, as it would suddenly swerve off the runway without any provocation.

... On 4 April 1939, I took off for a training flight in preparation for the speed record attempt in the second prototype, the Me 209V2. After a few tiring minutes of heaving the unwieldy controls, I turned in for a landing approach. I was accustomed to lowering the undercarriage as I reached Siebentischwald, a forest near the airfield at Haunstetten, but on that day, without warning (everything happened without warning in the Me 209) the lubricating system packed up, and immediately the pistons were grinding in the cylinders and the airscrew was standing as stiff as a poker. With a hell of a jolt, the plane virtually pulled up in mid-air, the result of the combined drag of the lowered undercarriage and the unfeathered airscrew. The

Above: The Me 209V1 was, despite German propaganda, an entirely new aircraft. (*Wolfgang Mühlbauer/DEHLA Archives*)

Left: Willy Messerschmitt discusses the finer points of the Me 209V1 with the test pilot, Fritz Wendel. (*Wolfgang Mühlbauer/DEHLA Archives*)

> vicious little brute started dropping like a stone, and below me was that damned forest. I strained on the stick with all I had and, to my surprise, the plane responded. I screamed over the last row of trees bordering the Haunstetterstrasse, and was even more surprised to find myself staggering away, relatively unhurt, from the heap of twisted metal that seconds before had been a Me 209.[1]

Just over three weeks later, on 26 April, Wendel achieved an average speed of 755.138 kph (469 mph) in the Me 209 V1, beating Hans Dieterle's record set on 30 March in the Heinkel He 100 V 8. Remarkably, Wendel's record remained unbroken for more than thirty years—it was not until 16 August 1968 that US pilot Darryl Greenamyer reached an average speed of 776.449 kph (482.533 mph) in a highly modified Grumman F8F Bearcat.

A third Me 209, D-IVFP, took to the air on 26 April 1939. It was followed by the fourth prototype, D-IRND, which flew on 12 May. D-IRND eventually received the code CE+BW and was used as a test vehicle in developing the basic Me 209 design into a fighter. The addition of armament and other military equipment meant that performance was considerably reduced. Interestingly, one Me 209 was ordered by the USSR, but this was, in all likelihood, not delivered. The Me 209 V1 was set aside for preservation at the *Deutschen Luftfahrt Sammlung* in Berlin, eventually being dismantled and moved away from Berlin to avoid destruction in Allied bomb raids. The fuselage of this historic aircraft remains in storage with the Polish Aviation Museum in Kraków.

In a rare occurrence within RLM aircraft designation policy, the Me 209 designation was re-used. The resulting aircraft was a new design that incorporated major components of the Bf 109G. One prototype, designated Me 209 V 5 (coded SP+LJ), was flown for the first time on 3 November 1943. Initially, a DB 603A engine was fitted. This was eventually replaced by a DB 603G, requiring an increase in the size of the fin and rudder. Further prototypes were completed, with two production variants—the Me 209A-1 and A-2—planned. The Me 209A armament

The Me 209 V4. (W Nr 1188) was an attempt at creating a new fighter. The poor flight and handling characteristics resulted in further development being cancelled in September 1940. Of interest is the red snake that adorned both sides of the fuselage. (*Wolfgang Mühlbauer/DEHLA Archives*)

Apart from the designation, the Me 209V5 had little in common with the pre-war Me 209 racer. (*Wolfgang Mühlbauer/DEHLA Archives*)

was to have consisted of one 30-mm MK 108 cannon and two 20-mm MG 151/20s. The performance of the Me 209 was essentially similar to that of the Fw 190D-9. It was, however, determined that large-scale manufacture of the latter involved less organisational changes at the aircraft production centres. A high-altitude variant, known as the Me 209H, was completed in mid-1944. With the advent of the Messerschmitt Me 262 jet fighter, the Me 209 did not enter production. Additionally, replacing the Bf 109G with the Me 209A would have caused severe disruption to an already overstretched German aircraft industry.

Messerschmitt Me 309

In early 1941, design work on an eventual replacement for the Bf 109 was initiated. The major drawback of the Bf 109 was its short range, something which had been made abundantly clear during the Battle of Britain. Thus, the new fighter was to have an increased range by some 85 per cent, as well as 25 per cent more speed than the Bf 109. One major departure for Messerschmitt designers was that the Me 309 was to feature a tricycle undercarriage similar to that of the Bell P-39 and P-63, as well as a reversible pitch propeller. Although the RLM did not foresee the replacement of the Bf 109, design work was allowed to proceed. Some of the design features were tested on Bf 109Fs. The first prototype, the Me 309V 1 (coded GE+CU), had been completed by mid-1942. It was powered by a DB 603 inline engine.

When taxiing trials began on 27 June, the nose wheel undercarriage showed a marked tendency to shimmy. The problems continued when the Me 309V 1 took to the air for the first time on 18 July; the test pilot, Karl Baur, reported severe

The Me 309 V1 GE+CU. Note the Me 262 prototype, still fitted with a tailwheel, sitting in the left background. (*Wolfgang Mühlbauer/DEHLA Archives*)

A close-up of the Me 309 V. (*Wolfgang Mühlbauer/DEHLA Archives*)

directional stability issues. Additionally, engine cooling was insufficient, and upon landing the nose wheel collapsed.

On 28 November, a second prototype, the Me 309V 2 (coded GE+CV), flew for the first time. However, the nose wheel undercarriage again collapsed on landing, severely damaging the aircraft. In the meantime, the Me 309V 1 had been repaired, and comparative trials between a Bf 109G and the Me 309V 1 showed that the former, although slower, could outturn the Me 309 with ease.

Two more prototypes, the Me 309V 3 (GE+CW) and V 4 (GE+CX), joined the test programme in early 1943. By this time it had become painfully obvious that the Me 309 was too problematic for the RLM to consider series production. Planned production variants included the Me 309A-2 *Zerstörer*, which had a powerful armament consisting of no less than four MG 131s, two MG 151/20s, and two MK 108 cannons, the Me 309B dive bomber, and the Me 609Z *Zwilling*.

Development of the Me 309 was subsequently abandoned, with the Me 309V1 and V3 subsequently being utilised for test flights in the Me 262 programme and reversible propeller-pitch tests.

Messerschmitt Me 409

In 1942, work began on a high-altitude fighter powered by one 1,750-hp DB 603 engine. The Me 409 did not proceed beyond the drawing board, although the basic wing design would reappear on the Me 155B.

3

Into Service

During the Second World War, the Bf 109 was the most numerous single-seat fighter used by the Luftwaffe. It saw service on every front (apart from a brief Luftwaffe sojourn into northern Iraq in April and May 1941), seeing use as a day fighter, night fighter, fighter-bomber, ground-attack aircraft, reconnaissance aircraft, advanced trainer, and, during the final stages of the war, a transport aircraft. Hundreds of Luftwaffe *Experten* (fighter aces) accumulated huge numbers of aerial victories against Allied aircraft. Between 1939 and 1945, 104 Luftwaffe pilots achieved more than 100 aerial victories. The majority of these aces flew Bf 109s for at least part of their career. The Bf 109 was also the mount of Bulgarian, Croatian, Finnish, Hungarian, and Romanian fighter aces.

Following the end of the First World War and the signing of the Treaty of Versailles, the German Imperial armed forces were largely disbanded. Military flying was banned, so too the production of military aircraft. Aircraft production in Germany was subsequently limited to gliders, sailplanes, low-powered civilian

Jumo 210-powered Bf 109s of an unidentified unit, seen during a pre-war exercise. (*NMUSAF*)

aircraft, and airliners. The establishment of the *Deutsche Luftsportverband* resulted in thousands of young German men and women learning to fly gliders and low-powered aircraft. The DLV would eventually have more than 50,000 members, making Germany one of the most air-minded nations in Europe. Following a 1925 agreement with the USSR, a large number of German pilots underwent flight training in utmost secrecy and in full cooperation with Soviet authorities. Ironically, several high-ranking Luftwaffe officers learned their trade under Soviet guidance.

Following the Nazi rise to power in January 1933, the re-establishment of military aviation was deemed of highest importance. Even by 1 January 1934, Erhard Milch (one of the most important individuals within German aviation during the mid-war years) envisaged a future German air arm having no less than 4,000 in service by September 1935, which meant that a vast expansion of the aircraft manufacturing industry had to be implemented.

The first *Jägdgruppe* (Fighter Group) of the still-secret German air arm was activated at Döberitz-Elsgrund near Berlin on 1 April 1934. Named *Fliegergruppe Döberitz*, the unit was equipped with a few civilian-registered Ar 65 fighters and commanded by Maj. Robert Ritter von Greim who, in late April 1945, would become the last Commander-in-Chief of the Luftwaffe following *Reichsmarschall* Göring's attempt to enter peace negotiations with the Allies.

On 26 February 1935, the existence of the Luftwaffe was proclaimed. Incidentally, the term *Reichsluftwaffe* was the correct name, although this never caught on with the general public, or with latter-day aviation historians. The new German air arm consisted of some 20,000 men and 1,888 aircraft, with an average of 300 aircraft rolling off the assembly lines every month. With the German army and navy having a centuries-old history, the Luftwaffe was the baby of the armed services and formally established by the Nazi regime, causing Hitler to remark, 'I have a Christian Navy, a reactionary Army, and a National Socialist Luftwaffe.'

The *Fliegergruppe Döberitz* was renamed *Jägdgeschwader* Richthofen soon afterwards, in honour of Germany's highest scoring ace during the Great War. A few weeks later, several officers were transferred to Jüterbog-Damm to initiate the formation of a second *Jägdgruppe*. Commanded by Maj. Johann Rathiel, the *Jägdgruppe* was known as *Fliegergruppe Damm*. Both units would eventually receive He 51 fighters—one of the two types of biplane fighters entering large-scale Luftwaffe service in the mid-1930s, the other being the Ar 68 (a total of 514 Ar 68s and 616 He 51s were built, with the former still equipping a few front-line units in September 1939). On 24 February 1936, a third *Jägdgruppe* was formed, initially known as *Fliegergruppe Lippstadt*, with its pilots having been transferred from *Fliegergruppe Döberitz*.

These first two *Fliegergruppen* were responsible for specific tasks. Döberitz was assigned weapons testing and developing a ground organisation, while Damm was responsible for developing air combat tactics and initiating trials with the *Zerstörer* concept.

On 7 March 1936, German troops marched into the Rhineland that had, since the end of the First World War, been controlled by France, including a brief military occupation during the early 1920s. Following mediation by the League of Nations, a referendum was held in which an overwhelming majority voted for the area to be returned to Germany. Despite protests from France and Britain, Hitler succeeded in returning the economically vital region to the Fatherland in what was the first German military operation since the Nazi regime's rise to power. As a result, Hitler's popularity in Germany soared; the shameful injustice of the Treaty of Versailles had been avenged. Although aerial cover was provided by all three *Fliegergruppen*, no shots were fired. The fighter component had consisted of Heinkel He 51s. Most of these were, incidentally, unarmed. The Bf 109 would eventually fire its guns in anger for the first time sixteen months later in Spain.

The first Luftwaffe unit to receive the Bf 109 was II./JG 132 at Döberitz, with an initial batch of twenty-five Bf 109Bs having arrived by 15 March 1937. Apparently, the pilots of II./JG 132 celebrated the arrival of the new fighters by means of consuming 109 bottles of beer.

The introduction into service of the Bf 109B was not without its problems though. Several aircraft were lost in fatal, seemingly unexplainable accidents. When, on 29 May 1938, BFW test pilot Hermann Wurster was performing a series of terminal velocity dives, part of the stabiliser was ripped off in mid-air. Wurster managed to regain control of the Bf 109 and land safely. It was discovered that the front attachment fitting of the stabiliser buckled and gave away during the high-*g* load dive. This problem was easily rectified. The Bf 109Bs remained in service with II./JG 132 until the spring of 1938, being replaced by Bf 109D-1s. Two more units, I./JGr 234 and II./JGr 234 re-equipped with Bf 109s before the end of 1937. A list of pre-war Bf 109 fighter units appears in Appendix I.

During the *Anschluss* on 13 March 1938, Bf 109s of I./JG 132 flew as escort to Hitler, who arrived triumphantly in Vienna in a Ju 52/3m. A couple of days later, Bf 109s of JG 334 landed at Wiener-Neustadt, subsequently making a number of show-the-flag flights over the Austrian capital. Austria was renamed Ostmark shortly afterwards and fully incorporated into Germany. Following screening, some 3,100 Austrian airmen joined the ranks of the Luftwaffe, with some being dismissed due to various reasons, including being branded 'Austrian nationalists'. By the spring of 1938, two more *Jägdgruppen*, I./JG 131 based at Jesau near Königsberg (present-day Kaliningrad) and I./JG 334 had received Bf 109s.

On 21 April 1938, to mark the 20th anniversary of Manfred von Richthofen's death, a memorial to the Great War ace was unveiled at Döberitz by Göring, with members of the Richthofen family present. Apart from a Bf 109B of I./JG 132, an original Fokker Dr.I was also present.

With insufficient numbers of Bf 109s having reached the Luftwaffe *Jägdgeschwader*, some units were forced to retain their Ar 68s. During the Munich crisis of the autumn of 1938, one *Staffel* briefly operated He 112Bs, which were eventually sold to Japan. At the height of the Munich crisis, JG 334 was ordered to patrol the border with France.

The signing of the Munich agreement on 30 September saw British Prime Minister Neville Chamberlain proclaim 'peace in our time.' To appease Hitler and his seemingly never-ending appetite for new land, France and Britain had agreed to the partition and eventual dissolution of Czechoslovakia. Formed in

1918 from the ruins of the old Austro-Hungarian Empire, Czechoslovakia had a large percentage of ethnic Germans, most of whom resided in the Sudetenland. Although preparations had been made for a military invasion of Czechoslovakia, this was unnecessary; German forces entered the Sudetenland on 1 October 1938. Two *Jägdgruppen*, I./JG 132 and I./JG 334 were temporarily based at Karlsbad (Karlovy Vary) and Wiener-Neustadt to provide cover for the German ground troops. Due to its frequent moves, the latter unit was unofficially known as *Wanderzirkus Janke* (Janke's Wandering Circus) after its commanding officer, Hptm Johannes Janke.

Renamed from I./JG 132, I./JG 331 took part in the occupation of what remained of Czechoslovakia in March 1939, moving to Olmütz (Olomouc) on 17 March where they remained until 21 April. Another unit taking part was II./JG 333, which transferred to Eger (Cheb) in late March.

The Bf 109B enjoyed a comparatively brief front-line service, what with being rapidly supplanted by the Bf 109D and the Bf 109E in particular. On 26 September 1938, there were 985 fighters in service with twenty-three *Jägdgruppen*. Of these, no less than 864 were Bf 109s. By 1939, all *Jägdgeschwader* of the Luftwaffe were operating Bf 109s. During the autumn of 1939, a *Jägdgeschwader* had a nominal strength of 124 pilots and 2,200 ground staff. Each *Jägdgeschwader* consisted of one or two *Gruppen*, each with three *Staffeln*. Each *Staffel* had fifteen aircraft, including three reserves.

Fighter Pilot Training

All prospective Luftwaffe fighter pilots had to accumulate between 120 and 150 hours during elementary and basic flight training in low-powered biplane trainers such as the Bücker Bü 131 *Jungmann*, Fw 44 *Stieglitz*, or He 72 *Kadett*, with an additional fifty hours on conversion (including about ten hours on Bf 108s or Ar 96s) and gunnery training in the Bf 109. This meant that fighter pilots had accumulated some 200 flight hours when posted to a fighter squadron.

Despite a well-laid out and extensive pilot training syllabus, the Bf 109 could be difficult to master. With no two-seat Bf 109 available, the four-seat Bf 108 Taifun or the Arado Ar 96 two-seat basic trainer was the penultimate step before climbing into a Bf 109 for the first time. The highly manoeuvrable Ar 96 entered service in late 1939 and had several features also found on the Bf 109, including a retractable undercarriage and automatic slats.

One Luftwaffe pilot, Julius Neumann, considered the Bf 108 'docile and comfortable' while providing the student pilot with some experience of novelties such as a retractable undercarriage, enclosed cockpit, automatic slats, and a variable-pitch propeller. Neuman later wrote of the single-seat Bf 109:

The first idiosyncrasy encountered when learning to fly the Bf 109E was provided by the fighter's take-off—it demanded quite a lot of right rudder to hold it straight, the propeller torque resulting in a predilection for breaking left. Fortunately, one soon became accustomed to this tendency. The landing, too, presented something of a problem for novices. As one reduced speed for the approach, control sloppiness increased. At about 90 mph (145 kph), the wing slots opened automatically and one immediately felt the extra lift that they imparted. The stalling speed with undercarriage and flaps down was about 60 mph (90 kph), and below that speed, the *Emil* would drop a wing violently and without warning. Under such circumstances, the fighter fell like a stone and unless a reasonable amount of height was available there was no time to recover! It was vital to get both mainwheels on the ground simultaneously, or else the aircraft would swing in the direction of whatever wheel touched first, and as often as not, the result was a broken undercarriage leg.[1]

Training accidents occurred with alarming frequency, usually during take-offs and landings, with several pilots being killed or severely injured. However, once the pilot had learned to master the idiosyncrasies of the Bf 109, the accident rate was reduced. Future ace Günther Rall stated that, 'The demands of this powerful machine are quite unlike anything I have flown before … the Messerschmitt is no docile machine, but a highly-strung thoroughbred.' Another Luftwaffe pilot, Heinz Knoke, later wrote in his memoirs:

> We have spent several days on theoretical conversion training before flying the Messerschmitt Bf 109, which is difficult to handle and dangerous at first. We can now go through every movement in our sleep. This morning we brought out the first 109 and were ready to fly. Sergeant Schmidt was the first of us, by drawing lots … Schmidt came in to land after making one circuit, but he misjudged the speed, which was higher than that to which he was accustomed, and so he overshot the runway. He came round again, and the same thing happened.

The Bf 109 V16, registered as D-IPGS, seen following a ground loop. The undercarriage was notoriously weak, resulting in many landing accidents. (*NMUSAF*)

> We began to worry, for Sergeant Schmidt had obviously lost his nerve. He was coming in and making a final turn before flattening out to touch down, when the aircraft suddenly stalled because of insufficient speed and spun out of control, crashing into the ground and exploding a few hundred feet short of the end of the runway. We all raced like madmen over to the scene of the crash. I was the first to arrive. Schmidt had been thrown clear, and was lying several feet from the fuming wreckage. He was screaming like an animal, covered in blood. I stooped down over the body of my comrade, and saw that both legs were missing.

Sergeant Schmidt was one of many aspiring Luftwaffe fighter pilots to suffer when learning to fly the Bf 109. Nevertheless, when a pilot had learned to master the idiosyncrasies of the Bf 109, it would become the fighter of choice for many of the Luftwaffe's fighter aces. In the event, with a large cadre of Luftwaffe fighter pilots honing their fighting skills in Spanish skies, by early 1940 the Luftwaffe was the most combat experienced air force in the world. By this time, the Luftwaffe flying schools had a monthly output of some 800 pilots, making sure that the Bf 109 units would have a steady supply of fighter pilots.

Baptism of Fire in Spain

The Spanish Civil War began in the summer of 1936 when General Franco initiated an armed rebellion that Republican government forces were unable to suppress; fighting soon spreading across Spain. Germany and Italy supported Franco, with the Republican government receiving large-scale material assistance from Stalin's USSR. In Spain, combat aircraft, tanks, and other weapons were used in what was essentially a proving ground for new military technology—a dress rehearsal for the Second World War. Apart from the military hardware, aerial tactics were developed as well.

The German air component, named *Legion Condor*, consisted of bomber, reconnaissance, and fighter units, with the latter equipped with Heinkel He 51s. Powered by a 750-hp BMW VI inline engine and armed with a pair of MG 17s, the He 51 had a top speed of 320 kph and was proved to be outclassed by the Soviet Polikarpov I-15bis and I-16 fighters. A fighter of superior performance was urgently needed.

As a result, three of the Bf 109 prototypes, V 3, V 4 and V 6 respectively, were despatched to Spain in December 1936. They were accompanied by Wolfram von Richthofen, who was to supervise the prototype's trial in Spain. Upon arrival, the Bf 109s were issued with Spanish codes: 6.1 (V3, later reissued to the V4 prototype), 6.2 (V 3) and 6.3 (V6), with the first numeral being the type designator and the second numeral indicating the individual aircraft.

However, the intended combat evaluation was fraught with difficulties. The Bf 109 V3 was severely damaged in a take-off accident at Tablada when flown by Uffz Erich Kley, with the wreck subsequently being returned to Augsburg. On

14 December 1936, Hannes Trautloft made his first flight in the Bf 109 V4. In his diary, Trautloft had noted two days earlier that, 'the new Bf 109 simply looks fabulous. Alongside it the good old He 51 looks like a withered maiden, and yet only with a heavy heart can I part from her, grown grey in honour.' With little in the way of pre-flight briefing apart from a mechanic pointing out the various levers and instruments, Trautloft noted:

> The take-off certainly is unusual but as soon as I am in the air I feel at home in the new bird. Its flight characteristics are fantastic. When I am airborne I find an Italian Fiat (CR.32) fighter above the airfield. So far the Fiat has been reckoned the fastest of all Franco's fighters, but I get behind it and have overtaken it in a moment, leaving it far behind.[2]

Numerous technical malfunctions were encountered during the evaluation, including with the undercarriage locking mechanism and the Jumo 210 engines overheating on a number of occasions, resulting in forced landings. Formal operational evaluation did not begin until 14 January 1937, and no aerial combat ensued, meaning the Bf 109 V4 was quickly returned to Germany. On 11 February the Bf 109 V6 crashed, claiming the life of Lt Paul Rehahn.

Even if the operational evaluation of the Bf 109 had been both brief and inconclusive, the RLM hurriedly despatched sixteen early-production Bf 109As and Bs (including four spare aircraft) to Spain in March 1937 to join the *Legion Condor*, along with personnel from the first Luftwaffe unit to receive Bf 109s, JG 132 Richthofen. The new fighters were assigned to 2./J88, which had previously operated He 51s that were relegated to the role of ground attack.

The Commander of 2./J88, Oblt Günther 'Franzl' Lützow, initiated a thorough training course to make sure that the German pilots received necessary flight experience in the Bf 109 before being committed to combat. The final segment of flight training included two one-hour flights. No serious accidents ensued, although the majority of pilots expressed concern over the Bf 109Bs tendency to drop its port wing during take-offs and landings. Following completion of pilot conversion, 2./J88 flew its first operational sorties in late May, although few enemy aircraft were encountered. However, in early July 1937, 2./J88 hurriedly transferred from Matacán to Avila near Madrid. Republican forces were pushing towards Brunete, threatening to cut the Nationalist units located between Madrid and Toledo in half. The Bf 109s flew numerous escort sorties for the Ju 52/3m bombers of the *Legion Condor*, with Russian-built Polikarpov I-16 fighters being encountered.

The Bf 109B was found to be slightly faster than the I-16, also possessing a higher diving speed. On the other hand, the I-16 had a better rate of climb and superior manoeuvrability, being able to outturn the Messerschmitt fighter, with the Bf 109B having a better service ceiling. One Bf 109B was claimed shot down on 6 July over Brunete by a Yugoslav volunteer pilot, Bozhko Petrovich. This loss was not admitted by the Nationalists, nor was the Bf 109B claimed to have been shot down by Yevgeny S. Ptukhin and Bozhko Petrovich on 8 July. The first loss of a Bf 109

Two Legion Condor Bf 109Bs. Note the Ju 86D in the background. (*NMUSAF*)

appears to have occurred on 13 July, when Uffz Höness was shot down by I-16s of *1a Escuadrilla*. One week later, on 20 July, Uffz Harbach baled out over the front line. Avila was raided by Republican Tupolev SB-2 bombers on 23 July. Despite claims that the raid had destroyed no less than twenty Bf 109s on the ground, in reality no bombs hit the airfield.

On 30 July, 2./J88 returned to Herrera. Additional Bf 109Bs soon arrived, making it possible for 1./J88 to relinquish its He 51 biplanes for the Messerschmitt fighters during September 1937. To ease conversion training, Oblt Lützow was appointed as 1./J88's *Staffelkapitän*.

On 4 December, the Republican forces managed to obtain a Bf 109B-1, serial 6.15. Running low on fuel, Fw Polenz landed on a road between Azaila and Escatron. Surprised and delighted, the Republican Air Force Command allowed a French team to evaluate the Messerschmitt, with the aircraft being sent to the USSR shortly afterwards.

On 15 December, Republican forces launched an offensive against Teruél. The cold weather saw a reduction of aerial activity, with the Jumo 210 engines of the Bf 109Bs having to be continuously ground run to prevent seizure. Nationalist forces eventually managed to push back the Republican army units, with Teruél being recaptured on 21 February. Before this, on 7 February, the Bf 109s of *Legion Condor* downed no less than thirteen SB-2 bombers and two I-16s with no losses to themselves. Three of the SB-2s were shot down in quick succession by Lt Wilhelm Balthasar. In all, thirty aircraft were claimed by Bf 109s during the battle for Teruél.

In an attempt to reach the Mediterranean and split the Republican government forces in two, Nationalist forces began an offensive in early 1938, eventually reaching the coast on 15 April. The Bf 109s of J./88 were transferred to La Cenia near the River Ebro delta. The same month, five Bf 109Cs arrived. Having a slightly improved overall performance, the Bf 109C also featured a heavier armament consisting of four MG 17s. These fighters were destined for 3./J88, which was temporarily withdrawn from the front for Bf 109 conversion training. Simultaneously, 3./J88's *Staffelkommandeur* Adolf Galland was replaced by Oblt Werner Mölders.

On 14 June, two Bf 109's of 2./J88 were lost, with Lt Plieber managing to nurse his badly damaged aircraft back to La Cenia. The second Bf 109 was flown by Lt Henz, who was forced down near River Mijares. When Henz's intact fighter was being dismantled, half-a-dozen Bf 109's arrived overhead and destroyed the Messerschmitt. However, the Bf 109 pilots were accumulating a large number of victories. On 15 July, Werner Mölders claimed his first victory—Mölders would become the highest-scoring ace of the *Legion Condor*, downing ten I-16's and four I-15bis's in less than four months.

During a huge air battle on 18 July, five I-15bis and five I-16s were shot down by Bf 109s and Italian CR.32s. However, two Bf 109s were claimed shot down in a separate air battle on the same day. The second battle for the Ebro bridgehead began on 24 and 25 July, with the three Bf 109 *Staffeln* being heavily committed to bomber escort and *Frei Jägd* sorties. The aerial tactics were further improved by introducing the so-called *Vierfinger Schwarm* (finger-four formation). The smallest tactical formation until that time was the *Rotte*, consisting of two aircraft flying in loose formation about 200 metres apart with the wingman flying behind and slightly above the leader, which protected the latter from attacks from the rear. At the initiative of Oblt Mölders, 3./J88 adopted the Vierfinger *Schwarm*, which consisted of two pairs of fighters. These fighter combat tactics increased the flexibility of the Bf 109 and provided the foundation for fighter tactics for decades to come.

By the autumn of 1938, the Nationalist air arm had achieved aerial supremacy, largely due to the Messerschmitt fighters. However, combat losses and wear and tear had reduced the operational effectiveness of the *Legion Condor*. Five Bf 109D-1s arrived at La Cenia during the first days of August, all destined for 3./J88. Plans were initiated to replace the Jumo 210-powered Bf 109's with Bf 109E's, with the former to be transferred to the Nationalist air arm. By December 1938, fifty-five Bf 109's had reached Spain, thirty-seven of which were still operational. Around this time, the first of an eventual total of forty-four Bf 109Es (colloquially known as *Emils*) began to arrive. This took place despite strong protests from high-ranking Luftwaffe officers, whose priority was to see home-based fighter units receiving Bf 109Es rather than transferring any such fighters to Spain, where the war had, to all intents and purposes, already been won. However, as with the sales to Switzerland and Yugoslavia, the transfer of Bf 109's to Spain was due to the high-grade ore—of vital importance for the German war industry—offered in exchange. 2./J88 were able to convert to the Bf 109E at Saragossa. Before the end of the war on 29 March 1939, about twenty Bf 109Es had been assembled by German technicians.

During the final months of the Spanish Civil War, the three Bf 109 *Staffeln* of J88 were mainly committed to ground strafing and rarely encountered any aerial opposition. The Republican air arm was no longer capable of sustained, concentrated operations, with the final Bf 109 victory of the war (a Polikarpov I-15bis) occurring on 5 March 1939. The final operational sortie of the Bf 109 *Staffeln* took place in the early hours of 27 March escorting He 111 bombers, during which no Republican aircraft were encountered. The exact number of Luftwaffe fighter pilots that served with the *Legion Condor* is unknown—estimates range from 150 to 250. Most of the fighter pilots that flew in Spanish skies, such as Wilhelm Balthasar and Werner Mölders, racked up huge numbers of victories during the Second World War.

For the Luftwaffe, the Spanish Civil War had proved invaluable not only for testing new combat aircraft, but also for developing new tactics and providing both pilots and ground crews with operational experience. *Legion Condor* Bf 109 pilots accounted for 189 Republican aircraft, with about twenty Bf 109s lost to all causes.

The exact quantity of Bf 109s transferred to the *Legion Condor* is not known with certainty. Published sources differ between a low figure of ninety-six and a high figure of 144. According to German sources, thirty-nine Bf 109Bs and forty-four Bf 109Es reached Spain. It would appear that the surviving Bf 109Cs and 'Ds' were returned to Germany (possibly due to the limited number of aircraft involved), with only the older Jumo-engine Bf 109Bs and the modern Daimler-Benz-powered Bf 109Es being transferred to Spanish control in March 1939.

Mass Production

Although a BFW design, as was common practice in the German aircraft manufacturing industry, the Bf 109 was also built under licence by other German aircraft manufacturers including AGO, Arado, Erla, Fieseler, Focke-Wulf, and WNF. In 1938, it was decided to transfer Bf 109 production from Augsburg to Regensburg—the first Bf 109E rolled off the Regensburg assembly line in

A Bf 109E assembly line at Regensburg. (*Wolfgang Mühlbauer/ DEHLA Archives*)

January 1939, where nearly 11,000 Bf 109s would be built. However, in 1939, a mere 144 *Emils* were completed, with only twenty-five of these being delivered to the Luftwaffe. The remaining 119 aircraft were exported to Switzerland and Yugoslavia. Although the sale of the premier Luftwaffe fighter abroad brought much needed raw materials to the German war industry, this was nevertheless highly controversial. With the rapid expansion of the Luftwaffe, additional Bf 109Es were urgently required to re-equip the *Jägdwaffe* units.

One Bf 109E-3a (the suffix letter 'a' referred to *Ausland*, meaning 'foreign nation') destined for Yugoslavia crashed on 1 November 1939, killing the factory test pilot Mühlenhausen. Mühlenhausen was eventually replaced by Josef 'Sepp' Haid, who went on to perform pre-delivery check flights on more than 5,000 Bf 109s during the war.

During the war, the name Messerschmitt would become synonymous with Luftwaffe single-seat fighters and, to some extent, with the Luftwaffe as a whole.

The Polish Campaign

The expansionist policies of the Nazi regime meant that further land areas were to be incorporated into the Reich to create *Lebensraum* for the German population. Following the annexation of Austria and the breaking of Czechoslovakia, Poland was next in line. On 24 August, the Molotov-Ribbentrop Pact was signed, which effectively sealed the partition of Poland between Germany and the USSR. Two days earlier, Hitler delivered a speech at Obersalzburg to high ranking German officers: 'Destruction of Poland is our first aim. Our target is not to achieve some defined line, but to destroy the human force ... Have no mercy. Be brutal. Eighty million people must receive what they deserve, they deserve their existence secured.'

The assault on Poland, codenamed *Fall Weiss*, was initially planned to begin on 26 August. However, *Fall Weiss* was postponed due to Poland's signing of an alliance with Britain on 25 August.

The Polish armed forces consisted of 1.2 million men, 600 tanks, and 494 aircraft, of which 392 were combat aircraft. Out of these, 158 were fighters, 86 were bombers, and 148 army co-operation and reconnaissance aircraft. All of the combat aircraft were of indigenous design, with the most modern fighter being the 1935-vintage PZL P-11c gull-winged monoplane fighter. Armed with two or four 7.7-mm machine guns and having a 150 kph speed disadvantage compared to the Bf 109E, 112 PZL P-11cs were available to the *Lotnictwo Wojskowe* (Polish Air Force) on 31 August 1939. Two types of bombers were in service: the PZL P-23 Karas single-engine bombers (eighty-six serviceable), and the twin-engine PZL P-37 Los (thirty-six serviceable), with the latter being the most modern aircraft in the *Lotnictwo Wojskowe* service. Information on the performance of the Luftwaffe's combat aircraft, including Bf 109s, was not made available to Lotnictwo Wojskowe

Luftwaffe Bf 109 Unit Strength, 2 September 1939, Polish Campaign				
Unit	**Base**	**Total aircraft**	**No. of serviceable aircraft**	**Remarks**
I./JG 1	Gutenfeld	54 (Bf 109Es)	54	Unit withdrawn on 6 Sep. 1939
I./JG 21	Gutenfeld	27 (Bf 109Ds)	24	
II.(J)/186 (T)	Brüsterort	24 (Bf 109Bs)	24	Unit withdrawn on 6 Sep. 1939
II./ZG 1	Lichtenau	36 (Bf 109Es)	36	Unit withdrawn on 27 Sep. 1939
Stab LG 2	Nieder-Ellgut	3 (Bf 109Es)	3	Subordinated to I./ZG 2 until 21 Sep. 1939, then to I.(J)/LG 2. Unit withdrawn on 30 Sep. 1939
I.(J)/LG 2	Malzkow (1 *Staffel*), Lottin (*Stab*, 2 and 3 *Staffeln*)	36 (Bf 109Es)	32	Unit withdrawn on 30 Sep. 1939
I./ZG 2	Gross-Stein	44 (Bf 109Ds)	40	Unit withdrawn on 21 Sep. 1939
I./JG 76	Stubendorf	51 (Bf 109Es)	45	NB; data for 1 Sep. 1939. Unit withdrawn on 26 Sep. 1939
I./JG 77	Juliusburg-Nord	48 (Bf 109Es)	43	Unit withdrawn on 28 Sep. 1939

units until the last days of March 1939. This was, according to one Polish fighter pilot, '...a revelation for us, although unpleasant'.

On 1 September 1939, the Luftwaffe had 1,056 Bf 109s (thirty-six Bf 109Cs, 389 Bf 109Ds, and 631 Bf 109Es), with 946 of these being serviceable. Of the Bf 109Ds, 112 were used by night-fighter units. The main operational roles of the Bf 109 units were to provide escort for the bombers and *Stuka* units, as well as conducting *Freie Jägd* sorties.

The first action for the Bf 109 units occurred in the afternoon of 1 September, with I./JG 21 having been detailed to provide escort for He 111s of kg 27 during a bombing raid against Warsaw. Upon reaching the rendezvous point, the trigger-happy He 111 gunners opened fire against the Bf 109s, mistaking them for Polish fighters. With no radio communication available, the *Gruppenkommodore* of

I./JG 21, Maj. Martin Mettig, attempted to fire an identification flare—the barrel of the flare gun was fitted on the right-hand side of the cockpit, making it possible for the pilot to fire and reload the flare gun. This went badly wrong when the flare went astray inside the cockpit. Mettig and his *Rottenflieger* had to abort and return to base. No Bf 109s were hit, but the pilots 'remained well clear of the bombers' as the gunners continued to fire against them.

Upon reaching the Warsaw suburbs, Polish PZL P.11c fighters awaited the Germans as reported by Lt Bob Heinz-Ekkehard, a pilot of 3./JG 21.

> A ferocious fight began, which quickly developed into a series of one-*versus*-one engagements. Our formation was now in total disarray, but we managed to engage all enemy fighters, which meant they couldn't get to the Heinkels. However, the prolonged fight ate into our fuel reserves and by the time we reached Warsaw we had barely enough gas left to make it back to base. Since we were scatted all over the sky it was each man for himself to find the way back to Arys-Rostken. For many of the rookie pilots getting their bearings right turned out to be an impossible task. I had no such problems, and, having positively established my position, quickly found my way home. Just before 1800 hours and with little more than fumes in my fuel tank, I was the first pilot from the 3. *Staffel* to land back at Arys-Rostken.[3]

Out of the eight Bf 109D-1s from 3./JG 21, only two arrived back at Arys-Rostken. Although no Bf 109s had been shot down, five pilots were forced down behind the front line due to a lack of fuel; all became prisoners of war. Another pilot, Gefr. Werner Ahrendt of 3./JG 21, had to make an unscheduled arrival at Berznicki, Lithuania. Ahrendt was interned, eventually being allowed to return on 6 October. However, five PZL P.11cs (referred to as 'PZL P-24s' in the Luftwaffe post-action briefings) were claimed as destroyed. Only four of these victories were subsequently confirmed—the first of these PZL P.11cs fell to Lt Fritz Gutezeit of 3./JG 21 at 16.55.

In the event, the Bf 109 units did not play a major role in the Polish campaign. In fact, the Polish fighter pilots considered the twin-engine Bf 110 as being a more dangerous opponent than the single-seat Bf 109. The Bf 109s were usually operated in defence of Luftwaffe air bases. With little fighter opposition, the Bf 109s were eventually diverted to ground strafing. Two units, I./JG 1 and I./JG 21, were soon withdrawn from Poland.

On 11 September, PZL P.11c pilots of the 132 *Eskadra Mysliwska* scrambled from Luban when a number of Bf 109's arrived over their airfield, with the Luftwaffe fighters performing,

> [A] regular merry-go-round. The readiness section of the *Dywizjon* removed the masking branches and scrambled immediately. Other pilots jumped into their machines and after a couple of minutes seven fighters were airborne … the Germans engaged … Eventually a trail of smoke appeared behind one of the Bf 109s. The aircraft fell to the ground. A moment later another Bf 109 emitting

> heavy smoke dropped towards the front line, where it crashed near the only artillery battery at the line of combat.

The Bf 109s were credited to kpt. Franciszek Jastrebski and pchor. Stefan Wapniarek. It appears likely that the Bf 109's belonged to I./ZG 2, which reported two of its Bf 109D-1's being forced down on this day following combat, with the aircraft suffering 60 and 40 per cent damage respectively.

On 17 September, Soviet forces attacked eastern Poland. Although sporadic resistance in the air continued, the *Lotnictwo Wojskowe* was a spent force by late September. On 5 October, Poland surrendered. The Polish government went into exile, with many airmen and technical staff being evacuated to Romania. Many pilots managed to reach France and Britain, continuing the fight against Nazi Germany.

Even though the PZL P-11c was outclassed in almost every aspect by the Bf 109, Polish fighter pilots claimed five Bf 109s shot down, with another ten being claimed by PZL P-37 and P-23 crews. Nevertheless, the majority of the forty Bf 109s lost by the end of September was due to ground fire and operational accidents, particularly due to a lack of fuel. An additional thirty-one Bf 109s suffered repairable damage. The most successful Luftwaffe pilot of the Polish campaign was Hptm Johannes Gentzen, the *Gruppenkommandeur* of I./ZG 2. Genzen's score consisted of six PZL P.23 Karas light bombers and one PZL P.37 Los medium bomber.

The Phoney War

Although the Luftwaffe was making its presence felt over Poland, the war on the Western Front seemed almost non-existent. No huge formations of Luftwaffe bombers appeared over London where blackout had been implemented precisely in fear and expectation of just that. Soon after war had been declared, it appeared as if life was returning to normal. Apart from a French Army thrust across the border, the front line remained static. During the first months of the war, British, French, and German reconnaissance aircraft regularly crossed the border, with fighters clashing on a number of occasions. Even before the war, a light-bomber force consisting of 160 Fairey Battles were based on French airfields. The Battles formed the core of the RAF Advanced Air Striking Force (AASF), which would later be reinforced by additional bomber, fighter and reconnaissance squadrons.

Differentiating between civilian and military targets was deemed difficult during daytime and virtually impossible at night due to the imposed blackout and the lack of long-range navigational experience over enemy territory, resulting in RAF Bomber Command only flying leaflet sorties over mainland Germany and the occupied territories. Actual bomb raids were only allowed against German naval vessels at sea, albeit not alongside a dock in a port. Following the declaration of war on 3 September 1939, the RAF despatched photo reconnaissance aircraft against Wilhelmshaven.

The first encounter between the RAF and Bf 109s occurred on 4 September when fourteen twin-engine Vickers Wellingtons of 9 and 149 Squadrons attacked the cruisers *Gneisenau* and *Scharnhorst* off Brunsbüttel. Fifteen Blenheims of 107, 110, and 139 Squadrons were to bomb *Kriegsmarine* ships anchored at Schillig Roads, Wilhelmshaven. After depositing their bombs, the Wellingtons were attacked by Bf 109Es from II./JG 77. Two of the RAF bombers were shot down, with one each claimed by Fw Alfred Held and Fw Hans Troitsch. These Wellingtons would be the first of many RAF aircraft to fall to Luftwaffe Bf 109 pilots.

Moments later, ten of the Blenheims (five had turned back due to poor weather) were intercepted by Bf 109s of II./JG 77 and 2./ZG 26. Four of the Blenheims were shot down in quick succession, with one Bf 109D of 2./ZG 26 being forced to ditch due to engine trouble. The Bf 109 pilot, Lt Hans Falke, was killed, becoming the Luftwaffe's first combat casualty (albeit due to technical failure) on the Western Front.

The first time that Bf 109s clashed with Allied fighters over the Western Front occurred on 8 September, when half-a-dozen French Curtiss H-75A Hawks encountered four Bf 109s of I./JG 53. Leading the Luftwaffe fighters was Oblt Werner Mölders. Although three of the French pilots claimed to have brought down two of the Bf 109s, neither side suffered any losses. It would appear that the French claims were due to the black smoke emanating from the exhausts of the DB 601 engines when the Luftwaffe pilots dived away. However, Mölders' Bf 109 had indeed been hit, with Mölders being forced to land at Birkenfeld.

Less than two weeks later, on 20 September, Bf 109s of JGr 152 shot down three Fairey Battles that had been part of a force of nine despatched on an unescorted reconnaissance sortie. Although one Bf 109 was claimed shot down by one of the Battle gunners, this was 'probably unconfirmed and incorrect'. On 27 September, a Battle gunner of 103 Squadron was responsible for shooting down a JGr 152 Bf 109D-1 west of Hornbach. Having first suffered the ignominy of being attacked in error by French fighters, the three Battles were then jumped by three Bf 109s. The ensuing fight resulted in the Bf 109 flown by Gefr Josef Scherm being hit by return fire. Moments earlier, Scherm had claimed another Battle shot down. Scherm died when his fighter crashed near Bockweiler at 12.30, marking the first time a Luftwaffe aircraft had been shot down by the RAF during the Second World War.

Although the majority of Bf 109 *Jägdgeschwader* operated during daytime, a few were also used as night fighters from early 1939 and mid-1940—in 1943 and 1944, Bf 109s were operated by several *Jägdgeschwader* using *Wilde Sau* ('wild boar') tactics. During the first months of 1939, the night fighter unit 10.(N)/JG 132 received Bf 109D-1s as replacement for their aging Ar 68s. This unit was eventually redesignated 10.(N)/NJG 2 and, along with 10.(N)/JG 26, operated a mix of Bf 109D-1s (nine aircraft with each unit) and Ar 68s by September 1939. Another two night-fighter *Staffeln* were part of JG 72, having a total of thirty-three Ar 68s. These four *Staffeln* formed the entire night-fighter element of the Luftwaffe at the outbreak of war. A few fighter units were not entirely unaccustomed to night-fighter operations, with some II./JG 132 pilots remarking that whenever Hitler made demands for more territory, the unit was ordered to undertake night-flight training exercises the week before.

During the autumn, personnel from 11./JG 72 were transferred to the newly formed 5./JG 52. Despite strong objections from 5./JG 52's *Staffelkapitän*, Oblt August Schumann, the unit was obliged to accept ancient Heinkel He 51s for night-fighter operations. For a brief period, 5./JG 52 pilots flew He 51s during the night and Bf 109s during the day.

When the air raid sirens sounded in Berlin during the night of 16–17 September, two fighters took off. Both fighters, one Ar 68 and one Bf 109, of I./JG 2 crashed fatally. It was thought that the pilots had been blinded by the powerful search lights; an inauspicious beginning for the Luftwaffe's night-fighter force. The distinction of being the first Allied bomber to actually drop bombs on Berlin belongs to a French Centre NC.223.4, which arrived over the German capital on the night of 7–8 June. During this epic sortie, about two tons of bombs were dropped, with the crew landing back at Paris-Orly after remaining airborne for 13.5 hours.)

A reconnaissance sortie flown on 30 September resulted in the loss of five Battles at the hands of 2./JG 53 Bf 109 pilots. Although two Bf 109's—flown by Stab Fw Prestele and Oblt Rolf Pingel—had suffered slight damage, the RAF cancelled all future Battle sorties across the lines. Two Hurricane squadrons, 1 and 73, were subsequently assigned escort duties.

The heaviest air combat on the Western front to date occurred on 30 September, with several separate clashes taking place during the day. The French Air Force sent two Potez 637's accompanied by a heavy fighter escort to photograph the area around Merzig—the French formation was intercepted by Bf 109s of I. and II./JG 53. When the dust had settled, the French had lost six aircraft and four pilots against four Bf 109s shot down, with three of the German pilots losing their lives.

With the coming winter aerial operations declined, although reconnaissance flights continued on a regular basis. On 30 October, Plt Off. Mould of 1 Squadron shot down a photo reconnaissance Do 17P. However, the first encounter with the Bf 109 was still some time away for the RAF's fighter squadrons.

With Poland conquered, a number of Luftwaffe fighter units were transferred to the Western Front. One such unit was I./ZG 2, which had been redesignated JGr 102 in the meantime. During the Polish campaign, the pilots of I./ZG 2 had claimed twenty-nine aircraft shot down, with another forty-nine being destroyed on the ground. On 6 November, JGr 102 clashed with French Curtiss H-75 Hawks of GC II/5. The Jumo 210-powered Bf 109D-1 proved inferior to the H-75 Hawk, with JGr 102 losing five aircraft and two pilots killed; two more pilots became prisoners of war. Three of the French fighters had suffered repairable damage. It was the worst defeat experienced by the Luftwaffe fighter units on the Western Front. As future events would prove, it was a gloriously isolated success for the French Air Force. On the same day, JGr 102 Bf 109s encountered a 73 Squadron Hurricane flown by Plt Off. Ayerst. In the event, Ayerst managed to escape, landing at Nancy. In all, ten bullet holes were found in the Hurricane's tail section in what appears to have been the first occasion that a RAF fighter met Bf 109s in the air during the war. During one clash on 22 November, a Bf 109E-1 of 1./JG 76 was forced to land at Goersdorf. The Bf 109 (W Nr 1304) was restored to airworthy condition, eventually being evaluated in France, Britain, and the USA. Due to the prevailing poor weather, air operations during December were limited to a reconnaissance flights. Several aircraft were damaged or written off in accidents, with weather being a contributing cause in some of the cases.

The Heligoland Raids

Following the declaration of war, the RAF would continue to raid German shipping, as well as fly a number of leaflet raids over mainland Germany. On 3 December, a force of twenty-four Wellingtons of 38, 115, and 149 Squadrons attacked a number of ships off Heligoland. One ship, claimed to be a cruiser, was hit, although it transpired that the Wellingtons sank a trawler. The bombers were then intercepted by Bf 109D's of I./ZG 26. One of the Luftwaffe pilots, Oblt Günther Specht, was shot down by return fire.[4]

This level of success boded well for the future. However, four subsequent anti-shipping raids failed to locate any *Kriegsmarine* vessels. Another daylight raid against shipping in the Heligoland Bight was carried out on 14 December. This time, a dozen 99 Squadron Wellingtons located a convoy in the Schillig Roads off Wilhelmshaven. They were met by Bf 109Es of 5./JG 77 and II.(J) 186 (T) as well as four Bf 110s of 1./ZG 26. No less than five Wellingtons were shot down by the Luftwaffe for the loss of one Bf 109. Officialdom found it difficult to comprehend that single-seat fighters were able to wreak such havoc on RAF bombers. Instead, the losses were attributed to heavy and accurate flak. Air Vice-Marshal Bottomley stated: 'It is by no means certain that enemy fighters did, in fact, succeeded in shooting down any of the Wellingtons.' It would appear that all of the Wellingtons shot down fell to pilots of 5./JG 77. It is worth noting that the Bf 109E's of this unit were only armed with 7.92-mm MG 17s, which lacked the punch of the 20-mm MG FF cannon.

Two small-scale raids on 15 and 17 December failed to locate any shipping. The following raid, on 18 December, would have far reaching consequences for the RAF. Despite the heavy losses on 14 December, a further raid against shipping north of Wilhelmshaven took place only four days later, on 18 December. A force of twenty-four Wellingtons was despatched, with twenty-two reaching the target area. The RAF bombers had been detected through an experimental Freya radar station at Wangerooge, allowing ample time to scramble Bf 109's of II./JG 77 and 10.(N)/JG 26, as well as a few Bf 110s. The sky was cloudless, and the lumbering Wellingtons were cut down by the Luftwaffe fighters. When the carnage was over, no less than ten of the Wellingtons had been shot down, with another two having to ditch on their way back due to battle damage. It was obvious that unescorted daytime bomb raids over Germany risked annihilation at the hands of Luftwaffe Bf 109s. The air battle had not been entirely one-sided; three Bf 109s (one Bf 109D-1 and two Bf 109Es) had been lost with two of the pilots killed. Another three were damaged in varying degrees.

A Bf 109E of 1./JG 20. This *Staffel* was redesignated 7./JG 51 soon afterwards. (*NMUSAF*)

On the Western Front, the first year of the war ended quietly. The winter curtailed any large-scale air operations, although reconnaissance sorties and sporadic dogfights occurred during the first months of 1940. In spite of the difficulties imposed by the cold and snowy weather conditions, the German High Command had planned to initiate *Fall Gelb* (Operation Yellow) on 17 January, which involved marching through Belgium and the Netherlands. Already postponed due to the prevailing poor weather, German units were preparing for *Fall Gelb* when a Luftwaffe Bf 108 force landed due to faulty navigation in Belgium on 10 January. One of the two officers aboard carried a copy of the *Fall Gelb* invasion plans with him. In the event, the Melchen incident, as it became known, resulted in the German invasion of the Low Countries and France being postponed yet again.

Long-range (and unarmed) photo reconnaissance Supermarine Spitfires began flying over Germany in November 1939. The first loss occurred on 22 March when Plt Off. Whitley was intercepted and shot down by Lt Jung of I./JG 20. Whitley unsuccessfully baled out, with the Spitfire (RAF serial N3069) coming down at Lobith—this was quite likely the first Spitfire to fall to the guns of a Bf 109.

Since September 1939, the number of Bf 109s written off or seriously damaged in accidents greatly outnumbered the operational losses over Poland and France. As a result, in March 1940 the RLM requisitioned seventy-five Bf 109Es destined for export customers. A new front of the war was about to be opened.

Denmark and Norway

Following the Soviet attack against Finland on 30 November 1939, Britain and France promised to send aircraft and other war materials to the small Nordic country—it must be remembered that at this time the USSR was an ally of Nazi Germany. Sweden had declared itself a non-combatant and sent as much military aid to Finland that could be spared. However, when it was suggested that British and French forces would be allowed to travel through Norway and Sweden to Finland, this was vehemently opposed by the Norwegian and Swedish governments. It was suspected that the Allied contingent would seize the Swedish high-grade iron ore mines, thus putting a stop to the lucrative export of iron ore to Germany, about one-third of which was shipped through the Norwegian town of Narvik. Iron ore was of utmost importance to the German war industry.

On 1 March, a directive regarding the invasion of Denmark and Norway was issued. The Luftwaffe's *X. Fliegerkorps* formed the airborne component of Operation Weserübung. Only one Bf 109 unit, II./JG 77, with thirty-eight aircraft, was to take part due to the distances involved, but also due to the expectation that the small Danish and Norwegian air arms would be unable to put up any long-term resistance.[5]

Interestingly, a RAF reconnaissance Spitfire flown by Flt Lt Maurice Longbottom, observed numerous Ju 52/3m's at Holtenau near Kiel on 7 April. The RAF photo interpreters were unable to unravel the true meaning of this, although all became clear two days later.

In the early hours of 9 April, Operation Weserübung began. Denmark was swiftly overrun, with II./JG 77 transferring from Husum on the German-Danish border to Esbjerg in the morning. On 10 April, the II./JG 77 pilots continued to Kristiansand-Kjevik on the southern tip of Norway; the ground personnel and equipment arrived the following day. The first Bf 109 air-to-air victory during the Norwegian campaign occurred on 12 April when Ofw Robert Menge shot down a Hudson of 224 Squadron. Shortly after noon, a force of RAF Hampdens appeared off Kristiansand. The fierce battle saw six of the Hampdens shot down by the Bf 109 pilots, including two claimed by Menge. However, II./JG 77 lost four pilots killed, with a fifth pilot being rescued after ditching in the sea. Further RAF raids against Kristiansand followed in the afternoon, but these were met by Bf 110s and Ju 88Cs.

Soon afterwards, II./JG 77 moved to Stavanger-Sola, with a Wellington of 38 Squadron being shot down by Lt Heinz Demes in the early hours of 15 April. On 24 April, two Hudsons of 220 Squadron were shot down off Stavanger. The last day of April saw further RAF raids, with six Blenheims of 110 Squadron and sixteen Wellingtons of 9, 37, and 99 Squadrons attacking Stavanger-Sola in separate waves. Four Bf 109's—flown by Fw Erwin Sawallisch, Helmut Henz (rank unknown), Lt Demes, and Fw Harbach—intercepted the Blenheims, shooting down two of the bombers. The second wave arrived less two hours later and was initially erroneously reported as consisting of eighty bombers. The four Bf 109s had been re-armed and refuelled, and, joined by a pair of I./ZG 76 Bf 110s, took off to intercept the RAF bombers. Out of the thirteen Wellingtons that reached Stavanger-Sola, four were shot down. However, Lt Demes was hit by return fire, crashing in flames into the sea.

By early May, II./JG 77 transferred to Værnes near Trondheim. By this time, fighting was concentrated to central and northern Norway. On 27 May, a pair of Blenheims of 254 Squadron strafed Stavanger-Sola, claiming to have damaged twenty Bf 109's on the ground, although it would in fact appear that none were damaged. One 6./JG 77 pilot, Hpt Franz-Heinz Lange, took off and shot down one of the Blenheims, although his Bf 109 was hit by return fire and Lange was injured. II./JG 77 saw no further action before Norway surrendered on 10 June. However, one Bf 109 was written off on 3 June at Oslo-Fornebu in an emergency landing.

During the British retreat from Norway, disaster struck on 8 June when the aircraft carrier HMS *Glorious* was sunk by the German cruiser *Scharnhorst*. During the battle, the *Scharnhorst* had suffered some damage and sought refuge at Trondheim. Both the RAF and Fleet Air Arm (FAA) attempted to sink the *Scharnhorst*, with twelve Hudsons of 269 Squadron making an attack on 11 June. Apart from a heavy barrage of flak, the Hudsons were met by four Bf 109s and one Bf 110 of 3./ZG 76. Two of the Hudsons were claimed shot down by II./JG 77 pilots. During the evening of 12 June, the RAF returned to Trondheim, with one Blenheim of 254 Squadron shot down by Oblt Walther of 1./ZG 76. The biggest raid took place on 13 June, when fifteen FAA Blackburn Skuas attacked the *Scharnhorst*. The hapless Skuas were met by flak and Luftwaffe fighters, with eight being shot down, including four by II./JG 77 pilots; Ofw Hans-Jacob Arnoldy claimed one Skua, Fw Menge two, and Fw Sawallisch one.

II./JG 77 saw further action during June and July, with the unit being joined by III./JG 77 (redesignated from II(J)./TrGr 186) in early July. During one heavy RAF raid on 9 July, seven Blenheims of 21 and 57 Squadrons were shot down, including two each by Fw Menge and Lt Horst Carganico. The battle was not entirely one-sided, though, with one 5./JG 77 pilot, Uffz Gerhard Weber, being shot down and killed.

II./JG 77 remained in Scandinavia until early 1941 when the unit was transferred to Romania in anticipation of the invasion of Greece and Crete. Later on, II./JG 77 fought on the Eastern Front.

During a training flight, a Bf 109E of 4./JG 77 ended up on the trotting course at Karlstad, Sweden. The pilot, Uffz Fröba, was soon repatriated, while his fighter was thoroughly examined by the aircraft manufacturer Saab. (*Arlanda Civil Aviation Collection*)

France and the Low Countries

The German invasion of Denmark and Norway meant increased tension along the Western Front. However, only a few Luftwaffe sorties were flown, with a Bf 109E of 4./JG 51 being severely damaged by flak over Kehl on 9 April. Two days later, RAF Hurricanes clashed inconclusively with Bf 109s of JG 53. One rather embarrassing friendly-fire incident took place on 17 April when I./JG 20 Bf 109s intercepted a Fw 58 of *Jägdfliegerführer* 2, eventually forcing down the twin-engine aircraft and its injured crew near Orsey.

The following day proved to be a particularly costly one for the Bf 109 units, with no less than six aircraft being written off and another two damaged. None of these losses were attributable to enemy action, however. The cause of the accidents were two III./JG 52 Bf 109E-3s colliding in mid-air south of Mannheim (one pilot killed and one baled out safely), one Bf 109E-1 of 2./JG 54 destroyed in a forced landing near Böblingen (the pilot survived), one Bf 109D-1 of 8./JG 3 crashing fatally upon return from an operational sortie, a Bf 109E-3 of 8./JG 3 destroyed in a forced landing at Recklinghausen, and one Bf 109E of I./JG 27 destroyed in a landing accident at Siegen. Finally, two Bf 109E-1s of II./JG 52 collided on take-off from Speyer.

Increased aerial activity resulted in several encounters between the RAF and the Luftwaffe. On 20 April, 1 Squadron Hurricanes intercepted a He 111 with an escort of four III./JG 2 Bf 109's. Even though three of the Bf 109's were claimed as shot down (one being reported as a Heinkel He 113), it would appear that none were lost. Later the same day, four 1 Squadron Hurricanes clashed with nine Bf 109's of JG 53. Flt Lt Walker claimed one Bf 109 (flown by Lt Sievers of 7./JG 53) with a second Messerschmitt being claimed by Fg Off. Drake. 1 Squadron suffered no losses.

On 3 May, a captured Bf 109E (W Nr 1304) was demonstrated at Amiens to a number of 1 Squadron pilots. The Bf 109E was also pitted in mock combat against a Hurricane, with the former being flown by Fg Off. Brown. The day before, 1 Squadron had received an initial batch of four Hurricanes fitted with three-blade constant-speed propellers. This propeller gave the Hurricane improved performance over the older, two-blade fixed-pitch wooden propellers. It was discovered that the Hurricane was, in fact, more manoeuvrable than the Bf 109, also being slightly faster at low altitude.

During early May, additional RAF squadrons arrived in France. No Spitfire squadrons were based in France; the RAF fighter squadrons were equipped with Gloster Gladiators and Hawker Hurricanes. There were few encounters with the Luftwaffe in what was the calm before the storm.

Blitzkrieg

On 10 May 1940, no fewer than 1,286 Bf 109s were in Luftwaffe service, of which 951 were serviceable. On this day, the invasion of France and the Low Countries began. The same *Blitzkrieg* tactics that had been employed during the Polish campaign saw armoured columns supported by Ju 87 dive bombers spearheading the invasion, with large-scale paratroop drops taking place over the Netherlands. The Duchy of Luxembourg was soon overwhelmed, with Belgian and Dutch defences succumbing to the might of the German armed forces.

The follow tables denote Luftwaffe Bf 109 units on the Western Front on 10 May 1940 (except where noted, all aircraft are Bf 109Es).

***JägdFliegerführer* 2, Dortmund**			
Unit	**Total no. of aircraft**	**Serviceable aircraft**	**Based**
Stab Jafü 2	4	2	Dortmund
Stab JG 26	4	3	Dortmund
II./JG 26	47	36	Dortmund
III./JG 26	42	22	Essen-Mülheim
III./JG 3	37	25	Hopsten
Stab JG 51	4	3	Bönninghardt
I./JG 20	48	36	Bönninghardt
I./JG 26	44	35	Bönninghardt
II./JG 27	32	23	Wesel
5./JG 27	16	12	Bönninghardt
I./JG 51	47	38	Krefeld
Total:	325	235	

VIII. *Fliegerkorps*, Grevenbroich			
Unit	**Total no. of aircraft**	**Serviceable aircraft**	**Based**
Stab JG 27	4	4	Mönchengladbach
I./JG 27	48	38	Mönchengladbach
I./JG 1	48	36	Gymnich
I./JG 21	46	37	Mönchengladbach
Total:	146	115	

I. *Fliegerkorps*, Cologne			
Unit	**Total no. of aircraft**	**Serviceable aircraft**	**Based**
Stab JG 77	4	3	Pepperhoven
I./JG 77	48	35	Odendorf
Stab I./JG 3	4	3	Bonn-Hangelar
1./JG 3	16	12	Pepperhoven

2./JG 3	16	12	Vogelsang
3./JG 3	16	11	Dünstekoven
Total:	104	76	

V. *Fliegerkorps*, Gersthofen			
Unit	**Total no. of aircraft**	**Serviceable aircraft**	**Based**
Stab JG 52	4	3	Mannheim-Sandhofen
I./JG 52	48	36	Lachen-Speyerdorf
II./JG 52	38	33	Speyer
Stab JG 54	4	4	Böblingen
I./JG 54	48	29	Eutingen
II./JG 51	48	35	Böblingen
Total:	200	140	

***JägdFliegerführer* 3, Wiesbaden**			
Unit	**Total no. of aircraft**	**Serviceable aircraft**	**Based**
Stab JG 2	4	4	Frankfurt-Rebstock
I./JG 2	48	39	Bassenheim
III./JG 2	38	23	Frankrurt-Rebstock
I./JG 76	48	43	Ober-Olm
Stab JG 53	4	4	Wiesbaden-Erbenheim
I./JG 53	48	40	Darmstadt-Griesheim
II./JG 53	48	45	Mannheim-Sandhofen
III./JG 53	48	38	Trier-Euren
III./JG 52	48	30	Mannheim-Sandhofen
Total:	344	266	

***JägdFliegerführer* Deutsche Bucht, Jever**			
Unit	**Total no. of aircraft**	**Serviceable aircraft**	**Based**
Stab JG 1	4	4	Jever
II./JG 2	47	35	Nordholz
Stab IV.(N)/JG 2	4	3	Hopsten (Bf 109D-1)
10.(N)/JG 2	16	10	Hopsten (Bf 109D-1)
I.(J)/LG 2	32	21	Wyk auf Föhr
3.(J)/LG 2	16	11	Esbjerg, Denmark
II.(J) TrGr 186	48	35	Wangerooge
Total:	167	119	

Allied Air Defences

The *Aéronautique Militaire Belge* (AMB) was equipped with three different types of fighter aircraft—twenty-five Fiat CR.42s, fourteen Gloster Gladiator Is, and less than twenty Hawker Hurricanes. Initial attacks on AMB air bases saw fourteen Fiat CR.42s and eleven Hurricanes destroyed. One CR 42 pilot did, however, claim one Bf 109 (flown by Lt Dutel of 2./JG 1.) shot down. Dutel managed to coax his damaged fighter across the border and take to his parachute over Aachen-Mätzdorf. The 1/1/2 Aé (Comet) Squadron, based at Schaffen with fourteen Gladiators, fared better. With only minutes to spare before a Luftwaffe raid against Schaffen at 4.32 a.m., fourteen Gladiators managed to take-off, with two more being destroyed.

At 09.15 a.m. on 10 May, a large formation of Bf 109s clashed with AMB Gladiators, claiming five shot down for the loss of one Luftwaffe fighter. Three Fairey Fox biplanes were quickly shot down, although Lt Dufossez managed to down one Bf 109. On 11 May, nine BAF Battles attacked the bridges over the Albert channel; escort was provided by six Gladiators. The Battles were intercepted before they reached their targets, with one being shot down by a Bf 109 of I./JG 27, and six more by the ever-present flak. Bf 109s of JG 1 were also involved, shooting down four Gladiators. One Bf 109 was claimed by First Sergeant Henri Winand, and another one damaged by First Sergeant Denis Rolin. On 14 May, Fiat CR.42s shot down one Bf 109 of 8./JG 53 and damaged another. However, Belgian resistance in the air was essentially over, with the few remaining aircraft being evacuated to France. On 28 May the Belgian King, against the advice of his government ministers, elected to surrender rather than go into exile.

On 10 May, the *Militaire Luchtvaart* (Dutch Air Force, ML) had a total of thirty-three Fokker D.XXI fighters, of which twenty-eight were operational. First flown on 27 March 1936 (almost exactly ten months after the Bf 109), the Fokker D.XXI was of orthodox construction, featuring a fixed undercarriage and enclosed cockpit. Powered by an 830-hp Bristol Mercury VIII engine and with armament

One of the Bf 109Es lost over the Netherlands in mid-May 1940. (*NMUSAF*)

consisting of four 7.9-mm machine guns, the Fokker D.XXI had a maximum speed of 480 kph. The rugged Fokker D.XXI was more manoeuvrable than the Bf 109E, although inferior in most other respects. The ML Fokker D.XXIs were divided among three squadrons based at De Kooy, Schiphol, and Ypenburg. Also in service were twenty-three twin-engine Fokker G.I heavy fighters.

The invasion began in the early hours of 10 May, with Fokker D.XXIs meeting Bf 109s over Den Helder. Despite being severely outnumbered, MLD pilots claimed two Bf 109s. Upon being shot down over De Kooy at 5.40 a.m. by 2Lt Overvest, one Bf 109 pilot, Hptm D. Robitzsch of 5./JGr. 186, incredulously asked his Dutch captors, '*warum leisten sie denn wiederstand*?' ('why do you oppose us?') Although no Fokker D.XXIs had been lost, most had been damaged during the fight. There was little respite, with the Bf 109s returning to strafe De Kooy at 8.40 a.m., destroying or damaging six D.XXI's. Further combat took place during the day, with Oblt Seifert of 3./JG 26 and Lt Neumann of 6./JG 27 claiming one Fokker D.XXI each. As with the Belgian Air Force, the MLD fighter pilots were unable to continue operations for more than a few days. However, before the Durch surrender on 15 May, the MLD Fokker D.XXI pilots had shot down seven Bf 109s.

The theoretical strength of the *Armée de l'Air* on 10 May was 210 squadrons. Out of these, there were twenty-six fighter squadrons equipped with Bloch 151/152s, C.714s, D.520s, MS 406s, or American-built H-75A Hawks. Of these, only the H-75A Hawk and the D.520 were able to hold their own against the Bf 109E, and very few D.520s were serving with front-line fighter squadrons in early May 1940. In addition, there existed a number of local defence flights, often referred to as 'chimney flights', defending industrial sites. However, due to a number of reasons (including ongoing re-equipment with more modern aircraft, insufficient training and such forth), only 119 squadrons were operational, with only some 25 per cent of these initially being committed to combat.

During the first day of the invasion, twenty-one French aircraft were shot down, with another fifty-seven destroyed in bomb raids or strafing attacks against airfields. The Bf 109 units flew numerous close-support sorties, also providing escort for the Ju 87 *Stuka*s. Only twelve Bf 109s were lost on 10 May, with another eleven aircraft suffering varying degrees of damage. RAF and *Armée de l'Air* fighters were frequently encountered however, although many of the Bf 109 pilots were relative newcomers, they held the tactical advantage over the Allied fighters on account of the latter's adherence to rigid three- or five-aircraft Vics that compared badly to the *Rotten* and *Schwarm* tactics of the Luftwaffe. Indeed, one JG 2 pilot, Wilhelm Balthasar, managed to achieve victories for twenty-one consecutive days during the French campaign.

On 12 May, the recently-appointed *Geschwader Adjutant* of JG 27, Adolf Galland, claimed his first victories, which he subsequently reported as Belgian Air Force Hurricanes. As all Belgian Hurricanes had been destroyed on 10 and 11 May, Galland's victories were most likely RAF Hurricanes or French MS 406s. Having served as *Staffelkapitän* with 4./LG 2, a Hs 123 unit, during the brief Polish campaign, Adolf Galland would eventually rise to command of the Luftwaffe's fighter arm at the age of twenty-nine. During the summer of 1940, Galland was to become one of the best known *Experten* of the Luftwaffe.

RAF Spitfires (of 66 Squadron) clashed with Bf 109s for the first time on 13 May, claiming one Bf 109 of 5./JG 26 shot down along with four Ju 87s. The Bf 109 was flown by Lt Borris, who abandoned his aircraft west of Dordrecht. Defiants of 264 Squadron also took part in the battle. Seven of the RAF fighters were lost, with six of the Defiants shot down. In this context it can be said that Luftwaffe Bf 109 pilots initially confused the Defiant with the Hurricane. A two-seat fighter armed with a gun turret with four 0.30-inch machine guns, the Defiant showed itself effective against bombers, but the Luftwaffe quickly learned of its drawbacks, making it an easy target for roving Bf 109 pilots.

One Spitfire (N3027) had been badly damaged during the battle, with Plt Off. Brown coming down at Aalter at 6 a.m. In their turn, the 5./JG 26 pilots claimed seven Spitfires and one Defiant. During the latter stages of the battle of France, Bf 109 pilots appeared to develop a high regard for the Supermarine Spitfire. It would seem that scoring a victory over a Spitfire ranked far higher than over a Hurricane. Being shot down by a Spitfire was no shame, but by a Hurricane... Nevertheless, aircraft recognition in the heat of battle was difficult.

The following day saw several waves of RAF bombers attack the bridges across the River Meuse. Out of seventy-one aircraft committed, thirty-seven were lost to flak and fighters—the highest loss rate in RAF history.

With fighting in the Netherlands largely over by 15 May, the Germans concentrated their efforts on breaking through the Belgian defence lines and advancing rapidly into northern France. During the first six days of the invasion, the RAF had lost a large number of aircraft. The decision to reinforce the RAF fighter squadrons based in France was addressed by Air Chief Marshal Dowding, who wrote on 16 May:

> I must point out that within the last few days the equivalent of ten squadrons have been sent to France, that the Hurricane squadrons remaining in this country are seriously depleted, and that the more squadrons which are sent to France the higher will be the wastage and the more insistent the demands for reinforcements ... I believe that, if an adequate fighter force is kept in this country, if the fleet remains in being, and if Home Forces are suitably organised to resist invasion, we should be able to carry on the war single-handed for some time, if not indefinitely. But, if the Home Defence Force is drained away in desperate attempts to remedy the situation in France, defeat in France will involve the final, complete and irremediable defeat of this country.[6]

In other words, Dowding foresaw the defeat of France and urged for immediate preparations for the impending Battle of Britain. In the event, Prime Minister Churchill took Dowding's advice that no additional RAF fighters should be sent to France, stating that, 'it makes no difference whether we strike down German bombers here or in France'. It was simply too late to stem the tide of the German *Panzers* and *Stukas*. Nevertheless, RAF fighter squadrons based in southern England would fly numerous sorties over the Low Countries and France until late May 1940.

On 21 May, the German forces broke through the front line, reaching Abbeville and the English Channel to drive a wedge between the Allied armies. In the north-east, British and French troops were encircled in the Dunkirk pocket. *Reichsmarschall* Göring was adamant that, 'this [was] a wonderful opportunity for the Luftwaffe' to deliver the final punch to the British and French forces on the continent. Göring eventually managed to persuade Hitler that the Luftwaffe, instead of the *Panzers*, would annihilate the enemy in the Dunkirk pocket.

By the end of May, a few RAF fighter squadrons, including 19 and 54 Squadrons, began copying the Luftwaffe *Rotten* and *Schwarm* tactics.

On 25 May, the decision was taken to evacuate the remaining British and French forces via the harbour at Dunkirk. Three days later, RAF Fighter Command received instructions to 'ensure the protection of Dunkirk beaches (three miles on either side) from first light until darkness by continuous fighter patrols in strength'. This resulted in a reduced RAF presence over other areas of France. Nevertheless, raids by Luftwaffe *Stuka*s and twin-engine bombers against the evacuation fleet resulted in many ships being sunk or heavily damaged. On 29 May, ferocious dogfights over Dunkirk resulted in seven Bf 109s, five He 111s, four Ju 87s, and three Ju 88s being shot down by RAF Spitfires and Defiants.

In the event, Operation Dynamo, the 'Miracle of Dunkirk' was successfully concluded on 4 June. A total of 338,226 British and French troops had been rescued by a vast flotilla of ships. Most of their weapons and equipment had to be left behind.

On 5 June, Oblt Mölders was shot down by a French fighter. Mölders later recalled the beginning of his two-week experience as a prisoner of war.

> Hanging under the parachute I look round for my adversary but I can only see 109s which are circling me. I am silently floating towards the ground, ground that is still being held by the enemy as I am 60 kilometres behind the front line, west of Compiègne. I draw my pistol and having cocked it put it into the pocket of my trousers.
>
> The ground is coming up so fast so I bend my knees slightly and the impact is relatively soft. I immediately free myself from the parachute and run towards a wood. Frenchmen are running towards me from all sides and as I reach the edge of the wood a bullet flies past my ears. I throw away my fur-lined flight jacket and run breathlessly to the other end of the wood. A large field of lupins lies in front of me so I crawl into it.
>
> Suddenly I hear a powerful explosion nearby and I see a thick cloud of blue smoke rising. My aircraft, having caught fire as it crashed, has just blown up and been completely destroyed. For about an hour I manage to stay hidden but suddenly I realise that this field is being searched too and the men are closing in. I lie totally flat and a farmer walks past ten metres away without seeing me. I am already believing that I am out of danger when I am challenged from behind. I stand up and raise my arms. Only now do I see soldiers and farmers everywhere. While I am standing still one of the *Poilus* (French soldiers) fires again but without hitting me.

> In the twinkling of an eye I am surrounded by about fifty people with five bayonets menacingly pointing towards me. Eventually an officer arrives who relieves me of all my possessions, including my *Ritterkreutz*, but fortunately I don't have much on me. Wearing a shirt and sleeveless sweater I am standing in the middle of a growing number of troops and the mood is hardly friendly. I explain that I am an Air Force officer and I have barely turned round to walk towards a road when the first kick lands on my rear. I think 'Stay calm' as I receive another blow in the small of my back. A little gnome of a farmer walking beside me berates me in no uncertain words until the officer intervenes and they escort me to a car with a few last blows.[7]

Interestingly, the French authorities seemed to have failed to recognise the propaganda value of having the highest-scoring Luftwaffe ace in their custody. Only a week before his capture, Mölders had become the first Luftwaffe fighter pilot to receive the *Ritterkreutz* (Knight's Cross).[8] Mölders subsequently returned to III./JG 53 following the French surrender, which took place on 25 June.

France was divided into two parts, with Germany occupying the northern and western parts of the country, including the Atlantic coastline, with a German puppet regime, Vichy France, being established in the southern areas of France. Within six weeks, Germany had defeated Belgium, the Netherlands, and France—something they had been unable to achieve during the First World War of 1914–1918.

In retrospect, it is worth noting that French fighter pilots averaged one sortie each day, with some Luftwaffe Bf 109 units managing to conduct up to four sorties per day. During the advance into France, the *Jägdgeschwader* were supported by a highly

A Bf 109E of 8./JG 51, with a mechanic hand-cranking the engine inertia starter. (*NMUSAF*)

efficient ground-support organisation. When a new airfield or landing ground (occasionally little more than a sufficiently flat grass strip of sufficient length) was occupied, telephone and teleprinter equipment was soon into place, with the ever-present Ju 52/3m transports bringing everything from mechanics, fuel, ammunition and tents. This meant that the Bf 109 pilots could resume operations within less than a day after arriving at a newly captured airfield.

During the German invasion, more than 400 *Armée de l'Air* fighters were destroyed either in air combat or during Luftwaffe raids on French airfields. Additionally, many unserviceable or damaged *Armée de l'Air* and RAF aircraft were abandoned during the retreat. French and RAF squadrons had the disadvantage of being forced to fight while on the retreat, constantly moving from one airfield to another, which put great strains on the supply and command chain. RAF fighter squadrons were too few in number to be able to influence the outcome of the Battle of France, with the RAF as a whole losing 949 aircraft, including 477 precious fighters, between 10 May and 24 June. Nearly 200 fighter pilots were killed, wounded or missing—a horrific number that included twenty-nine hard-to-replace squadron and flight commanders. Nevertheless, the Luftwaffe had lost nearly 1,500 aircraft, including some 200 Bf 109s since 10 May.

Even though the *Blitzkrieg* tactics had worked successfully in the Low Countries and France, the operational experience showed that the Bf 109 did indeed possess some clear disadvantages. The most serious of these was the lack of range, which, in the event, would not be properly addressed until late August. An internal fuel capacity of 400 litres gave the Bf 109E an endurance of about fifty-five minutes at an altitude of 5,000 metres with a continuous maximum engine output of 2,400 rpm, giving a true airspeed of 520 kph with the range being 460 km. Range and endurance could, of course, be increased through fuel economy, but naturally

Following the end of the Battle of France, a Bf 109E was placed on display in central Berlin. (*Author's collection*)

A line-up of JG 52 Bf 109Es, most likely in Belgium or the Netherlands. The three-engine aircraft in the left background is a Fokker F.VII/3m. (*NMUSAF*)

this would considerably reduce the combat value of the Messerschmitt fighter. Other deficiencies included the lack of armour protection for the pilot, which was eventually solved by adding 8-mm thick seat armour.

The Battle of Britain

Following the conquest of France and the Low Countries, Britain stood alone against the overwhelming might of the Luftwaffe.

The Battle of Britain was about to begin. On 18 June, Churchill had stated that, 'the Battle of France is over, I expect that the Battle of Britain is about to begin.' Two days previously, Hitler had issued Directive 16, which concerned the invasion of the British Isles. Codenamed Operation Seelöwe (Operation Sea Lion), the invasion was to be preceded by heavy air attacks against British convoys. However, Hitler believed that Britain might surrender to the might of Germany before the invasion took place, with the Luftwaffe delivering a decisive blow—as had indeed occurred earlier in Poland and the Netherlands—and thus negating the necessity for an invasion: 'As England, despite the hopelessness of her military situation, has so far shown herself unwilling to come to any compromise, I have therefore decided to begin preparation for, and if necessary to carry out, an invasion of England.' It appeared that Hitler was reluctant to commit to an actual invasion of Britain.

Indeed, as late as 19 July, Hitler once more attempted to enter peace negotiations with Britain. However, attacks against shipping in the English Channel had already begun in earnest on 4 July. The attacks against British convoys were named *Kanalkampf* (Channel Battle) by the Germans. With heavy fighter escort, Luftwaffe

Ju 87 *Stukas* and twin-engine bombers attacked convoys off the southern coast of England. Air raids against British coastal towns and industrial centres also took place, with night raids beginning on 3 June.

Following consolidation and some vital rest and recuperation in the wake of the French surrender, the Luftwaffe Bf 109 units were once again committed to battle. The English Channel was not seen as much of an obstacle but something more akin to the moat of a medieval fortress. Crossing the Channel by air at its narrowest point took less than five minutes; establishing air superiority over the beaches of southern England would surely be swiftly accomplished against an RAF that had lost precious pilots and aircraft during the battle of France.

On 10 July, the 'official' start of the battle (at least, according to the RAF) was marked by a Bf 109E of 5./JG 51 downed over the Thames Estuary, killing Uffz Stöcker. Escort and *Freie Jägd* sorties over the southern English coast were flown with increasing frequency, with the barrage balloons protecting the coastal towns occasionally providing excellent opportunities for target practice for the Bf 109 pilots.

On 30 June, 1,107 Bf 109s were in Luftwaffe service, with the vast majority of these being based on the Western Front. On this day, German forces landed at Guernsey, with Jersey invaded on 1 July. The Channel Islands would remain under German occupation until May 1945. A number of Bf 109Es of JG 53 were eventually based at Villiaze and St Helier, with the Channel Islands airfields also serving as emergency landing strips for damaged Luftwaffe aircraft unable to reach France. JG 53 Bf 109s would remain in the Channel Islands until early 1941.

During July, the Bf 109 units of *Luftflotten* 2 and 3 arrived in the Pas-de-Calais, Normandy, and Brittany areas. JG 2 was based at Beaumont-le-Roger, Bernay, Granville, Mardyck, Octeville and Oye Plage; JG 3 at Colembert, Desvres, and

A Bf 109E either undergoing maintenance or having its guns synchronised in the summer of 1940. (*NMUSAF*)

Samer; JG 26 at Audembert, Caffiers, and Marquise; JG 27 at Carquebut, Crépon, Plumetot, and Théville; JG 51 at Pihen, St Omer, and Wissant; JG 52 at Coquelles and Peuplingues; JG 53 at Berck, Dinan, Etaples, La Villiaze, and Sempy; and LG 2 at Mardyck and Oye Plage. Arguably, the Battle of Britain was to be the zenith of the combat career of the Bf 109. At the time, it was the sole single-seat fighter of the Luftwaffe, being pitted against RAF Hurricanes and Spitfires of similar performance. Compared with the Hurricane Mk. I and Spitfire Mk. I, which each had an armament of eight .303 machine guns, the armament of the Bf 109E-3 consisted of a pair of 7.92-mm MG 17s and three 20-mm MG 151/20 cannons. The latter weapons in particular carried a considerable punch. However, the MG 151/20 cannon mounted in the engine caused severe problems. In the end, this cannon was often removed in service. Even if the performance of the Bf 109 and its RAF opponents were closely matched, the outcome in any air battle was usually down to 'height, sun, and surprise'. At this stage of the war, it must be said that the majority of the *Jägdwaffe* pilots had accumulated more combat experience than their RAF counterparts.

The inability of the Defiant crews to combat Bf 109Es on anything resembling equal terms was already well known. On 19 July, Bf 109s of III./JG 51 shot down five out of 141 Squadron's nine Defiants, seriously damaging another aircraft. One Bf 109E of 9./JG 51 was hit by return fire with its pilot, Fw Heilmann, managing to make it back to France. Fw Heilmann died of his wounds the following day.

On 27 July, having successfully returned from his brief sojourn as a French PoW, Maj. Werner Mölders succeeded Oblt Theodore Osterkamp as the *Geschwaderkommodore* of JG 51. Aged forty-eight, Osterkamp had served as a fighter pilot during the Great War, accumulating thirty-two victories. During the early stages of the Second World War, Osterkamp scored an additional six victories, also having the distinction of being one of the oldest Bf 109 fighter pilot. Promoted to *Generalmajor*, Osterkamp was forbidden to fly any further combat sorties. Air combat, particularly in single-seat fighters, was no business for old men.

A Bf 109E being pushed out of the assembly line. (*NMUSAF*)

On 30 July, Hitler ordered Göring to 'destroy the flying units, ground organisations and supply installations of the RAF and the British air armaments industry'. Three days later, on 2 August, Göring ordered the Luftwaffe to redirect its efforts from attacking convoys towards annihilating the RAF as a fighting force. Göring himself believed that it would take no more than four days to eliminate the RAF presence from southern England—the Battle of Britain was set to begin in earnest.

As mentioned previously, the short range of the Bf 109E was a major drawback when operating over southern England. On any raids north of London, the bombers were forced to continue unescorted. In his memoirs, Adolf Galland wrote:

> The short range of the Me 109 became more and more of a disadvantage. During a single sortie of my Wing we lost twelve fighter planes, not by enemy action, but simply because after two hours flying time the bombers we were escorting had not yet reached the mainland on their return journey. Five of these fighters managed to make a pancake landing on the French shore with their last drop of fuel, seven of them landing in the 'drink'.

If a Luftwaffe aircraft went down in the English Channel, its pilot or crew stood a fairly good chance of rescue. Among the Bf 109 pilot's gear was an inflatable dinghy; high-speed rescue launches would attempt to reach any downed aircraft. Additionally, a number of rescue floats were anchored at regular intervals with Heinkel He 59 *Seenotdienst* (Air Sea Rescue) floatplanes being active. During the initial stages of the battle, the He 59s were finished in Red Cross markings, eventually changing to regular Luftwaffe insignia. RAF fighters were shooting down any He 59 caught over the Channel. Later on, the *Seenotdienst* He 59s were provided with fighter escort, with the twin-engine Bf 110 being preferred over the Bf 109. This was due to the Bf 109s lack of range.

A posed propaganda shot showing a fighter pilot describing the sortie to a mechanic. (*NMUSAF*)

One unnamed *Jägdwaffe* pilot later described (reproduced in the Swedish aviation magazine *Flyg* in the January 1941 issue) his experiences trying to regain the French coast following an 'argument' with RAF fighters:

> The enemy is 'finished'. He goes down in flames, while I praise my good fortune. But my engine has stopped. [The propeller] is still turning slowly, stopping completely after two turns. The three propeller blades appear black and sinister against the horizon. I try to remain calm. I am still at an altitude of 4,800 metres. I have about 30 kilometres left to reach the Channel, with the Channel itself being some 40 kilometres wide in this direction. I am thinking: I will reach the Channel at least. While I am flying in this direction, I am feathering the propeller, i.e. with the least amount of air resistance. The fields and meadows of southern England are still below me. I can now discern the sharp coastline in front of me. I am flying as calmly as I can, with my right hand on the control column. I cannot make any sudden moves. Every metre is valuable. It is indeed a strange feeling gliding through the air without the noise of the engine.
>
> As a precaution, I release the cockpit canopy so that I will be able to quickly get out of the aircraft if I have to ditch. The minutes pass slowly. Ten long minutes! Here comes the Channel. I notice some German boats down there. I case I have to bale out, I keep one of them in sight to try to land as close as possible. When I passed over the coast, I had an altitude of 3,000 metres. The fighter slowly loses altitude and I try keep the aircraft from stalling. Long calculations does not help, I have to literally fly by the seat of my pants.
>
> I can now see the other coastline far ahead and below me. When I have passed half distance across the Channel, I know that I at least will be able to land close to the coast. I should get that far. I now become aware of a light down-wind breeze, on which my Me is floating toward land.
>
> At an altitude of about 50 metres I am crossing the French coast. On my right, I see a freshly ploughed field. I put my aircraft in a slight dive to the right and glides toward a belly landing. The aircraft settles fairly soft in the field, skids for ten metres before coming to a halt. I remain seated for a moment. This thing was not that easy. I wipe away the earth that has ended up in my face. Slowly, I release my parachute harness, and climbs out of the aircraft. The belly is slightly damaged, with the propeller naturally being completely bent out of shape. I walk around my ME, counting more than twenty hits, most of which are in the wings and fuselage. However, two stray bullets are lodged in the radiator. It was these that forced me down.

One huge advantage for the British was radar. Although the radar operators were unable to differentiate between fighters and bombers, they were able to provide information on the size, position, height, and course of the enemy formation. According to Adolf Galland, the information supplied to the Bf 109 pilots during the briefing 'was already three hours old (when they crossed the English coast)', the British only as many seconds old.

The Bf 109s were frequently misidentified by RAF pilots as 'Heinkel He 113s'. According to German propaganda, the He 113 fighter was in large-scale Luftwaffe service. The truth was the opposite with the He 113 being the propaganda designation for the He 100D. Similarly to the earlier He 112B, the He 100D was not ordered by the Luftwaffe. Of the fifteen He 100Ds built, three each were sold to Japan and the USSR. The remaining nine He 100Ds were retained at the Heinkel Rostock factory, never firing their guns in anger.

On 10 August 1940, 934 Bf 109s were available, of which 805 were serviceable. Göring declared this day to be *Adler Tag* (Eagle Day), the first in a series of large-scale attacks against RAF airfields. In the event, poor weather meant that only reconnaissance aircraft reached British shores, with a few Luftwaffe attacks against shipping taking place. However, 13 August saw the Luftwaffe committed to *Adler Tag*. This all-out effort included Bf 109s of JG 2, JG 3, JG 26, JG 27, JG 51, JG 52, JG 53, and JG 54 venturing across the English Channel. A total of 1,485 Luftwaffe sorties were flown on 13 August, attacking airfields and radar stations. The net result of *Adler Tag* was, for the Luftwaffe, disappointing. The RAF lost eighteen Hurricanes and two Spitfires, with others being damaged. Ten Bf 109s were lost, with another three being damaged.

Despite the best efforts of the Bf 109 pilots, the RAF fighters had managed to reach the bombers, resulting in five Do 17Zs, seven Ju 87s and eight Ju 88s being shot down or damaged beyond repair, with others suffering various degrees of damage. Additionally, seven twin-engine Bf 110 *Zerstörers* (Destroyers) had been lost. Two days later, the Luftwaffe was back in force, with the raids being directed against RAF airfields. The RAF flew 974 sorties, losing seventeen pilots killed and thirty-four aircraft destroyed. Nevertheless, the jubilant RAF pilots claimed 182 Luftwaffe aircraft shot down. In the event, the Luftwaffe lost seventy-five aircraft, including seven Bf 109s. One of the Bf 109s belonged *to 3./Erprobungsgruppe 210*, a special unit devoted to developing proper *Zerstörer* and *Jabo* tactics. Two of the unit's three *Staffeln* were flying the twin-engine Bf 110, with the third *Staffel* operating Bf 109E-4s.

What would become known as 'The Hardest Day' occurred on 18 August. With the weather forecast stating that Sunday 18 August was to be sunny with few clouds, maximum effort was undertaken. Nevertheless, the Luftwaffe bombers failed in its objective in destroying the RAF on the ground. During the day, nearly twenty Bf 109s were lost as well. One of the Bf 109s brought down was flown by Oblt Julius Neumann of 6./JG 27. Years later, Neumann recalled his final sortie of the war.

> Soon after crossing the British coastline I caught sight of a few small specks on the horizon: RAF fighters! In no time at all, a tremendous dogfight was in full swing as we endeavoured to keep the Spitfires and Hurricanes off the *Stukas*. I succeeded in getting on the tail on one of the enemy fighters and chased him in a high speed dive while he jinked from side to side to avoid my fire. We were soon down to about 165 feet (50 metres) above the sea and heading towards the Isle of Wight. I knew that I had scored some hits and my quarry began to leave a thin trail of black smoke. Now, I thought, I have him cold! I glanced aft to make sure that my tail was clear before going in for the kill and was startled to see two smoke trails behind us—a black one and a white one. The white trail was coming from my *Emil*!

> Although I had no idea that my aircraft had been hit, the glycol system had evidently been punctured. I glanced at the engine temperature and saw that the needle was hard against the upper stop, realising at the same time that the cockpit was getting uncomfortably hot. My engine began to splutter, so I broke off the chase and tried to gain height in order to bale out. At that moment, the engine cut dead and flame(s) began to appear from the joint in the cowling. I was only some 100 feet (30 metres) above the ground, jettisoned the canopy and prepared to crash land, side-slipping into a small field. The port wing struck the ground first and took the force of the landing, and my *Emil* spun round and slithered to a halt in a cloud of dust, my head receiving a hefty when it was jerked violently to one side.[9]

Evidently, the *Jägdwaffe* fighter pilots were to blame for these disasters. On 19 August, Göring declared that the *Jägdwaffe* Bf 109 pilots appeared more interested in adding to their personal victory scores than providing proper protection for the bombers. The fact that tying the fighters to close-escort sorties would rob the Bf 109s from *Frei Jägd* sorties was inconsequential. Göring also stated that if any fighter pilot had the nerve to abort an escort sortie on account of poor weather, he was to be summarily court-martialled. Older, 'complacent' commanding officers were subsequently replaced by younger fighter pilots who had gained considerable operational experience, like Adolf Galland, who was promoted to *Geschwaderkommodore* for JG 26, while Günther Lützow becoming *Geschwaderkommodore* for JG 3. The next day, 20 August, a directive regarding the task ahead for the Luftwaffe was issued:

> To continue the fight against the enemy air force until further notice, with the aim of weakening the British fighter forces. The enemy is to be forced to use his fighters by means of ceaseless attacks. In addition, the aircraft industry and the ground organisation are to be attacked by individual aircraft by day and by night, if weather conditions do not permit the use of complete formations.

However, even putting aside the short endurance of the Bf 109, escorting bombers was a difficult task. Adolf Galland later recalled:

> … In 1940 at least, JG 26 was the best wing for escort. I organised this thing myself, because we didn't have any experience or rules to follow. I split up the escort between direct escorts, which flies in direct contact with the bombers, mostly at the same speed, which was much too low. This was about one-third of the total number—one *Gruppe*. They stayed with the bombers, and defended them – not the best way, but this was the way that the bombers wanted it. Better is the *erweiterte* ['detached'] escort, which keeps the bomber stream in sight, but can go to one side, and if it finds the enemy, can go [to] attack. Even so, after the combat, it must try to re-establish contact with the bombers after the fighting. And then we had the *Freie Jägd*, which flew in advance of the bombers. This was many times the most successful escort. Of course, it was not seen by the bombers, and the bomber crews didn't trust it. I discussed these tactics with the bombers many, many times, without success. They kept complaining to Göring, who listened to them.[10]

Bf 109Es flying close escort to He 111 bombers. This particular tactic of remaining close and within viewing distance of the bomber crews was thoroughly disliked by the *Jägdwaffe* pilots. (*NMUSAF*)

During the latter half of August, attacks against RAF airfields continued unabated. By late August, RAF Fighter Command was on its knees. The relentless Luftwaffe raids against the airfields saw RAF fighter pilots, 'the few', nearing the brink of physical exhaustion. The fighter pilots were regularly flying several sorties every day with little or no respite, while their airfields were being continuously raided. For instance, in just three days during late August and early September, Biggin Hill was hit six times, with most of the hangars and ground equipment destroyed or seriously damaged. However, fate (and faulty navigation) would change the course of the battle.

During the night of 24–25 August, Luftwaffe bombers hit London for the first time. Faulty navigation was to blame, but the RAF retaliated the following night, with some fifty bombers being despatched against Berlin. The RAF bomber crews found the German capital completely covered in cloud. Six of the bombers were lost, with three running out of fuel due to a strong headwind on the return flight. Many of the bombs hit farmland south of Berlin, with one wooden summer cottage being destroyed. Two people suffered slight injuries. However, the psychological effect of the raid would have far-reaching consequences. On 2 September, Hitler issued orders to initiate a bombing campaign against London. As a result, the airfields of Fighter Command, which had been continuously attacked by the Luftwaffe for more than three weeks, gained a much-needed respite.

Deliveries of Hurricanes and Spitfires to RAF Fighter Command continued with little interruption throughout the battle, with damaged aircraft being repaired at maintenance units or by the respective manufacturer. On 31 August,

A Bf 109E of 9./JG 54 seen on a field in southern England. (*NMUSAF*)

the Defiant was belatedly removed from daylight operations, except in areas where the RAF held complete air superiority. It would, however, prove a quite efficient night fighter.

The final days of August also saw the introduction into service of a new variant: the Bf 109E-7. Essentially similar to the earlier Bf 109E-4, the E-7 could be fitted with a 300-litre drop tank constructed of plywood and carried on an under-fuselage ETC 500 centreline rack. Tests were performed at Rechlin in June 1940 using an Erla-built Bf 109E-4 coded CA+NK (W Nr 1361), with this aircraft serving as the prototype for the E-7 and E-8 series. The addition of 300 litres of fuel greatly extended the range of the Bf 109E. However, the drop tank was rarely used, as it had a propensity to leak fuel and even catch fire. If the drop tank was not fitted, a 250 SC 250 bomb could be carried. Alternately, four 50 SC 50 bombs could be carried. A Revi C/12 d bomb sight was fitted as well, with the additional oil consumption being addressed through the fitting of a 9-litre oil tank in the engine compartment. The oil flow could be checked by the pilot by means of a valve.

The ability to carry a bomb meant that the operational use of the Bf 109E would soon include that of a fighter-bomber. Earlier Bf 109E variants were subsequently retrofitted as fighter bombers. A total of 229 Bf 109s were lost during August, with fifty-seven pilots being killed, forty-one wounded, eighty-four missing in action, and three becoming prisoners of war.

During a visit to Dover Castle on 28 August, Prime Minister Churchill witnessed the shooting down of several Luftwaffe aircraft, as later recalled by his bodyguard, W. H. Thompson:

Bf 109E-4 CA+NK seen during fighter-bomber trials at Rechlin. Note the very limited ground clearance for the 250-kg bomb. (*NMUSAF*)

> While at Dover Castle, an alert sounded and from the Cliffside we could see the approach of the German bombers and the resulting clash when our fighters attacked. The battle went over our heads for several moments. During the fighting, dodging and shooting, two German planes came down into the sea, perhaps half-a-mile from where we stood and watched. It thrilled us all to see the enemy in flames, a roar, a hiss and a fountain of exploding waters
>
> ... Driving from Dover to Ramsgate, we saw a fighter plane shot down and Churchill immediately asked our driver to take us as close to the point where it would crash as we could get. We arrived at the spot. Churchill jumped out and proceeded on foot with me at his side. This was an unnecessary risk as the Germans did a great deal of strafing and always shot off whatever they still had aboard before scooting for home again. Firemen had arrived just before us. Flames were shooting up. We had not been able to determine whether it was a German fighter or one of our own
>
> ... 'I hope to God it isn't a British plane!' Churchill remarked. He walked right up to the blazing craft. To the relief of us all, we found it was a German and that the pilot had baled out.[11]

The incident witnessed by Churchill involved a *Stab* I./JG 3 Bf 109E-4 (W Nr 0941), which crashed at Church Whitfield at 16.25. The pilot, Lt Landry, had been severely wounded and baled out of his stricken fighter; he died of his wounds on 23 September. It must be said that most Luftwaffe pilots that ended up in British captivity received good treatment. However, there were instances where civilians attempted to, so to speak, take matters into their own hands. During a

Frei Jägd sortie on 27 October, Lt Wilhelm Busch of I./JG 3 was shot down over Wickham Court Farm east of Croydon. Taking to his parachute, Lt Busch landed at New Addington Estate where he was 'set upon by a group of incensed housewives'. Lt Busch was eventually rescued by the arrival of a British army patrol.

The Battle of Britain came to its climax on 15 September. Two large-scale attacks against targets in southern England and the Greater London area, with the first raid including more than 100 *Frei Jägd* Bf 109s paving the way for the bombers, as well as twenty-one Bf 109 *Jabos* of JG 2 that were to strike against various railway targets across London. On 17 September, Hitler postponed Operation Seelöwe indefinitely. With winter rapidly approaching, an invasion force would not only have had to fight against the RAF, Royal Navy, and British Army, but also poor weather conditions. Ultimately, it was inability of the Luftwaffe to establish air superiority over southern England that resulted in the invasion being postponed and, in the end, cancelled.

The efforts and sacrifices of RAF's Fighter Command ensured the survival of Britain and an eventual victory over Nazi Germany. However, it was not until 31 October that the Battle of Britain officially came to an end. Nevertheless, Luftwaffe night raids against London and other cities would continue until May 1941. Additionally, an increasing number of Bf 109 *Jabo* sorties were flown against shipping and coastal cities. Between 1 July and 31 October, slightly more than 600 Bf 109s had been lost. Losses for the Bf 109 units continued, with the *Gruppenkommodore* of I./JG 2, Maj. Helmut Wick, shot down over the Solent on 28 November. Wick had accumulated fifty-five victories in little over a year.

An unidentified Bf 109E on public display in Bolton, Lancashire, 1940–41. (*NMUSAF*)

The Bf 109F Arrives

A new variant, the Bf 109F, began to reach operational units in late 1940, with *Stab* JG 51 being the first recipient in early October. Although the Bf 109F, or *Friedrich* as it became known, had a better overall performance than the Bf 109E, the armament had been reduced, resulting in severe criticism from many Luftwaffe pilots.

The JG 51 *Geschwaderkommodore*, Werner Mölders, flew the first operational Bf 109F sortie on 9 October, using Bf 109F-1 W Nr 5628. Two days later, Mölders shot down a 66 Squadron Spitfire. Additional Bf 109F-1s were delivered to I./JG 51 later the same month. The first operational loss of a Bf 109F occurred on 11 November when the I./JG 51 *Staffelkapitän*, Oblt Georg Clausen, was lost over the English Channel. On 5 December, Bf 109s of JG 26 escorted II.(J)/LG 2 on a fighter-bomber sweep over southern England.

In March 1941, the Air Ministry's Deputy Directorate of Air Tactics distributed information on different Luftwaffe combat aircraft, including the Bf 109.

> In this type, the pilot is very vulnerable to deflection attacks owing to the position of the armour, which is some 50 inches astern of his seat. The glycol, radiator and oil coolers are also very vulnerable to attack from below, and many aircraft have been brought down by having their cooling systems shot through. Me 109s frequently adopt dive and zoom tactics, which are not easy to follow and for Hurricane Is the best counter measure seem to be to attempt to make surprise attacks. If the Me 109s form defensive circles, it is best to attack them by flying round inside the circle in the opposite direction. When Me 109s are escorting bomber formations and form defensive circles, it is best for the fighters to make feint attacks to try and occupy the attention of the fighters while allowing the bombers to proceed unescorted. Small numbers of fighters have successfully achieved this, allowing the greater concentration of our fighters to attack the

Bf 109 V24 code VK+AB was one of the prototypes for the Bf 109F series. (*NMUSAF*)

> enemy bombers. Me 109s seem to prefer avoiding combats where numbers are more or less equal, but sometimes go away to gain height and then return in an attempt to surprise our fighters.

In early 1941, the RAF took delivery of an initial batch of US-designed Bell Aircobras. It had been hoped that the Airacobra would be able to hold its own against the Bf 109, supplementing the RAF Spitfire MkV that had begun to roll off the assembly lines. During comparative trials, the Airacobra showed itself to have a superior turning radius and higher diving speed than the Bf 109. However, as one RAF pilot later put it, above an altitude of 6,000 metres, the Airacobra was 'utterly useless'. Only one squadron, No. 601, operated Airacobras, flying a single sortie across the Channel where 'nothing but flak' was encountered. Improved Airacobras would perform well in Soviet service against late-model Bf 109s.

No Longer a Pure Fighter

Specialised ground attack aircraft had been a feature of the First World War and operated with a high-degree of success in support of advancing troops. By the early 1930s, the concept of dive-bombing entered the minds of the RLM, and, in particular, with Ernst Udet. The Spanish Civil War made it possible for the Luftwaffe to develop and establish new tactics regarding close air support and dive-bombing. As a result, five dedicated *Schlachtfliegergruppen* (literally 'slaughter flight groups') were formed on 1 August 1938. Although these units initially used He 50s and Hs 123s, the Bf 109E would form the main equipment of II.(Schl)/LG 2 from mid-1940 until the early months of 1942.

During the summer of 1940, a number of fighter-bomber sorties using Bf 109Es had already been flown over Britain by *3./Erbrobungsgruppe 210*. As described previously, the Bf 109E-4 was fitted with an external bomb rack and was thus able to carry either one SC 250 bomb or four SC 50 bombs. This involved a new role for the Bf 109, namely, that of the fighter-bomber (*Jägdbomber*, usually shortened to *Jabo*). With the aerial offensive against Britain continuing during the spring of 1941, a new tactic, known as 'tip and run', was introduced. One unit, II.(Schl)/LG 2, had flown *Jabo* sorties against London and the south coast of England since late August 1940. Its final appearance over the British Isles occurred in March 1941, with one Bf 109E being shot down when caught by three Hurricanes. In March 1941, the decision was taken to devote 2, 6, and 7./JG 2 (i.e. one *Staffel* from each Gruppe) to the role of *Jabo*. These units did, however, continue to operate in the pure fighter role as well.

The first *Jabo* sortie was flown on 26 April (by 2./JG 2). This, and subsequent attacks, were mostly directed against convoys, with the *Jabo*s claiming two freight ships and a tanker sunk after one month of operations. Such raids showed enough promise that a dedicated *Jabostaffel*, 13./JG 2, was formed on 10 November 1941. The

A 250-kg bomb being loaded onto a Bf 109E. Note the Junkers W 34 in the left background. (*NMUSAF*)

tactics were devised by Oblt Frank Liesendahl. This involved approaching the target at an extremely low altitude, then climb to a maximum altitude of 500 metres when the target was at a distance of 1,800 metres before levelling off before entering a shallow dive. The pilot would then drop the bomb on the target and turn away. This tactic was known as the Liesendahl *Verfahren* (Liesendahl process).

Training and refining the tip-and-run tactics continued well into the new year. Although 13./JG 2 did not become operational until 4 March 1942, the unit had completed a number of sorties prior to this date. A steamer had been sunk on 10 February to give further impetus to the tip-and-run tactics. Apart from 13./JG 2 (eventually redesignated 10./JG 2), a second *Jabostaffel*, 10./JG 26, was formed. The pilots of the latter unit had not received much training in the tip-and-run tactics, which, along with a certain unwillingness exhibited by a few pilots, did not bode well for a resounding success. Nevertheless, tip-and-run raids were formally authorised in March 1942. The following month, 156 tip-and-run sorties were flown against convoys, harbours, and high-value inland targets—the latter included the Telecommunications and Research Establishment (TRE) in Dorset, which was attacked twice, forcing its relocation to Malvern in Worcestershire. The tip-and-run raids did prove successful, with the RAF having no effective countermeasure. With the Bf 109s approaching both low and fast, they were difficult to catch for the RAF fighters. Both 10./JG 2 and 10./JG 26 began to receive Fw 190s during the summer of 1942, which, in the event, was a far more suitable aircraft for low-level fighter-bomber sorties.

A close-up of the bomb rack carrying four SC 50. (50 kg) bombs. (*NMUSAF*)

Re-equipping with the Bf 109F lasted well into the summer of 1941. Units based in France and those destined to participate in Operation Barbarossa had priority for deliveries of the new Bf 109 variant. The first flight in a Bf 109F for Adolf Galland took place on 15 April 1941. Later the same day, Galland took off in the same fighter, having been invited to celebrate Theo Osterkamp's birthday. Bringing along bottles of champagne and some lobsters, Galland and his *Rottenflieger*, Obfw Westphal, decided to make a detour over southern England before heading for Le Touquet. Encountering a number of Spitfires, Galland claimed three of the RAF fighters shot down. The Luftwaffe pilots eventually dived away, heading for France. As it turned out, Galland's Bf 109F was considerably slower than the one flown by Westphal. Entering the landing pattern over Le Touquet, Galland extended the undercarriage, or so he thought. He was met with red flares and ground crew waving frantically. Following the clash with the RAF Spitfires, Galland had inadvertently extended his undercarriage, which considerably reduced the speed of his Messerschmitt. During the flight, he had had to consistently re-adjust the trim rudder to keep the Bf 109 straight and level. In the event, Galland managed to land safely with the undercarriage extended.

By the spring of 1941, Bf 109Fs had largely replaced the faithful *Emils* of JG 51, I./JG 3, III./JG 26, and JG 53, with JG 54 following a few months later. The higher performance Bf 109F did not receive unanimous praise from all Luftwaffe pilots. The armament was considered insufficient, with the engine cooling proving to be problematical. As related before, several early-production Bf 109Fs had been lost in seemingly unexplainable accidents. It was eventually determined that the tail section would separate from the rear fuselage during high-*g* manoeuvres, which was eventually resolved by fitting metal strips between the rear fuselage and tail section.

A poor but nevertheless interesting photo of a Bf 109F. (*NMUSAF*)

The introduction into service of the Bf 109F was plagued by difficulties. Severe criticism was raised against its weak armament, as well as its unfortunate tendency of shedding its tail section during high-*g* manoeuvres. In early April 1941, *Generalfeldmarschall* Albert Kesselring, Commander of *Luftflotte* 2, sent a telegram to Ernst Udet (who forwarded it to Willy Messerschmitt on 4 April) regarding no less than twenty-five deficiencies found in the Bf 109F. Apart from the problems with the tail section, Kesselring also mentioned that the pilot seat was located too far forward, making it impossible for a pilot in full flying kit 'to move the control column fully backwards and one result of this is that only wheel landings are possible'. The oxygen breathing gear was said to be wholly inadequate; the ammunition containers in the wings came loose (small wooden blocks were fitted as a temporary remedy); the automatic propeller pitch control needed to be fixed; the main wheel tyres endured extremely high wear and tear due to 'pronounced toe-in' when landing on concrete runways and required replacement after twenty landings; the fuel consumption of Arado-built aircraft was 70 litres more per hour than Bf 109Fs manufactured by other companies—and such forth.

Accidents continued to occur during the summer of 1941.

> On 4 June 1941, shortly after we had received our new Bf 109F-2 aircraft, the *Staffelkapitän*, Oblt Hein, took the entire *Staffel* in tight formation up to maximum altitude. We were flying over the North Sea at 12,500 metres and dived down steeply in formation, our airspeed indicators registering the maximum, about 1,000 kph. We had dived to about 5,000 metres, when the *Kapitän* ordered us to pull out slowly. We gradually eased back on our control columns in order to bring the aircraft to a normal attitude, but one excited voice over the radio stated that his aircraft would not pull out. It was Harry Krause. The *Kapitän* told him to keep

calm and to slowly but firmly pull back on his stick, but we heard Krause crying: 'It's not responding, it's not responding!'

At this point, the *Staffelkapitän* told him to bale out. We saw Krause's canopy come away but, to our horror, saw two separate dots falling down followed by one loosely fluttering parachute. (Krause) had pulled his ripcord immediately after he'd left his aircraft, but due to the high speed of his fall, the straps of his parachute had been torn apart and he plummeted to his death. His body was later discovered in a sand dune. Only his flight suit kept him in one piece; there was not a single bone unbroken.[12]

Yugoslavia and Greece

Expecting a quick and easy victory, Italy invaded Greece on 28 October 1940. However, the Italian forces met fierce resistance both on the ground and in the air. On 4 November, Hitler, anxious not to see Mussolini embarrassed or even suffer a humiliating defeat at the hands of the numerically inferior Greek forces, issued a directive to investigate options to send German reinforcements to assist the struggling Italian army. Initially, Luftwaffe Ju 52/3ms ferried Italian troops and supplies to the front while plans for further German involvement were discussed. With planning for the invasion of the USSR well underway, an invasion of Greece would have to be concluded in a swift manner. However, due to political and military reasons, Greece would have to wait until 1 April 1941.

During the first months of 1941, Luftwaffe units of *Luftflotte* 4 and VIII. *Fliegerkorps* were transferred to bases in Austria, Bulgaria, and Romania in anticipation of an invasion of Greece, which put additional political and military pressure on Yugoslavia. With Bulgaria and Romania already under German dominance, the Yugoslav government were asked (or rather, bullied) into signing the Tripartite Pact with Germany. Following some deliberation, the actual signing took place on 25 March, which resulted in an anti-German *coup d'état* two days later. Swift action was necessary. While Greece, and Yugoslavia were dealt with, the invasion of the USSR had to be postponed for four weeks. On 6 April, German forces, supported by Italy, Bulgaria, and Hungary, invaded Yugoslavia.

Luftwaffe Bf 109 units, 5 April 1941				
Unit	**Base**	**Total no. of aircraft**	**Serviceable aircraft**	**Remarks**
II./JG 54	Graz, Austria			*Fliegerführer* Graz
I./JG 27	Graz, Austria			*Fliegerführer* Graz
III./JG 54	Arad, Romania			*Fliegerführer* Arad
4./JG 54	Arad, Romania			*Fliegerführer* Arad

Stab JG 77	Arad, Romania			*Fliegerführer* Arad
II./JG 77	Arad, Romania			*Fliegerführer* Arad
III./JG 77	Arad, Romania			*Fliegerführer* Arad
Stab JG 27	Belica & Sofia-Vrba, Bulgaria			VIII. *Fliegerkorps*
II./JG 27	Belica & Sofia-Vrba, Bulgaria			VIII. *Fliegerkorps*
III./JG 27	Belica & Sofia-Vrba, Bulgaria			VIII. *Fliegerkorps*
I.(J)/LG 2	Sofia-Vrazdebna, Bulgaria			VIII. *Fliegerkorps*
II.(Sch)/LG 2	Sofia-Vrazdebna, Bulgaria	29	23	VIII. *Fliegerkorps*

It was inevitable that the Luftwaffe Bf 109 units would encounter Bf 109Es flown by the Yugoslav air arm. In an attempt to avoid 'friendly-fire' incidents, the forward fuselages of the Luftwaffe Bf 109s were painted yellow. Even if the VVKJ possessed a large number of modern combat aircraft purchased from a disparate number of countries, including Bf 109Es, Hurricanes, Blenheims, and SM 79s, several factors reduced their operational value and efficiency, including a lack of flying hours for its pilots, orthodox tactics, and a poor supply of spare parts.

During the first day of the invasion, the Bf 109 units were heavily engaged in bomber-escort and ground strafing sorties, mainly against airfields. Around 06.00, seventeen Bf 109s, including aircraft belonging to I.(J)/LG 2, strafed Rezanovacka Kosa airfield, destroying several aircraft on the ground before shooting down no less than eleven Furies that had been preparing to take-off during the initial attack. Only one I.(J)/LG 2 Bf 109 was lost, with three more force-landing upon return to their bases in Bulgaria. During another strafing attack, Hpt Herbert Ihlefeld of I.(J)/LG 2 was shot down over Nis, becoming a PoW.

The first encounter between Bf 109Es flown by opposing sides took place in the air above Prjnavor, when a total of thirty-four Yugoslav Air Force (VVKJ) fighters, including twenty-nine Bf 109s, engaged a large Luftwaffe formation, which included Bf 109s of JG 77. During the brief but fierce fight, nine VVKJ fighters were shot down or severely damaged. During the day, several raids against Belgrade took place, claiming the destruction of dozens of VVKJ aircraft for the loss of only one Bf 109E of *Stab* JG 54.

On 6 April, Luftwaffe Bf 109s conducted strafing raids against VVKJ airfields across Yugoslavia, as well as Yugoslav army troop columns. One of the JG 27 pilots strafing Ljubljana airfield was Hans-Joachim Marseille, who managed to collect an anti-aircraft shell in the fuselage of his aircraft. Nevertheless, Marseille managed to make a safe return to Graz. During the second day of the invasion, 4./JG 54 Bf 109s clashed with VVKJ B 109s, claiming four shot down for no loss. By this time, the Luftwaffe had secured complete aerial supremacy over Yugoslavia, with few VVKJ fighters remaining airworthy. On 17 April, an unconditional surrender was signed. Nevertheless, Yugoslavian partisan forces would cause much trouble for the occupying German and Italian forces.

A number of RAF squadrons were based in Greece, reinforcing the meagre Greek Air Force, which was composed of a heterogeneous mix of fighters, including Polish PZL P.24s, British Gladiators, and French Bloch 151s. In the early hours of 6 April, a German troop column entered the Rupel Pass. A dozen Hurricanes of 33 Squadron, led by Sqn Ldr Marmaduke Thomas St John 'Pat' Pattle, met Bf 109Es of 8./JG 27. During a brief but fierce combat, four Bf 109s were shot down, including two by Sqn Ldr Pattle. Although Luftwaffe raids against Greek airfields and shipping continued, Yugoslavia remained the primary objective. Meanwhile, RAF Blenheims, usually escorted by Hurricanes, conducted a number of raids against German troop concentrations in Yugoslavia. One unescorted raid on 13 April ended in disaster when three Bf 109s of 6./JG 27 shot down six Blenheims.

With Yugoslav resistance at an end, the Luftwaffe turned its attention toward Greece. On 14 April, many Yugoslav aircraft began to arrive at Paramythia, provoking repeated Axis strafing attacks against both Paramythia and Larissa. At Larissa, eight Bf 109s of II./JG 77 shot approximately fifteen RAF and Greek aircraft, as well as shooting down two out of three 33 Squadron Hurricanes that had just managed to get airborne prior to the attack. However, two of the Bf 109s were lost, including the one flown by Lt Jacob Arnoldy, who was mortally wounded before baling out over the airfield. Remarkably, Arnoldy's Bf 109E managed a near-perfect pilotless belly landing, with only two bullet holes being discovered, both located just below the canopy. However, worse was to come for the RAF squadrons in Greece.

On 19 April, most of the remaining Greek fighters were destroyed in a strafing attack against Amphiklia-Lodi. During the afternoon, Sqn Ldr Pattle claimed at least one Bf 109 destroyed, although these losses cannot be verified by German records. During the morning of the following day, thirty-six Bf 109s of JG 77—including five bomb-carrying aircraft—attacked ships in Athens harbour, claiming hits or near misses on two vessels as well as strafing Menidi airfield. Further raids against the area around Athens followed, during which several RAF aircraft were destroyed or seriously damaged. A strafing attack against Eleusis by II./JG 27 was later recalled by Roald Dahl, then a Hurricane pilot with 33 Squadron.

> There were many 109s circling the aerodrome, and one by one they straightened out and dived past the hangars, spraying the ground with their guns. But they did something else. They slid back their cockpit hoods and threw out small bombs which exploded when they hit the ground and fiercely flung quantities of large lead balls in every direction ... Then I saw the men, the ground crews, standing up in their slit trenches firing at the Messerschmitts with their rifles, reloading and firing as fast as they could, cursing and shouting as they shot, aiming ludicrously, hopelessly, aiming at an aeroplane with just a rifle. At Eleusis there were no other defences. Suddenly the Messerschmitts all turned and headed for home, all except one, which glided down and made a smooth landing on the aerodrome. Then there was chaos. The Greeks around us raised a shout and jumped on to the fire

> tender and headed out towards the crashed German aeroplane. At the same time more Greeks streamed out from every corner of the field, shouting and yelling and crying for the blood of the pilot. It was a mob intent on vengeance and one could not blame them.[13]

The 4./JG 27 pilot was Ofw Fritz Röckel, who was extremely fortunate that RAF personnel were the first ones to reach the crash site and thus prevented a near-certain lynching. Röckel was transported to a RAF Medical Officer for treatment, eventually returning to his unit.

During the afternoon, Sqn Ldr Pattle was shot down and killed. During the Greek campaign, Sqn Ldr Pattle, DFC and Bar, had been credited with an incredible 50 2/3 victories—the vast majority scored during April 1941—making him the most successful RAF (and indeed Allied) fighter pilot of the war. During the air battles of 20 April, the RAF lost eight Hurricanes, with two pilots being killed, for a total of twenty-two Luftwaffe aircraft being claimed as shot down. However, further Luftwaffe raids against RAF airfields in the Athens area took place on 21 and 22 April. On the latter day, thirty-one JG 77 Bf 109s attacked Menidi.

> Messerschmitt fighters over Menidi put on an aerobatic display which would have drawn a crowd in times of peace. Yellow-nosed 109s skimmed around the perimeter, making daisy-cutting turns, chasing stray airmen down the trenches, and firing at everything and everybody. Twice forming line-astern they roared flat-out across the grass towards the hangars, stood on one wing, and sped like letters through a letter-box through the gap between the sheds. Messerschmitts appeared suddenly from below hedges, among tents, and round hangar corners. Airmen in tree-tops and trenches, firing at them, stood in admiration of their flying skill(s).[14]

The evacuation of remaining RAF units and army personnel to Crete and Egypt began in earnest on 21 April. Two days later, Bf 109s of JG 77 struck Argos only moments after the arrival of five replacement Hurricanes. During several strafing raids against Argos, no less than fifty-three RAF and Greek aircraft were destroyed, including thirteen Hurricanes, leaving a mere seven flyable Hurricanes for air defence and convoy protection.

On 26 April, Bf 109s of II.(Schl)/LG 2 flew in support of airborne troop landings at the Corinth Canal. The following day, the Luftwaffe held a victory parade over Athens, where the Swastika flew from the Acropolis. Of the 200 aircraft involved, fifty were Bf 109s. The fighting in Greece was almost over, with the evacuation of British and Commonwealth troops being completed on 1 May. The German victory over Yugoslavia and Greece had indeed been swift and made the most of the *Blitzkrieg* tactics. However, precious time had been lost, with the intended invasion of the USSR having to be postponed until mid- to late June.

A total of fifty-four Bf 109Es were lost during the brief Yugoslav-Greek campaign. However, there remained one obstacle to German dominance of the eastern Mediterranean.

Crete and Malta

On the eve of the invasion of Crete, code-named Operation Merkur (Operation Mercury), 119 Bf 109s of II./JG 77, III./JG 77, and I.(J)/LG 2 were based at Molaoi. With the distance involved between mainland Greece and Crete exceeding that of the range of a bomb-carrying Bf 109E, II.(Schl)/LG 2 did not participate in the invasion, instead being transferred to Praschnitz (Przasnysz, in present-day Poland) in anticipation of Operation Barbarossa.

The invasion began on 20 May, with hundreds of Ju 52/3ms towing DFS 230 assault gliders. With few RAF and FAA fighters available, the biggest threat to the Luftwaffe was anti-aircraft artillery. Before the Ju 52/3ms with their load of paratroops arrived, the Allied defence positions were repeatedly strafed by Bf 109s and Bf 110s. Three JG 77 aircraft were shot down in quick succession by intense small-arms fire while attacking Maleme airfield. All three pilots, Oblt Berthold Jung, Oblt Gerhard Rahm and Ofw Werner Petermann survived, with one of them having his ring finger hacked off by a woman. A further three Bf 109s were brought down near Maleme during the day, with one of the pilots, Fw Dietrich Saake, becoming a prisoner of war. By the end of 20 May, German paratroopers had managed to gain a foothold on the island, despite fierce resistance from British, Anzac, and Greek forces. Fighting would continue for more than a week, with the German forces eventually securing the strategically important island.

On 21 May, the warship HMS *Warspite* was attacked by a pair of 8./JG 77 Bf 109s, with their 250-kg bombs striking some of the battleship's gun positions. An evacuation to Egypt of all remaining British, Anzac, and Greek troops was approved on 27 May. Between 13 May and 1 June, fifty-five Bf 109s were lost in combat, with others sustaining irreparable damage in accidents.

Malta had been under attack by the *Regia Aeronautica* since 11 June 1940. The first Luftwaffe Bf 109 unit to arrive in the area was 7./JG 26, led by Oblt Joachim Müncheberg. Having arrived at Gela, Sicily, on 8 February 1941 with a dozen Bf 109E-7s, the first sortie over Malta was flown four days later. Escorting a trio of Ju 88s, the Bf 109s were intercepted by six Hurricanes. In the event, three of the Hurricanes were shot down, one by Müncheberg for his twenty-fourth victory, and two by Fw Leibing. No Bf 109s were lost. Apart from escort sorties, many *Freie Jägd* sorties were flown. The tactics employed during the latter involved arriving over Malta at 6,000 metres then dive sharply, attack, and then head north towards Sicily. With their superior performance, the Bf 109 pilots were able to enter and break off combat at will, although turning dogfights had to be avoided. Occasionally, Müncheberg reverted to the pre-war three-aircraft formation *Kette* (similar to the RAF's 'V' formation), presumably to conserve flight hours for his Bf 109Es.

Apart from a brief transfer to Taranto in southern Italy to support the invasion of Yugoslavia, 7./JG 26 remained based at Gela until 25 May, claiming the destruction of no less than forty-four Hurricanes, two Sunderlands, one Blenheim, and one Wellington for no own losses. During the final sortie on 25 May, five Hurricanes were destroyed on the ground at RAF Takali. In October 1941, II./JG 53 and III./JG 53 arrived in Sicily from the Eastern Front, being reinforced two months later by I./JG 53. By March 1942, the Luftwaffe raids against Malta saw the RAF defenders almost on their knees. The Hurricanes had proved themselves unable to enter combat with the Bf 109Fs on equal terms. However, a total of thirty-two Spitfire Mk Vs arrived during the month, although most of these were quickly neutralised by the Luftwaffe. During just nine days, 20–28 March, the Bf 109 units flew no fewer than 5,667 sorties over Malta.

Occasionally, Bf 109Fs were brought down over the beleaguered island. One such victim was Lt Herman Neuhoff of 7./JG 53.

> On 10 April, I led a *Schwarm* over Malta. The other *Schwarm* of my *Staffel* unexpectedly drifted off and was nowhere to be found. We ran into three Spitfires and I opened fire at the machine crossing my flight path. Suddenly something thudded into my aircraft. Lt. Schöw called out his first victory—unfortunately, it was me. He mistook me for a Hurricane!
>
> I resolved to stay in the cockpit since I knew that ditching the aircraft would increase [*sic*] my chances of survival. However, when the flames began to sear into the cockpit, I jettisoned the canopy. Seconds later my 109 blew up. Luckily, I had undone my seat belts and got rid of the canopy. I was thrown clear of the aircraft at a height of 2,500 metres. At 400 metres I pulled the rip chord and landed safely near Luqa.

The stubborn British defences in Malta were a hindrance to German supply routes to North Africa. With the Luftwaffe having failed to break the island's defences, a German plan to invade Malta, codenamed Operation Herkules (Hercules), was to be implemented in July–August 1942. Thus, strengthening Malta's air defences was of vital importance. In the event, fifty-nine Spitfire Mk Vs flew from the decks of aircraft carriers and reached Malta on 9 May. The following day, thirteen Hurricanes and thirty-seven Spitfires were airborne to intercept a large force of Luftwaffe Bf 109s and Ju 88s. The subsequent air battle was the turning point in the battle of Malta. No less than fifty-seven Luftwaffe aircraft were claimed shot down; the *Times of Malta* claimed that, 'the sea between Malta and Sicily [was] so full of rubber dinghies and shot-down aircraft that it looked like Henley on Regatta Day.'

Malta was out of danger. With the Allied victory in North Africa in May 1943 and subsequent landings on Sicily a few weeks later, the war on the Mediterranean Front appeared lost for Germany.

North Africa

Although the first Luftwaffe units had arrived at Benghazi already in mid-January 1941, Bf 109s would not appear over North Africa until three months later. Fresh from operations over Malta and Yugoslavia, I./JG 27 arrived in North Africa on 14 April. Having experienced multiple transfers during the previous weeks, the unit arrived at Benghazi without any tropical kit. Suitable gear had to be hastily acquired from a Jewish clothes pedlar in Tripoli.

The Commander of I./JG 27, Hptm Eduard 'Edu' Neumann, was as colourful as his pilots, having brought along a circus caravan as his living quarters. The first operational sortie took place on 19 April. The sortie involved 1./JG 27, escorting Ju 88s of III./KG 30, on a raid against British ships in Tobruk harbour.

> Intercepted by Hurricane Mk Is of 274 Squadron, the Bf 109 pilots proceeded to shoot down two of their Hurricanes. Having previously fought against Italian Fiat CR 42s and Macchi C.200s, against which the Hurricane I enjoyed a slight superiority, encountering Luftwaffe Bf 109s was a profound shock.

One of the Hurricane pilots, Sqn Ldr Lapsey, later wrote:

> The impact of the Messerschmitts was very great. These aircraft had a very significantly [*sic*] better performance than the Hurricane in climbing, diving and level speed. The manoeuvrability of the two aircraft was comparable. Our results against the Italians had been so good that perhaps we were a little over-confident and had not sufficiently absorbed the tactical lessons of the war in Europe. This all combined to give us a very rough time for the first few weeks after the Messerschmitts arrived.

One of the II./JG 27 pilots was Hans-Joachim Marseille, who was to become the leading Luftwaffe ace in North Africa. Entering flight training in late 1938,

Although a well-known photo, this graphically shows the effectiveness of the desert camouflage scheme. (*NMUSAF*)

Marseille's flying career was littered with controversy. An incorrigible womaniser, Marseille also loved American Jazz (considered degenerate by the Nazis) and had severe difficulty adapting to military regulations. A naturally gifted pilot, Marseille shot down a RAF fighter on his first operational sortie on 24 August 1940. Nevertheless, he was also considered reckless, baling out of battle-damaged Bf 109s on a number of occasions. Upon his transfer to JG 27, Marseille was initially treated with suspicion by his fellow pilots and superiors. Marseille had shot down 158 Allied aircraft—becoming the highest-scoring ace on the Western Front—when he died on 30 September 1942 unsuccessfully baling out of his Bf 109G-2 trop following engine failure.

The Bf 109Es sent to Africa were fitted with desert equipment, including a dust filter for the supercharger air intake. This reduced the overall performance of the Bf 109 by about 5 per cent. It must be said, however, that the RAF Hurricanes and Spitfires had the Vokes sand filter fitted, comparably reducing their performance. Most dogfights occurred at low and medium altitudes; British ground commanders were adamant that RAF fighters were to stay close to any column of vehicles. Flying in close formation at low speed and at low altitude, such RAF aircraft gave Bf 109 pilots ample opportunities of scoring aerial victories.

Beginning on 14 June, Operation Battleaxe was designed to break the siege of Tobruk. However, Battleaxe ran out of steam after a few days. Also on 14 June 1941, 7./JG 26 arrived at Ain el Gazala with six Bf 109E-7s. Upon arrival, the 7./JG 26 pilots were welcomed with 'splendid hospitality' by the *Gruppenkommandeur* of I./JG 27, Hptm Edu Neumann. Neumann later recalled that Oblt Müncheberg and his pilots were 'allowed to plan and carry out his *Staffel*'s operations without hindrance from me'. As it turned out, 7./JG 26 suffered severe operational difficulties during their brief North African sojourn, particularly with regards to the DB 601 N engines of the aircraft. Nevertheless, 7./JG 26's *Staffelkommandeur*, Oblt Joachim Müncheberg, scored his first victory on 20 June, shooting down a Hurricane of 6 Squadron.

On 24 July, 7./JG 26 reported only seven serviceable Bf 109s out of a total of thirteen aircraft. The last known 7./JG 26 sortie over North Africa took place on 21 August, with a pair of Martin Maryland light bombers shot down. Oblt Müncheberg had, incidentally, pleaded for some weeks for his *Staffel* to be allowed to re-join the rest of JG 26. In little over six months, 7./JG 26 pilots had destroyed sixty-six aircraft while losing two Bf 109s and no pilots.

On 14 September, II./JG 27 began to arrive in North Africa fresh from the Eastern Front. Incessant sand storms initially hindered operations, with the first II./JG 27 sortie (flown by 4./JG 27) flown on 26 September. On 17 November, Ofw Otto Schulz of 4./JG 27 scrambled when a RAF Bristol Bombay transport was spotted passing near the airfield. Within three minutes, Schulz had taken off, shot down the hapless Bombay and landed, earning him the moniker '*Eins-zwei-drei*-Schulze'.

Operation Crusader was launched the following day, 18 November, with Rommel's *Afrika Korps* retreating under the pressure from the British 8th Army. On 7 December, the JG 27 airfield at Gazala was abandoned and the unit relocated

JG 27 personnel resting between sorties. (*NMUSAF*)

to Tmimi. By the end of December 1941, the wrecks of 458 Axis aircraft had been found at different airfields—at least twenty-six of these were Bf 109s.

Reinforcement units arrived in early December, with III./JG 53 flew their first sorties on 11 December, with III./JG 27 following suit the next day. By mid-1942, USAAF Lockheed P-38 Lightning and Curtiss P-40 Warhawk fighter squadrons began to arrive in North Africa. With the RAF operating considerable numbers of the earlier Kittyhawk, the *Jägdwaffe* pilots were well aware of the performance of this fighter, particularly its incredible turning radius. Nevertheless, some *Jägdwaffe* pilots, including Oblt Hans-Joachim Marseille, managed to shoot down large quantities of Kittyhawks. On 3 June 1942, Oblt Marseille clashed with Kittyhawks of 5 Squadron SAAF. Marseille's wingman, Fw Rainer Pöttgen, later described the dogfight.

> All the enemy fighters were brought down in a turning engagement. Marseille was a master of deflection shooting and he instinctively knew when to press the triggers. When he opened up, one could simply watch and enjoy the fireworks as the slugs impacted against an enemy aircraft. The hits he scored could be seen flashing over the engine cowling, running down the fuselage, and disappearing around the cockpit area. Marseille could not explain how he managed to lay off the right deflection with such ease. Watching him at work, I noticed that during dogfights he used to throttle back, which enabled him to outturn his opponent. Then one burst was enough to send the enemy crashing down in flames.[15]

The twin-engine Lockheed P-38 Lightning was another matter. Hans Pichler, a seventy-five-victory ace, later recalled:

> Over Tunisia, my flight encountered four P-38s and we slipped behind them, virtually unnoticed. Although our *Gustavs* gave all they could, the distance between us and the Lightnings hardly diminished. At a distance of about 500 metres, I fired all my guns, but my shells exploded behind one of the P-38s. After several more ineffective bursts, the U.S. pilots obviously sensed danger. Applying full war-emergency power, they disappeared, leaving us with our mouths open. The five-minute chase caused my engine to seize. One of the connecting rods pushed itself right through the cowling...

An interesting incident that took place during the first week of July 1942 involved elements of the Royal Egyptian Air Force (REAF) being less than pleased with British rule in Egypt. A plan was hatched by some REAF officers (including future President Anwar Sadat) to offer co-operation with Germany following the *Afrika Korps*' victory in North Africa (which, at the time, was a distinct possibility). A 'treaty' was to be delivered to Rommel, with the document in question to be handed over by Plt Off. Ahmad Sa'ūdū Husaynm, who was to fly a REAF Gladiator and land behind the German lines. However, during the morning of 7 July, Plt Off. Husaynm was intercepted by a pair of Bf 109Fs of I./JG 27 and promptly shot

A Bf 109G found by US forces at Montesquieu, Algeria, following Operation *Torch* in November 1942. A pair of P-40s sits in the background. (*NMUSAF*)

A number of Bf 109s and Bf 110s in various states of disrepair at a North African airfield. (*NMUSAF*)

down by Lt Stahlschmidt. Another more successful attempt was made the following day, with the REAF pilot being quickly despatched to Berlin. As a result of this episode, the entire REAF was grounded for a considerable time.

With the Allied landings in Algeria (controlled by the pro-German Vichy French regime) in November 1942, the days of an Axis presence in North Africa were numbered. During April 1943, large numbers of Ju 52/3m and Me 323 transports were shot down by Allied fighters. Flying in large formations, a small fighter escort was usually available. On 18 April, no less than thirty-three Ju 52/3ms were shot down out of a formation of sixty-eight transports that were escorted by a small number of Bf 109s, Bf 110s, and Italian Macchi C.202s. On 12 May, the remaining Axis forces in Tunisia surrendered. Losses to the Bf 109 units had been considerable, with more than 100 Bf 109s being found in various stages of disrepair on Tunisian airfields.

Operation Barbarossa

The German invasion of the USSR, Operation Barbarossa, began on 22 June 1941. Supporting the invasion were a number of Bf 109 units, including II./JG 53 and I. to III./JG 54 (*Luftflotte* 1 operating on the northern front), II. and III./JG 27, I. to

IV./JG 51, II./JG 52, I. and III./JG 53 (*Luftflotte* 2 operating on the central front), I. to III./JG 3, I./JG 52, II., III. and *Ergänzung* JG 77, as well as the dedicated ground-attack unit I.(*Jabo*) LG 2 (*Luftflotte* 4 operating on the southern front). Although a number of these units, including JG 77, were operating Bf 109Es, most had been re-equipped with the Bf 109F.

The Soviet forces appeared completely unprepared for the German onslaught. One 7./JG 54 pilot, Lt Max-Hellmut Ostermann, recalled the moments before strafing the Soviet airfields: 'As we flew above the enemy's country, everything below seemed to be asleep. No anti-aircraft fire, no movement, and no enemy aircraft were present to confront us.'

The first Luftwaffe victory over a *Voyenno-Vosdushnye Sily* (Soviet Military Air Force, V-VS) aircraft was scored by Oblt Robert Olejnik of II./JG 3. Post-war, Olejnik recalled the initial moments of Operation Barbarossa:

> On 19 June, the complete II./JG 3 left with all its Bf 109F-2s for the airstrip at Dub, some 8 km from the Polish town of Zamosc, which lay 80 km south-east of Lublin, and about 50 km from the nearest Russian soil. On the occasion of the Midsummer Night celebrations, we lit a huge bonfire and had the usual cold drinks. Then around midnight there came a telephone call from the *Geschwader*: 'All unit commanders immediately to the command post.' There each received an envelope with a mission order, but it was only to be opened when the code word 'Barbarossa' was given. It was impossible to think about sleep; though we all lay down in our tents to rest, we were excited and full of tension. On 22 June 1941, at about 02.30, the password came through. I opened my envelope and found that an attack against the Soviet Union was about to begin.
>
> Everybody in the *Geschwader* knew that I was an early riser and that I liked the first missions at dawn, so I made the first take-off. About 03.30, I took off with my *Rottenflieger* to reconnoitre Russian airfields near the border, watching for enemy fighters. In doing so I discovered that on every enemy airfield two or three Russian fighters were stood at the ready. After flying over several airfields, and on the way back, I again flew over the first airfield I'd seen. As I got nearer I saw that two aircraft were already manned by pilots. At a height of 700–800 metres I flew a wide turn round the airfield and watched closely. After one and a half circuits, I saw the Russians start their engines and taxi out, then take off immediately. As they were obviously looking for a fight, I attacked the first '*Rata*' with a height advantage of 300–400 metres, and succeeded in shooting it down with only a few rounds in my first attack. Comparing times with my *Rottenflieger* later, this happened at 03.58 on 22 June 1941. The second fighter was probably shocked by seeing one of his unit going down burning and flew away, because I could no longer find him. Returning over our own airfield, I waggled my wings three times. Unbelieving, my comrades shook their heads—most of them had only just woken [up] and were peering sleepily from their tents.[16]

Although modern fighters such as the LaGG-3, MiG-3, and Yak-1 were beginning to enter service, the V-VS was still operating huge numbers of Polikarpov I-153 and

The victor and the vanquished. A Polikarpov I-16 Rata sits alongside a Bf 109F soon after the commencement of Operation Barbarossa. (*NMUSAF*)

I-16 fighters. Similarly to the Luftwaffe, the V-VS was essentially a tactical air arm, with operations being concentrated to supporting army units. This meant that most air combat took place below an altitude of 3,000 metres. Interestingly, much effort had been devoted during the 1930s in establishing a strategic bomber force, with a limited strategic bombing capacity remaining throughout the war.

During the first day, a staggering 1,489 aircraft were claimed destroyed during strafing attacks, with another 322 being shot down by fighters and flak. An incredulous Göring, prone to grand exaggeration, ordered a recount. In the event, on the airfields captured by the advancing German panzer columns, in excess of 2,000 destroyed aircraft were located. According to Soviet sources, nearly 4,000 aircraft were lost during the first three days of the invasion. As had been the case in Poland and France, the *Jägdwaffe* Bf 109 units transferred between different airfields with the aid of Ju 52/3ms, which hauled mechanics and ground support equipment.

The battle was not entirely one-sided, though. Even if the Polikarpov I-153 and I-16s equipping the majority of the V-VS fighter units lacked the overall performance of the Bf 109, the Soviet fighters were more manoeuvrable in a turning dogfight. One of the Luftwaffe pilots lost on the first day of the invasion was the *Geschwaderkommodore* of JG 27, Maj. Wolfgang Schellmann. While attacking an I-16 *Rata*, Schellmann's Bf 109 was hit by shrapnel, forcing him to bale out over Soviet-held territory. It is presumed that Schellmann was executed by the Russians, who treated all German troops as war criminals. By mid-July, the Luftwaffe had lost nearly 1,300 aircraft destroyed or damaged, resulting in many units being severely decimated.

On 15 July 1941, Werner Mölders achieved his 100th and 101st victories, having earlier been the first Luftwaffe pilot to reach and surpass the score of the famed

Great War ace Manfred von Richthofen. Mölders was also the first Luftwaffe fighter pilot to reach 100 victories during the war. As related earlier, Mölders had accumulated fourteen victories during the Spanish Civil War. Mölders was awarded the Knight's Cross with Swords and Diamonds and was immediately grounded as he was deemed far too valuable to lose in combat. Mölders was promoted to *Oberst*, being appointed *General der Flieger* (Inspector General for Fighters). Upon returning to Germany to attend Erich Udet's funeral in October 1941, his He 111 crashed near Breslau, killing him and the crew. In his honour, JG 51 would become known as *Jägdgeschwader* Mölders. Soon after Mölders death, rumours appeared claiming that he had, in fact, been killed because of his severe criticism of the Nazi regime.

Little more than two-and-a-half months into Operation Barbarossa, the number of victories accumulated by individual *Jägdwaffe* pilots had risen considerably. Indeed, JG 51 pilots reached 2,000 victories during late August, with JG 3 pilots reaching 1,000 victories on 30 August. It seemed as if the *Blitzkrieg* tactics would once again tip the scale in the German's favour. German forces were fast approaching Moscow, St Petersburg, and other Russian cities, with millions of Soviet troops becoming prisoners of war.

Having scored relatively few victories on the Western Front, the JG 52 pilots began to find success over Russia in June 1941. On 2 December 1941, Oblt Johannes Steinhoff of 4./JG 52 became the first JG 52 pilot to reach fifty victories. In the event, JG 52 would end the war as the most successful fighter unit of all time, scoring in excess of 10,000 victories.

By December 1941, roughly two-thirds of the Luftwaffe's combat strength was serving on the Eastern Front. The arrival of the Russian winter resulted in severe difficulties for Luftwaffe operations. With temperatures reaching below minus-40° Celsius, the Bf 109 engines seized, resulting in barely operational units. In January 1942, the pilots of one Bf 109F unit, II./JG 52, were ordered to fight as regular ground troops when Russian forces approached their base at Klin. When Klin was captured, six unserviceable Bf 109Fs were found.

The problem of having engines seizing due to the freezing temperature was eventually solved by diluting the engine lubricating oil with petrol. Although this increased the risk of fire when starting up the engine, it worked well enough, with any remaining petrol quickly evaporating. Apparently this method was introduced follow the interrogations of captured V-VS pilots and mechanics. Another high-risk method of starting the engine was to place a tray of petrol underneath the engine and then set the petrol alight; the heat generated by the burning petrol assisted in getting the engine running. Machine-gun mechanisms were equally affected by the Russian winter, with the lubricating oil or grease having to be wiped clean using either petrol or boiling water. It is highly likely that these methods increased the wear and tear on both engines and armament.

Other *Jägdwaffe* units were more fortunate. Based in the Leningrad area, I./JG 54 claimed ninety-nine Soviet aircraft shot down during 1,152 sorties in January 1942. Protecting the Ju 52/3m airlift into the Demyansk pocket was assigned to I./JG 51, which flew countless escort and ground-support sorties between January and April 1942.

A JG 54 Bf 109F with a horse-sled transport in front. (*NMUSAF*)

A new tactic was introduced during the spring of 1942, which involved catching V-VS fighters during take-offs or landings. As recalled by a LaGG-3 pilot:

> The Germans blocked our airfields … They flew in pairs, particularly near the fighter regiment's airdromes at Gremyachevo, Serebrennitsa, and Budogoschch … It's hard to talk about this today, but our commander took no counteractive measures to counter the blockade of our airfields … Our passivity encouraged the German pilots, and they became most impudent … We paid a high price for poor command planning… On one of those days I witnessed the death of *Kapitan* Thikomirov (of the 41 IAP Fighter Squadron) over the airfield at Gremyachevo. He was returning to base after completing a mission and was out of ammunition when the hunters fell upon him. Thikomirov was a very skilful and experienced pilot, but without any ammunition there wasn't much he could do against the Me 109 hunters.

This Luftwaffe tactic was similar to that employed by the RAF in early 1945 to catch Me 262 jet fighters during the landing phase. The spring of 1942 brought with it severe operational difficulties both for the Luftwaffe and the V-VS. The airfields became muddy strips, reducing operational effectiveness considerably. In spite of Soviet counter-offensives along the 3,000-km front line, the German High Command were planning to advance into Caucasus, where a large percentage of the Soviet oil fields were located, as well as the industrial city of Stalingrad on the banks of the Volga River. Reaching the latter objective was deemed of utmost importance both for strategic and psychological reasons. By this time, new Soviet fighters such as the La-5 and Yak-9 were reaching the V-VS fighter squadrons. The performance of both the La-5 and Yak-9 largely matched that of the Bf 109F-4 and Bf 109G-2 variants. One of the most dangerous of all Soviet aircraft however, was the Polikarpov U-2. A low-powered two-seat biplane dating back from the late 1920s, the U-2 was used in night-harassment raids. Often flown by female crews, dubbed *Nachthexen* ('night witches') by II./JG 52 pilots, the U-2s caused comparatively little material damage. However, being unable to light fires to stay warm and the inability to fall asleep comfortably affected the morale of the German troops.

On 8 October 1942, a new replacement pilot joined 7./JG 52, based in the Stalingrad area. Following an inauspicious beginning, the pilot, Lt Erich Hartmann, scored his first victory, an Ilyushin Il-2 Shturmovik, on 5 November. Hartmann would finish the war with 352 victories, all while flying successive variants of the Bf 109G.

Having occupied parts of Stalingrad, German troops were unable to reach the Volga and stop Soviet reinforcements from arriving. On 17 November, a Soviet counter-offensive resulted in the German 6th Army inside the Stalingrad pocket becoming encircled. Supplying the troops required many tons of materiel airlifted into Stalingrad by Ju 52/3ms and other transport aircraft. For the protection of the airlift, a small detachment of Bf 109s, led by Hptm Rudolf Germeroth, was based at Pitomnik. This was named *Platzschutzstaffel* Pitomnik (Local Protection Squadron Pitomnik) and consisted of aircraft drawn from JG 3. Other units were committed to escorting and clearing the way for the Ju 52/3m transports. One II./JG 52 pilot later recalled that the Ju 52/3m crews seemed unable to trust the Bf 109 escorts, claiming that the Ju 52/3m pilots preferred to fly at extreme low level, literally hugging the ground, and then climbing to an altitude of 1,000 metres upon reaching the front line.

On 15 January, seventeen Soviet aircraft, including five Lisunov Li-2s, were claimed as shot down over Stalingrad. The following day, five Bf 109s were flown from Pitomnik to Gumrak ahead of Soviet tanks. A dozen unserviceable aircraft had to be left behind. Upon reaching Gumrak, four of the five Bf 109s crashed when attempting to land on the unprepared runway.

On 2 February 1943, the German 6th Army surrendered; the seemingly invincible German forces suffering a humiliating defeat. The outcome of the battles of Stalingrad and El Alamein a few months earlier finally saw the tide turn in favour of the Allies. Even with the introduction of the improved Bf 109G-6, the *Jägdwaffe* units on the Eastern Front found themselves unable to contain the increasing number of V-VS fighters and bombers.

The Kuban peninsula was where German forces attempted to stem the Soviet push westwards. Intense Soviet air attacks resulted in many *Jägdwaffe* pilots adding to their scores. However, there was a price to pay. The crack *Jägdwaffe* unit JG 52 lost twenty-three pilots killed or missing, and fourteen wounded, between April and June 1943. The, final, major German offensive (as it turned out) on the Eastern Front, Operation Zitadelle, resulted in the largest tank battle in history. Aerial activity was great, with some 400 Soviet aircraft being claimed as destroyed in the air on 5 July, the first day of Operation Zitadelle. The top-scorer was the *Gruppenkommandeur* of

I./JG 52, Hptm Johannes Wiese, who claimed no less than twelve V-VS aircraft shot down. Nevertheless, with North Africa abandoned and Allied troops wading ashore on Sicily, Hitler reluctantly ordered the end of Operation Zitadelle. From then on, the Red Army would be continuously on the offensive toward Germany.

During fierce air battles over the Crimean peninsula in April 1944, no less than 1,010 Soviet aircraft were claimed destroyed. On 8 May, German forces began withdrawing from Crimea. With the increasing air raids on Germany, many *Jägdgeschwader* became part of the *Reichsverteidigung*, i.e. Defence of the Reich. Despite the urgent needs on the Eastern Front, by late 1944, the only remaining Bf 109 unit remaining was JG 52. For JG 52, the war came to an end at Deutsch Brod in present-day Czech Republic on 8 May 1945. Prior to the end of hostilities, Hptm Erich Hartmann claimed a Yak-11 (most likely a Yak-3) shot down for his 352nd victory. Having accumulated approximately 10,600 air-to-air victories between 8 September 1939 and 8 May 1945, JG 52 was the most successful fighter unit in history, with thirty-two of its pilots scoring more than 100 victories. However, JG 52 had lost 679 pilots, including 262 killed in combat, 142 wounded in combat, 142 missing and forty-one taken PoW.

Ground-attack units

As described earlier, Bf 109s fitted with an external bomb rack were used as fighter-bombers over southern England. Organised within the VIII. *Fliegerkorps*, II.(Schl)/LG 2 played an important role during the invasion with its bomb carrying Bf 109Es and Hs 123s. Based at Praschnitz (Przasnysz in present-day Poland) on 22 June 1941, II.(Schl)/LG 2 flew a large number close air support sorties, following closely on the heels of the advancing Panzer columns. Carrying one SC 250 bomb or four SC 50 bombs, the tactic was to arrive at low altitude, attempting to hit armoured vehicles by dropping the bomb(s) on them. Shortly after the Germans reached Smolensk in August, II.(Schl)/LG 2 was transferred to the northern front, flying in support of German forces during the conquest of Novgorod, with a pair of Bf 109Es being destroyed in a Russian air raid. On 29 August, II.(Schl)/LG 2 transferred to Lyuban near Leningrad. Conditions at Lyuban were less than ideal, resulting in a number of accidents. In late September, II.(Schl)/LG 2 moved south again, supporting the advance towards Moscow. During the intense air operations in the second half of 1941, the Bf 109E's had proved themselves rather troublesome, with the engine and undercarriage in particular being the source of many problems. Even though II.(Schl)/LG 2 had a nominal strength of thirty-six Bf 109s, barely a dozen were usually available at any one time. In contrast, the aging Hs 123 seemed able to accommodate any kind of environment.

On 13 January 1942, II.(Schl)/LG 2 was redesignated as I. *Gruppe Schlachtgeschwader* 1 (I./Schl.G 1), becoming the first dedicated close air support unit of the Luftwaffe. At the time the unit was based at Dugino, eventually being withdrawn from the front in March for rest and recuperation. A second *Gruppe*, II./Schl.G 1, had also been formed on 13 January, receiving Hs 129s. Transferring to Gramatikovo in Crimea in early May, I./Schl.G 1 had a nominal strength of 120 Bf 109Es and fifteen Hs 123s. The first operational sortie was flown on 7 May. When a Soviet counter-offensive in southern Ukraine began on 25 May, I./Schl.G 1 was hurriedly transferred to Kharkov-Rogan. Flying multiple daily sorties, the pilots of SchlG 1 managed to stop the offensive in its tracks.

Although the primary role of I./SchlG 1 was close air support for the troops, an increasing number of Soviet fighters were encountered. A few of the pilots, including Obfw Otto Dommeratzky, did not mind such challenges. According to Dommeratzky's *Rottenflieger*, this could lead to trouble.

> The *Kommandeur* was not at all happy at Otto's insatiable appetite for dogfighting; that he simply dumped his bombs. Our role, after all, was to attack ground targets and support our own ground forces. Despite the chief's instructions, Otto never passed up an opportunity. He just couldn't do otherwise.
>
> One day, Otto and I headed north out of Slavyansk on an infantry-support mission. We bombed an enemy mortar position as ordered and were on our way back when we bumped into a gaggle of Soviet LaGG-3 fighters—fifteen or twenty of them. We were at about 1,500 metres, but Otto had already waded in. Utter confusion: we were not only in the minority, but this time at a real disadvantage. We had spotted them too late—more correctly, I should say that I had not spotted them at all!
>
> Otto was weaving in and out like a madman. It was all I could do not to lose him, my machine surrounded by nothing but Red Stars. The dogfight had lasted five or six minutes when suddenly Otto's machine took some hits and burst into flames. He baled out but I didn't see what happened after that as I was concentrating on escaping southwards at low level.
>
> Somehow I made it back to base. I had learned another hard lesson. We'd been taken completely by surprise by the sudden appearance of the LaGGs—eyes open, always keep your eyes open!
>
> The chief was not exactly overjoyed at my reporting Otto missing. Division was informed. And the army unit we had been supporting. About an hour later they got back to us: Otto had come down unhurt in the lines of a mountain regiment 40 km to the north of us and could we please send someone to pick him up!

Otto Dommeratzky eventually accumulated some 600 operational sorties and approximately thirty-eight victories before being killed in action on 13 October 1944.

By 1 September, I./Schl.G 1 was based at Tuzov, about 100 km west of Stalingrad, with thirty-seven Bf 109s. Operations continued until 19 November when the Soviet army initiated a counter-offensive, resulting in a move to Oblivskaya. Despite atrocious weather conditions, I./Schl.G 1 continued to fly support missions. Soviet fighters were occasionally encountered, with the unit claiming six aircraft shot down during December.

During the first weeks of 1943, operations over Stalingrad continued until the surrender of the German 6th Army. By mid-February, Soviet forces entered Kharkov before German forces eventually recaptured the city two weeks later, with I./Schl.G 1 being heavily involved in support operations.

In the end, the Bf 109 was not the ideal aircraft for ground-attack and close air-support duties. It was too delicate, and its narrow undercarriage was the source of many accidents. Additionally, its DB 601 inline engine was susceptible to damage from small-arms fire. Following some deliberation, a replacement was found in the Fw 190. I./Schl.G 1 initiated conversion training in the spring of 1943. In the event, the Fw 190 was to prove far more suited, with dedicated ground-attack variants entering production.

Apart from II.(Schl)/LG 2 and I./Schl.G 1, Bf 109s were also operated in the ground-attack role by the *Sonderstaffel Gamringer* and *Einsatzkommando Liedtke*, both on the Eastern Front.

The Western Front

By mid-1941, the Bf 109E had been largely replaced by the improved Bf 109F. Additionally, the first Fw 190A-1s began to arrive in August 1941. With the impending invasion of the USSR, most Luftwaffe units were transferred to the

A Bf 109E-7 of an unidentified unit. (*NMUSAF*)

Eastern Front. JG 2, JG 26 and I./JG 52 remained based in France and Belgium—the latter unit was soon to be transferred to the Eastern Front. By the end of the year, only a few Bf 109Es remained with reconnaissance units. On 7 January 1942, a Bf 109E-7/Z (W Nr 4970) of 1.(F)/123 crashed near Buckfastleigh, Devon, due to engine failure. It was the last *Emil* to make an unscheduled arrival in Britain.

As mentioned previously, Oblt Galland had been highly critical of the limited armament of the Bf 109F. He subsequently ordered the modification of a standard Bf 109F-2 by fitting heavier armament. Galland was to score his final victory in this aircraft on 18 November while serving with JG 26.

Throughout 1941 and into 1942, JG 2 and JG 26 pilots became increasingly accustomed to adopting a defensive role. From late 1940, RAF Fighter Command adopted a set of new fighter-sweep tactics. The first of these was called rhubarb, which involved sending a limited number of fighters on ground-strafing sorties against military targets of opportunity along the French coast. Larger fighter sweeps were code-named rodeos, while circuses (first flown on 10 January 1941) involved a large number of fighters along with a few bombers to lure the Bf 109 units into action. Ramrod sorties involved RAF bombers escorted by a strong force of RAF fighters. RAF bombers also continued with small-scale raids against shipping in raids known as roadsteads. This RAF 'non-stop offensive' soon acquired the derogatory term 'nonsense offensive' by German propaganda.

With the death of Ob Mölders in October 1941, Adolf Galland was appointed as the new *General der Jägdflieger*. Galland would continuously make inspection trips to the various *Jägdgeschwader*, keeping himself up-to-date with the day-to-day operations on all fronts.

By early 1942, plans to move the battle cruisers *Gneisenau* and *Scharnhorst,* as well as the heavy cruiser *Prinz Eugen*, to Norway from their anchorage at Brest were initiated. This involved sailing through the English Channel, well within reach of the RAF and Royal Navy. The battleships were to remain under continuous Luftwaffe escort during the entire journey, with a number of auxiliary airfields along the French, Belgian, and Dutch coastlines receiving fuel and ammunition supplies. The move had been expected by the British High Command, but it had been anticipated that the Germans would carry it out during cover of darkness. As it turned out, the newly-appointed *General der Jägdflieger*, Adolf Galland, successfully argued that moving three huge battlecruisers through the Straits of Dover was the best possible option as this, Galland correctly assumed, would be completely unexpected by the British. Galland was supremely confident that his fighters would be able to cover the battleship's journey northwards. At his disposal, Galland had 252 Bf 109s and Fw 190s from JG 1, JG 2, and JG 26. A few aircraft of a fighter-training unit based in Paris were also involved, as were some Bf 110 night fighters. The Operation was codenamed Donnerkeil (Thunderbolt), but is today better known as the 'Channel Dash'. In the event, *Gneisenau*, *Scharnhorst*, and *Prinz Eugen* left Brest during the night of 12 February.

Owing to various reasons, their departure went unobserved to the British. Not until 11.25 a.m. on 12 February were the *Kriegsmarine* vessels observed by two

Spitfires of 91 Squadron. With radio silence ordered, the Spitfire pilots did not report the presence of the cruisers until ten minutes later, with the radio message being intercepted by the Germans. The British response was slow and uncoordinated. In all, forty-three British aircraft were lost, including six Swordfishes performing an extremely brave low-level torpedo attack against an overwhelming force of Luftwaffe fighters and flak. Ironically, the only damage suffered to the German fleet occurred during the evening when *Gneisenau* and *Scharnhorst* suffered slight damage when they struck mines.

Even though Operation Donnelkeil was a successful and brilliantly executed tactical operation—Galland would refer to Operation Donnerkeil as his greatest wartime success—it also meant that the three cruisers would remain in home waters or in Norway, rarely seeing action during the remainder of the war.

On 17 April 1942, RAF Bomber Command despatched twelve Lancasters on a low-level daylight raid against the MAN diesel engine factory at Augsburg. Large-scale diversionary raids were conducted, with the Luftwaffe becoming aware of the raid when half a dozen Lancasters passed directly over JG 2's airfield at Beaumont le Roger. Otto Happel, a JG 2 pilot, later recalled:

> It was late in the afternoon of 17 April at Beaumont le Roger. Our fighters had been up on their last operation of the day, and the first of them were just returning and coming in to land when somebody yelled: Vietmots flying low over the field!
>
> I immediately warned our incoming fighters of the danger over the R/T. Maj. Walther Oesau shot passed me like greased lightning, heading for his Me 109—which was always held at instant readiness. Without further ado, he set off after the departing bombers … We later learned that four of the bombers had been shot down. *Unteroffizier* Pohl's victim was the *Geschwader*'s 1000th kill, and Maj. Oesau's was his 101st. It was common knowledge that *Kommodore* Oesau had received a *Startverbot* [i.e. had been banned from operational flying after achieving his 'century' the previous October], but his excuse was a classic. He immediately informed his superiors that he had been up on a routine test flight when these monsters suddenly appeared out of nowhere and [that] he had been forced to shown a Lancaster purely out of self-defence. A perfectly believable story to anybody who did not know the true facts.[17]

On 19 August 1942, a large-scale raid against Dieppe saw the 'fiercest fighting in the air since the Battle of Britain'. Code-named Operation Jubilee, 6,000 British and Canadian troops were to wade ashore at Dieppe supported by tanks and RAF air cover. The operation was designed as a test for the forthcoming invasion of France. In all, 115 fighters of JG 2 and JG 26 were available, the majority of which were Fw 190s. Only the two *Höhenjägerstaffeln* (high-altitude squadrons), 11.(H)/JG 2 and 11.(H)/JG 26 were operating Bf 109G-1s. Also available were a number of Do 217E and Ju 88 medium bombers. When the invasion fleet arrived at Dieppe, they were met by intense fire from the German batteries. The Hurricanes providing ground support for the first wave suffered seven aircraft shot down by flak. The operation soon went awry, with only 3,623 troops arriving back on British shores. Despite outnumbering the Luftwaffe by 3:1, the RAF lost 106 aircraft, with 11.(H)/JG 26 accounting for five Spitfires. The Luftwaffe lost twenty fighters, including two Bf 109G-1s, and 28 Do 217s.

Even though the Luftwaffe had won a clear tactical victory, a severe problem immediately arose, namely that of fuel supply. Due to logistical problems, replacement fuel did not arrive at JG 2 and JG 26 until a few days after 19 August; lack of fuel was to increasingly plague Luftwaffe operations until the end of the war.

Intercepting Allied Bombers

The strategic daylight bomb raids against Germany flown by USAAF B-17 Flying Fortresses and B-24 Liberators are well known. However, the RAF had already flown a number of daylight raids using B-17C Flying Fortresses in mid-1941. With twenty early-production B-17Cs handed over through Lend-Lease, 90 Squadron was assigned the task of establishing the operational procedures of high-altitude daylight raids. Many problems were encountered, with both crews and equipment suffering badly from the cold at 9,750 metres (32,000 feet). Nevertheless, the first Fortress daylight raid was flown on 8 July against the submarine base at Wilhelmshaven—the Luftwaffe did not attempt to intercept the RAF Fortresses.

The next raid, on 23 July, intended to hit Berlin, but had to be aborted due to technical problems. However, the Luftwaffe was now aware of the presence of the four-engine high-flying RAF bombers. During a raid against Kiel on 2 August, one Fortress (serial AN530) received slight damage when intercepted by a pair of Bf 109Fs. Two weeks later, on 16 August, two 90 Squadron Fortresses paid a visit to Brest, the target being the cruiser *Gneisenau*. One of the Fortresses was attacked by five Bf 109Fs of I./JG 2, as well as two He 113s, with the Luftwaffe pilots making no less than twenty-six firing passes at the Fortress. The attacks began at 9,750 metres (32,000 feet), with the RAF pilots descending to 2,440 metres (8,000 feet), finally ending some 48 km (30 miles) off the English coast. Plt Off. F. W. Sturmey managed to bring the heavily damaged Fortress to a forced landing at Roborough near Plymouth.

During a raid against Oslo harbour on 6 September, the Fortresses could not see the target, the battlecruiser *Admiral Scheer*. A second raid against the same target two days later ended in disaster when one Fortress (RAF serial AN525) was shot down and another severely damaged by Lt Jakobi and his *Rottenflieger* Lt Steinecke of I./JG 77. During the fight, two single-engine aircraft were observed at a great distance, which Lt Steinecke (erroneously) identified as Defiants. Jakobi's first attack saw smoke pouring from the left outer engine. Prior to the second attack, the Fortress crew dropped their load of bombs while turning left. Jakobi fired again, with return fire from the Fortress striking the right wing of his Bf 109. However, the left wing of the Fortress was on fire, with smoke emanating from the cockpit. The doomed Fortress then entered a spiralling dive, coming down 75 km north of Kristiansand. A few days later, an RLM team arrived, eagerly searching through the wreckage of the first Fortress to be shot down by the Luftwaffe.

The RAF would eventually abandon the high-altitude daylight raids to concentrate instead on night raids. Following the US entry into the war on 7 December 1941, huge numbers of USAAF B-17 Flying Fortress and B-24 Liberator heavy bombers were based in the UK and North Africa, initiating a daylight strategic bombing campaign against the German Reich. The Bf 109 was to become one of the most important weapons in combating the USAAF B-17s and B-24s, and, to a lesser extent, the RAF night bombers.

By May 1942, production of the Bf 109F ended and was replaced by the Bf 109G. With the Bf 109G having been cleared for operations, an initial batch of Erla-built Bf 109G-1s was delivered to 11./JG 2 in May and June 1942. This *Staffel* was to specifically operate against high-flying Allied aircraft. Another early recipient of Bf 109G-1s was 2./JG 1. The Bf 109Gs, fitted with cockpit pressurisation, were not always popular with its pilots. When activated, the compressor was noisy and made the windows prone to icing at high altitudes. Incidentally, this was a common occurrence to all Bf 109Gs—pressurised or not—operating at high altitudes, usually caused by deficient insulation.

The first USAAF raid against occupied Europe took place on 4 July 1942 (a date chosen for obvious reasons), using borrowed Douglas Boston light bombers that had originally been delivered under Lend-Lease to the RAF. The raid, flown together with 226 Squadron RAF, was not a success. Two US-flown Boston were downed by flak, while one RAF aircraft was shot down by Uffz Johannes Rathenow of IV./JG 1. One 10./JG 2 pilot, Uffz Erwin Grütz, was hit by return fire and crashed fatally when attempting to land at Bergen.

The Bf 109G-1 was developed specifically to counter high-flying Allied aircraft. Equipped with a pressurised cockpit, the Bf 109G-1 had an absolute service ceiling of 12,100 metres, more than enough to intercept USAAF bomber formations as well as solitary reconnaissance aircraft. Only three sub-variants of the *Gustav* were equipped with a pressurised cockpit: the Bf 109G-1, the G-3, and the G-5. Gerhard Barkhorn later wrote that 'there was no heating in the aircraft and I had to wear goggles. They froze and I could see nothing at this altitude.' Barkhorn eventually requested a transfer back to his own unit, JG 52.

One weapon introduced in 1943 was the 21-cm air mortar, or *Wurfgranate* 21. The mortar rockets had a considerable punch, and a range of 1.2 km, far beyond the bomber's machine gun defences. However, the mortar rockets were unguided, with the pilot having to depend more on luck than skill in bringing down a bomber. These mortar rockets were used operationally by Bf 109, Bf 110, Fw 190, and Me 410 units, to little effect. The Bf 109G could carry two of these weapons, one underneath each wing. The additional weight and air resistance caused by the air mortars reduced airspeed by about 50 kph, also making the Bf 109 cumbersome and easy prey for Allied fighters. The pilot's opinion of the rockets may be judged from the name bestowed on it: *Dödel* (idiot).

A close-up of the 21-cm air mortar tube. (*NMUSAF*)

Another weapon evaluated on the Bf 109 was the Rheinmetall-Borsig RZ 65 air-to-air missile. A Bf 109F-2 was tested in 1943 at E-Stelle Tarnewitz, but the RZ 65 was not adopted for the Bf 109. (*NMUSAF*)

Defending the Reich

The first USAAF 8 AF raid on Germany took place on 27 January 1943. The target for the eighty-four B-17 Fortresses and seven B-24 Liberators was Wilhelmshaven, with a pair of B-17s performing a diversion raid against Emden. In all, JG 1 lost eight fighters, including five Bf 109G-1s, with two pilots killed, two wounded, and one missing. Only three of the B-17s had been brought down, with many others damaged. However, at this time, the USAAF lacked long-range fighters that could accompany the bombers on deep penetration raids over Germany. Upon crossing the German coastline, the P-47D Thunderbolts were forced to return to England. With the addition of drop tanks, the range of the fighters would increase substantially—this was some months away, though.

The Luftwaffe fighter pilots would refer to the four-engine heavy bombers as '*Dicke Autos*' ('fat cars') and the single-engine fighters as '*Kleine Indianer*' ('tiny Indians').

With the introduction of Window (strips of 27 cm × 6 cm black paper with thin aluminium foil pasted to one side), the German network of radar stations and night fighters were effectively blinded. When bundles of Window were dropped during night raids, the amount of radar signatures multiplied, making it very difficult to differentiate the false echoes from the echoes of real bombers. Window was also adopted by the USAAF, being referred to as 'Chaff'.

In June 1943, Maj. Hajo Hermann proposed a new tactic to counter RAF night bombers. Hermann's idea was to literally 'leave the lights on' in German cities under threat of attack. Powerful searchlights would be employed to spot approaching RAF bombers, making them easy targets for Luftwaffe fighters. To avoid the risk of shooting down any Luftwaffe fighters, the flak guns would only fire up to a predetermined altitude, thus giving the Luftwaffe free rein. Göring immediately approved the new tactic, which was named *Wilde Sau* (Wild Boar). The first *Wilde Sau* sortie, on 3–4 July, nearly ended in failure when the RAF bombed Cologne instead of the city predicted where the Luftwaffe pilots were waiting for them. Quickly diverting to Cologne, the *Wilde Sau* pilots shot down twelve bombers for the loss of one fighter. Post-raid briefings stated that four of the bombers were fired upon by other RAF aircraft. This was almost certainly due to the presence of Hermann's Bf 109s. The Cologne flak defences also claimed a dozen RAF bombers. In the end, the RAF aircraft confirmed shot down were shared evenly between the flak units and the Luftwaffe.

This level of success resulted in three new *Jägdgeschwader*—JG 300, JG 301, and JG 302—being formed specifically for *Wilde Sau* operations, all becoming part of the 30. *Jägddivision*. A specific Bf 109 night-fighter variant was also developed. Known as the Bf 109G-6/U4N ('N' denoting *Nacht*, meaning 'night'), few were built, primarily being flown by NJG 11 and JG 300. Featuring increased armament and flame dampeners for engine exhausts, the Bf 109G-6/U4N also had a FuG 350 Naxos Z radar fitted in the rear fuselage behind the pilot. The associated ADF rotating loop antenna was fitted in the lower rear fuselage. With the Naxos Z radar picking up emissions from the RAF bombers' H2S radars, the Bf 109 pilots would

Although showing a Bf 109F, probably in early 1941, the difficulties operating Bf 109s as night fighters late in the war can easily be imagined. (*NMUSAF*)

be able to locate and shoot down their victims. However, the workload of flying and operating the radar at the same time proved too much, with the Bf 109G-6/U4N also being sluggish and difficult to operate during night conditions. Interestingly, at least one Bf 109G-14, flown by Maj. Friedrich Müller of II./NJG 11, was modified by having two MG 151/20 cannons mounted in the rear fuselage firing upwards at a 70° angle. Known as *Schräge Musik*, ('slanted music'), this was a common feature on twin-engine night fighters.

Despite initial success, the 30. *Jägddivision* was disbanded in March 1944, with JG 300, 301, and 302 being used for daylight operations against USAAF raids. Losses of *Wilde Sau* pilots and aircraft had been great.

On 17 August 1943, the USAAF sent 376 B-17 Flying Fortresses against the ball-bearing factory at Schweinfurt and the Messerschmitt factory at Regensburg. Escort was provided by P-47 Thunderbolts of four Fighter Groups. Of the B-17 bombers, 230 would raid Schweinfurt, and 146 Regensburg, with the latter force set to fly south to North Africa. Due to poor planning and weather issues, the bombers had to fly unescorted for most of the time while over Germany. When the carnage was over, no less than sixty B-17s had been shot down, with 168 more being damaged, many of them barely reaching England. The intensity of the battle came as a shock to USAAF commanders. During the night of 17–18 August, the RAF struck the rocket weapon's test site at Peenemünde. As a result of the USAAF and RAF raids, the Luftwaffe's Chief of Staff committed suicide.

A second raid against Schweinfurt was flown on 14 October. This day would become known as 'Black Thursday'. A total of 291 Fortresses set off from England.

The raid cost the USAAF another sixty B-17s shot down, with seven more so badly damaged that they had to be scrapped. Poor weather on the return flight prevented further losses. Such heavy losses (more than 20 per cent) were unacceptable. Following the huge losses of aircrew and aircraft, the 8 AF did not return to full strength until two months later.

A battle of attrition developed. Having single-engine escort fighters accompanying the bombers on daylight raids over Germany became a high-priority issue. The daylight raid had seen a maximum effort both from the Luftwaffe and the USAAF. Luftwaffe fighter pilots flew 833 sorties, with thirty-eight fighters being lost.

With the increased number of Allied bomb raids, Luftwaffe fighter pilots became accustomed to waiting for the signal to scramble. It was the wait rather than actual combat that wore down some of even the most experienced pilots, as described succinctly by JG 3 pilot, Lt Hans Iffland.

> For me, the minutes between being ordered to cockpit readiness and receiving the order to take-off was the most terrible of all. After the order came to get airborne one was too busy to think about one's possible fate; but waiting to go, with nothing to do but think about what might happen, that was the worst time. My own greatest fear was that I might be seriously wounded with permanent injuries. Death was of course a fear but that would have been an end. But the thought of being a cripple for the rest of my life, that held the greatest terror of all to me.

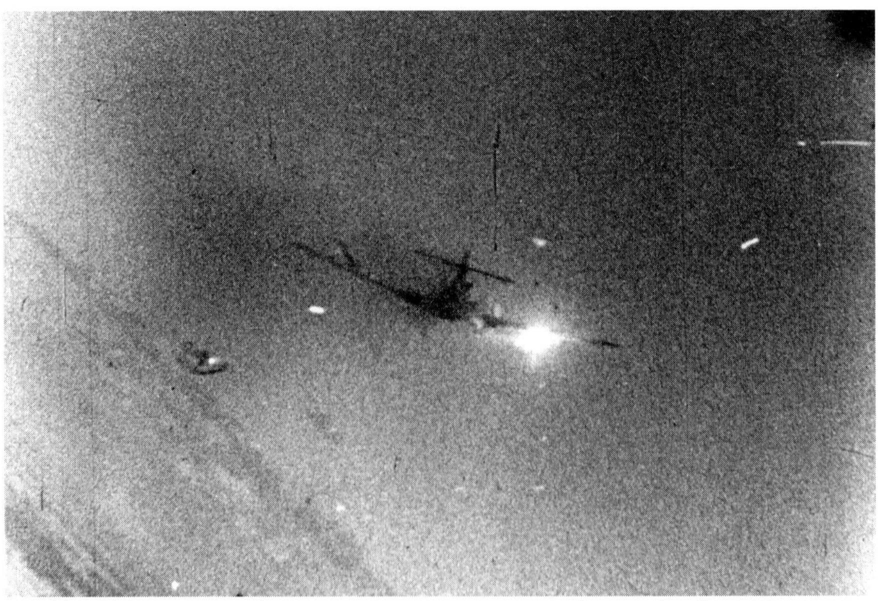

A Luftwaffe Bf 109 caught by a USAAF fighter flown by Major George I Ruddell of the 406 FG, 514 FS over Germany on 8 October 1944. (*NMUSAF*)

Protecting the south-eastern Mediterranean was the *Luftwaffenkommando Süd-Ost* based in Greece. On 31 August 1943, *Stab* JG 27 and IV./JG 27 were based at Athens-Tanagra with the close-range reconnaissance units *Stab* NAGr 2 and 2./NAGr 2 having a total of nineteen Bf 109G-4s (fifteen serviceable). 2.(F)/123 was based at Crete, which operated a mix of Bf 109G-4s, Ju 86R-1s, and Ju 88D-1s for long-range reconnaissance.

The Italian Front

On 8 September 1943, Italy declared an armistice. By late May 1944, Allied forces were advancing towards Rome, entering the Eternal City on 4 June. NAGr 12, with its Bf 109Gs, was charged with photographing the southern Italian harbours, attempting to keep a close eye on Allied shipping. On 31 May, *Luftflotte* 2 included four Bf 109G units—NAGr 11 with fifteen Bf 109G-5/6/8s (eight serviceable), JG 4 with thirteen Bf 109G-6s (ten serviceable), JG 53 with twenty-one Bf 10G-6s (fourteen serviceable), and JG 77 with seventy-six Bf 109G-6s (fifty-two serviceable).

Although the USAAF's 15 AF were able to strike against targets in southern Germany from bases in Italy, the *Jägdwaffe* units had been withdrawn from

A JG 53 Bf 109G-6 seen in Italy in late 1943. (*NMUSAF*)

Italy by the autumn of 1944. The air defence of Italy was, to all intents and purposes, left to the *Aeronautica Nazionale Repubblicana* (ANR), the air arm of the Fascist puppet regime in northern Italy. The NAGr 11 pilots continued to fly until April 1945 when, on 27 April, the unit's Bf 109Gs at Campoformido were intentionally destroyed to avoid capture. The end of the war was only days away.

Reichsverteidigung

With Allied forces approaching Germany, many units were withdrawn from other fronts. Apart from the fighters of the *Luftflotte* Reich, more than 20,000 anti-aircraft guns, including 6,220 guns with 88-mm or larger calibres, were guarding the Reich against Allied bombers.

By early 1944, Adolf Galland complained that the fighter defences were being continually drained of both pilots and aircraft.

> Not a high enough priority had been given to fighter production, the training of pilots or to air defense [*sic*] in general. At this time Hitler's thinking was still on the offensive; he paid much more attention to an attack by fifty of our bombers on England, than one by 500 enemy bombers on Germany. And of the fighter types which were built we lost many to other arms of the Luftwaffe. For example, ground attack units received large numbers of Focke-Wulf Fw 190s and reconnaissance units received both FW 190s and Messerschmitt 109s. The fighter force did not receive the best pilots from training schools and there were never enough of them anyway.[18]

The continual development of the Bf 109 meant that the basic airframe, although fitted with a more powerful engine, was burdened with heavier armament, which increased weight and reduced overall performance according to Hptm Rudolf Sinner of JG 54.

> [The Bf 109G] with its liquid-cooled engine ... was too vulnerable to enemy fire. Even with the two additional 20-mm cannon it had insufficient fire power to engage enemy heavy bombers and these cannon reduced performance to such an extent that the Me 109 became too vulnerable to enemy fighters.

Nevertheless, mass production and continuous development of the Bf 109 would continue until the end of the war.

The German aircraft industry was a high-priority target for Allied bombers. On 20 February 1944, the USAAF initiated Operation Argument (also known as 'Big Week'), which involved raids against aircraft factories across Germany. Regensburg was hit twice, on 22 and 25 February.

Having scrambled to intercept USAAF bombers raiding Regensburg on 25 February, Lt Heinrich Freiherr von Rodewils of I./JG 5 recalled:

> As on 22 February, we arrived at the location (of the USAAF bombers) too late. Flying diagonally over the town, we attempted to connect up with the bombers. We were successful in attacking some of the B-24s that were flying away. After landing at Obertraubling at 12.30, our fighters that were returning one by one were immediately refuelled and re-armed. Our well-practised ground crew were absolutely first-class … Hardly were our aircraft ready for another sortie, when attacking bombers were again announced. We said to ourselves: 'That just can't be!' But not even fifteen minutes later, we were soon taught otherwise. Each one of us made a dash for his aircraft so as to be able to take-off as soon as possible. My Me 109 was parked on the concrete in front of one of the large hangars at the *Fliegerhorst*. Quickly into the aircraft, I strapped myself in and closed the canopy. The second mechanic was already cranking the starting handle, and when the revolutions reached the maximum figure, I activated the clutch. The airscrew made three or four turns, but the engine did not start. A new attempt was then made with the power lever almost at full load. Again the same thing; the otherwise reliable DB 605 engine showed no sign of life. The other aircraft had long since taken off. Even after we had made several attempts, the engine did not turn. From the time the first alarm siren had gone off, some 10 to 12 minutes had passed when the first bombers were recognisable in the blue sky. Now there was nothing for it but to get out of my Me 109 and head for the cover! … The entire Fleigerhorst meanwhile lay beneath a thick pall of smoke. After the last bombers had departed, I headed back to my Me 109, but it was completely destroyed. The *Fliegerhorst* had been badly hit in all areas and almost all of our equipment had been destroyed. Our quarters had also suffered heavy damage. We pilots were thus re-quartered in the Park Hotel Maximilian in Regensburg. A few days later, we relocated to Herzogenraurach, but it was only on 16 March that I./JG 5 could report itself ready for operations.

Operation Argument was eventually cancelled on 26 February due to poor weather.

The next target for the 8 AF was Berlin, which between 18 November 1943 and 30 January 1944 had been the target of numerous RAF Bomber Command night raids. During these raids, Bomber Command had lost nearly 400 aircraft. Daylight raids against the German capital had been avoided due to the distance involved, as well as the large number of flak guns and fighters defending Berlin. Although USAAF bombers appeared over Berlin on 3 March, the first big raid took place three days later, on 6 March.

In all, more than 700 B-17 Flying Fortresses and B-24 Liberators, escorted by P-38 Lightnings, P-47 Thunderbolts, and the newly-introduced P-51B Mustang fighters appeared over the German capitol. The range of the escort fighters had been greatly enhanced with the use of external drop tanks, making it possible for the USAAF fighter pilots to remain with the bombers on deep penetrating missions over German-occupied Europe. The twin-engine P-38 Lightning was considered the least suitable escort fighter as it suffered from continuous engine problems, as well as having a lower diving speed than either the Bf 109 or Fw 190. According to Colonel 'Hub' Zemke, Commander of the 56th Fighter Group, the P-47 Thunderbolt (which weighed twice as much as a Bf 109G) was not particularly suitable at lower altitudes: 'To try to engage 109s and 190s in dogfights below 15,000 feet could be suicidal—that was not playing the game our way.' Powered by a Packard-built Rolls-Royce Merlin engine, the P-51B Mustang had the best overall performance and was arguably the best US fighter of the war.

Walter Krupinski, a 197-victory ace, later compared his experiences meeting both Russian and USAAF fighters.

> The Americans were eager to fight. The Russian pilots, up to the moment I left [in the spring of 1944], always gave the impression of trying to defend themselves rather than fight. The Americans were very different, they liked to take the initiative. We had to compromise our tactics to defend the 'heavy fighters' and so were not free to dogfight. On the first mission I flew with a group of twenty-two or so aircraft—I came back with twelve. They were not all dead, but those who had been shot down were scattered all over the country and had to be returned to the unit for the next mission, but then, of course, we could only send, for example, fifteen aircraft.

Of the many factories located in and around Berlin, mention must be made of the Daimler-Benz factory at Genshagen. Cloud cover saved Genshagen from major damage, with most of the bombs falling outside the factory area.

The USAAF paid a heavy price—sixty-nine heavy bombers and eleven escort fighters failed to return. Out of these, about forty-two of the bombers and five fighters were shot down by Luftwaffe fighters. Luftwaffe fighter units accumulated 528 sorties, with 369 engaging the USAAF aircraft. A total of sixty-six fighters, including twenty-two Bf 109s, were lost, with another thirteen Bf 109s suffering damage. It was, in essence, a battle of attrition that the Luftwaffe could not win.

Following the heavy raid against Berlin, a USAAF Spitfire PR XI was despatched to obtain post-raid photographs. The sortie was at the extreme of its range and required external drop tanks. The pilot, Major Walt Weitner, subsequently reported:

> As I climbed through 40,000 feet (12,200 metres) I could see that the German fighters behind me had split: one went on my right and two on my left, to box me in. And at that moment the engine coughed. I immediately selected internal fuel and the engine caught right away. At 41,500 feet (12,500 m) I levelled off and my indicated airspeed increased to 178 mph [286 kph—the true airspeed being around 360 mph or 580 kph]. After what seemed forever, but was probably only two or three minutes, the German fighters began to fall back and slid out of sight. Had they come any closer I should have gone to emergency boost, but it never got that desperate.

A late-model Bf 109G seen prior to taking off on another sortie. (*Gregory Alegi*)

Weitner stayed over Berlin for twenty-five minutes, making several photo runs, before eventually making it to Mount Farm with dry fuel tanks.

During the first months of 1944, the two-seat Bf 109G-12 advanced trainer began to reach Luftwaffe *Jägdfliegerschulen* (Fighter Training Schools). By now, a new fighter pilot did not have the luxury of accumulating 200 flight hours before being posted to a front-line unit. In order to speed-up fighter pilot training, a two-seat variant of the Bf 109G was developed. The Bf 109G-12 eventually served with thirteen *Jägdfliegerschulen* (Fighter Training Schools): JG 101 to JG 110, and JG 114 and JG 115. One of these, JG 102, began to receive Bf 109G-12s in mid-1944. By July 1944, I./JG 102 had transferred to Aalborg-Ost in Denmark. During the late summer, early-autumn of 1944, three Bf 109G-12s of I./JG 102 were destroyed or damaged in training accidents, with two pilots killed. One of the Bf 109G-12s was W Nr 19776, indicating a WNF-built Bf 109G-4 completed in the spring of 1943.

During the spring of 1944, a special *Einsatzstaffel* (literally, 'combat squadron') was formed at each of the *Jägdfliegerschulen*, and manned by flight instructors. Three of these *Einsatzstaffeln* were part of *Luftflotte* Reich, as indicated in the following table.

***Luftflotte* Reich Bf 109 units on 31 May 1944**			
Unit	**Total No. of aircraft**	**Serviceable aircraft**	**Remarks**
III./JG 1	48	21	
Stab JG 3	4	2	

I./JG 3	26	9	
II./JG 3	29	23	
III./JG 3	31	9	
I./JG 5	43	36	
II./JG 5	44	36	
Stab JG 11	4	3	
II./JG 11	31	14	
10./JG 11	10	7	Includes a few Fw 190s
Stab JG 27	4	4	
I./JG 27	41	31	
II./JG 27	24	12	
III./JG 27	26	20	
IV./JG 27	18	12	
II./JG 53	31	14	
JG 104	4	4	Flight training school, included one *Einsatzstaffel* manned by Flight Instructors
JG 106	5	3	Flight training school, included one *Einsatzstaffel* manned by Flight Instructors
JG 108	12	6	Flight training school, included one *Einsatzstaffel* manned by Flight Instructors
I./JG 300	29	19	Combined day and night fighter unit
III./JG 300	27	25	Combined day and night fighter unit
I./JG 301	25	21	
I./JG 302	27	11	
	543	342	

In addition, the NAGr 8 and NAGr 14 tactical-reconnaissance units had four Bf 109s between them, with only two being serviceable.

By the summer of 1944, Allied forces were closing in on the German Reich. Operation Overlord, the invasion of France, began on 6 June 1944. Few Luftwaffe units were available to oppose the Allied air supremacy. It is said that Oblt Paul-Adalbert Baerwolf of NAGr. 3./13 was the first Luftwaffe pilot to observe the invasion fleet from the air. (This remains unconfirmed, however.)

In anticipation of an Allied invasion of southern France, *Jägdgruppe* 200 was formed from *Jägdgruppe Süd* (becoming 1. and 2./JGr 200) and JG 101 (3./JGr 200) in early June 1944. In early August, Allied bombers began attacking targets in southern France. One of the few other Luftwaffe units in the area was NAGr 13, with a mix of Fw 190As and Bf 109G-8s. On 12 August, two Allied convoys, which included two aircraft carriers, were spotted off Ajaccio. Three days later, Operation Dragoon, the invasion of southern France, began. Although the Bf 109 pilots of *Jägdgruppe* 200 scored some victories, Allied air supremacy meant that the unit was quickly decimated.

Between 23 August and 9 September, Germany lost three of her allies: Romania, Finland, and Bulgaria. All three countries subsequently conducted air and ground operations against German forces, as described elsewhere in this book. However, it is worth mentioning that upon the Bulgarian declaration of war on 9 September 1944, six Luftwaffe Bf 109s strafed a VVNV fuel depot. The Bf 109s then tangled with Avia B.534 biplanes, shooting down one.[19]

In early October 1944, the first Bf 109K-4s arrived, with III./JG 27 becoming initial unit to receive the new variant. The Bf 109K-4 would be the final production variant of the Messerschmitt fighter, with most Bf 109 units standardising on the type.

Operation *Bodenplatte*

During the autumn of 1944, the Luftwaffe was losing hundreds of fighter pilots in continuous battles against RAF and USAAF bombers. The heaviest fighter losses during a single day occurred on 2 November, when 120 Bf 109s, Fw 190s, and Me 163s were lost during a USAAF raid. In all, seventy pilots were killed or missing in action, with an additional twenty-eight wounded. The hardest hit unit was JG 27, which lost twenty-seven pilots killed (including eleven from I./JG 27) and twelve wounded. USAAF losses consisted of forty bombers and sixteen fighters.

With the Allies closing in on Germany's borders, plans were put forward to initiate a large-scale ground and air offensive in the west. Under the codename of *Wacht am Rhein* (Watch on the Rhine), all available Luftwaffe fighters would strike against Allied airfields and support advancing *Panzers*. In the event, *Wacht am Rhein* would emerge as the Ardennes offensive, beginning on 16 December. Supported by the Luftwaffe, German ground units managed to push back American units. However, the intended attacks against sixteen Allied airfields in Belgium, France, and the Netherlands were not co-ordinated to occur simultaneously with the ground offensive. Instead, final attack orders were not received until the afternoon of 31 December, New Year's Eve. A great effort took place during the early hours of 1 January. New Year celebrations were, to the chagrin of most, effectively cancelled. During the briefing, recent aerial photographs of most of the airfields were distributed, although there was no such luxury for the sole French airfield to be attacked, Metz-Frescaty, where the available photographs dated from the German occupation. The *Geschwaderkommodore* of JG 6, Oblt Johann Kogler, managed to prepare scale sand models of the Dutch airfield Volkel.

It had initially been intended to strike at dawn. However, this would involve taking off, joining formation, and then finding the way to the respective designated targets in darkness. This could not be performed without severe losses, resulting in take-off being moved forward to around 8 a.m. The time set for a co-ordinated attack was 9.20 a.m. Navigation would be eased by having Ju 88s with master navigators leading each formation.

Bf 109 units taking part in Operation Bodenplatte			
Unit	**Bf 109 variant(s)**	**Base**	**Intended target(s)**
III./JG 1	Bf 109G-10, Bf 109G-14, Bf 109K-4	Rheine	
I./JG 3	Bf 109G-10, Bf 109G-14	Paderborn	Eindhoven/Gilze-Rijen
I./JG 27	Bf 109G-10, Bf 109G-14	Rheine	
II./JG 27	Bf 109G-10, Bf 109G-14, Bf 109K-4	Hopsten	
III./JG 27	Bf 109G-14, Bf 109K-4	Hesepe	
IV./JG 27	Bf 109G-10, Bf 109G-14, Bf 109K-4	Achmer	
II./JG 53	Bf 109G-14	Malmsheim	Metz-Frescaty
III./JG 53	Bf 109G-14, Bf 109K-4	Kirrlach	Metz-Frescaty
IV./JG 53	Bf 109G-14, Bf 109K-4	Stuttgart-Eschterdingen	Metz-Frescaty
I./JG 77	Bf 109G-14	Dortmund	
II./JG 77	Bf 109K-4	Bönninghardt	
III./JG 77	Bf 109K-4	Düsseldorf-Lohausen	

Trigger-happy German flak crews, believing such a large formation of fighters must either be American or British, shot down at least seventeen Bf 109s and Fw 190s. Nevertheless, complete surprise was achieved, with the Luftwaffe fighter pilots enjoying free rein over the respective airfields. At Eindhoven, two squadrons of RAF Typhoons were in the process of taking off when most aircraft were hit during repeated strafing runs. Brussels-Evère was targeted by the Second and Third *Gruppen* of JG 26. When the few light anti-aircraft guns ran out of ammunition, the Luftwaffe fighters turned the sortie into an air-to-ground practice flight and were able to make firing passes at the resident aircraft and hangars for some forty-five minutes at extreme low-level. After shooting down a solitary 416 Squadron Spitfire that had managed to get airborne at the start of the attack, twenty-two more

Spitfires were destroyed or damaged, as were several transport aircraft. However, with about sixty Spitfires resident at Brussels-Evére, the aim of the Luftwaffe pilots can only be considered as poor. Although hundreds of RAF and USAAF aircraft were destroyed or damaged, the Luftwaffe lost 271 fighters, with another sixty-five damaged. No less than 143 pilots were killed, twenty-one wounded, with seventy becoming prisoners of war. The Luftwaffe fighter units would never fully recover from the losses of highly experienced pilots and aircraft. In retrospect, Operation Baseplate was a failure, with the Allies being able to replace the aircraft that had been destroyed within days. Additionally, with the Ardennes offensive stopped in its tracks, Operation Baseplate had lost its strategic impetus. Simply put, it was a grand, futile gesture.

One important task of the Bf 109 units during the latter stages of the war was to provide protection for the Me 262 air bases. Although an excellent jet fighter, the Me 262 had one Achilles heel. At low speeds while on approach to land, with undercarriage and flaps extended, the Me 262 was a sitting duck to Allied fighters. On 2 March, JG 27 managed to get seventy-one Bf 109s into the air for defensive patrols around Rheine, a major Me 262 air base. A major clash with RAF fighters ensued, with the JG 27 pilots claiming two Tempest Vs and one Spitfire shot down. However, no less than eight Bf 109s had been downed, with five of the pilots killed.

With Bulgaria and Romania having changed sides in the late summer of 1944, Luftwaffe Bf 109 pilots occasionally found themselves fighting against enemy Bf 109s. On 25 February 1945, Hptm Helmut Lipfert of I./JG 53, encountered Romanian Bf 109s.

A destroyed Bf 109G hidden among trees in early 1945. (*NMUSAF*)

> Two Messerschmitts were coming towards me, so I climbed up into the clouds. Before entering (into the) cloud I recognised their Romanian markings. Perhaps the pilots were two of the Romanians I had instructed at Tiraspol. A unique situation, I wanted to see what they had learned. Coming out of the clouds, I descended to just above the ground. I saw two machines above and to my right and approached them from behind and below.
>
> With my speed I shot past them into the climb and once again noticed their Romanian markings. When we began turning, I concluded to my relief that these two definitely could not have been at Tiraspol, as they appeared to be very inexperienced. The enemy pilots seemed to be afraid to fly their aircraft to the limit and therefore made rather only gentle turns. Their aircraft also seemed to be rather slow, as I was able to get behind them on my first pass. After the first shots at the trailing Romanian, he immediately tried to dive away in the direction of the enemy lines. But I sat on his tail, blazing away with my one [working] machine gun. He took no evasive action, seeking safety in flight instead ... I didn't want to let this machine get away so easily. The other Romanian separated from his companion but did not come to his aid. Afterward I maintained an especially close watch behind and continued firing at the 'Me' in front of me. It was really smoking heavily and crashed into a hill. There was no fire.[20]

An interesting event on 6 March was the picking up a Bf 109 pilot of 1./NAG 4, which had force landed near Goschin, by helicopter. A few days earlier, the *Transportgruppe* 40 received orders to pick up three prisoners from the *Seydlitz Armee* (former German prisoners of war fighting on the Soviet side) held at Gradenz. A Fa 223 helicopter (code GW+PA) flown by Lt Hans Helmut Gerstenhauer would perform the pick up within 500 metres of Soviet troops. Having arrived at Danzig-Praust, Bf 109s of 1./NAG 4 were despatched to check the presence of Soviet flak over Gradenz. During one such reconnaissance flight, a Bf 109G-8 force-landed in German-held territory. Lt Gersternhauer was sent to pick up the Bf 109 pilot, which was accomplished with few problems. The flight to Gradenz was cancelled, though, as the risks involved were deemed too great.

Supplying the beleaguered city of Breslau demanded a large number of sorties for the Luftwaffe's diminishing number of Ju 52/3ms. As a result, Bf 109s flew 180 sorties between 16 March and 26 April, dropping a total of twenty-six, 56 tons of ammunition, as well as three light howizers and an infantry gun. However, only about 20 per cent of the ammunition containers fell within the German defence perimeter.

The Russian Liberation Army

One unique Bf 109 operator was the *Russkaja oswobodite'naja armija* (Russian Liberation Army, ROA). Following reluctant German approval, the ROA was formed in late 1944 under the command of General Andrei Vlassov.21 Many Russian prisoners of war, forced labourers, and immigrants were recruited to the

ROA ranks. On 16 September 1944, the Commander of the SS, Heinrich Himmler, ordered the establishment of an ROA aviation component, which included one *Jägdstaffel* with sixteen Bf 109G-10s.[22] This unit, designated *Jägdstaffel* 5, was named Ob Kazakow in honour of the Tzarist-Russian Great War ace. The ROA insignia, consisting of a blue St Andrew's cross superimposed on a white shield outlined in red and black with the Cyrillic letters 'POA' above, was painted on the aircraft.

Initially, the ROA aviation component had 2,594 men, of which some 1,800 were undergoing training. On 7 March 1945, four Bf 109Gs, four Ar 96s, and two Bü 181s of *Jägdstaffel* 5 arrived at Deutsch Brod (present-day Havlíčkuv Brod) in Bohemia. In early April, *Jägdstaffel* 5 was declared operational, with its first sorties flown in support of the 1 ROA Division against Soviet forces along the Oder. However, the war was already lost. In the final days of the war, Vlassov's forces turned their weapons on the Germans.

Mistel Operations

Originally developed as a method of transporting assault gliders into a combat zone by means of having a powered aircraft placed 'piggy-back style' on top of the glider, this concept was eventually used for the Mistel heavy bomber concept. Initial trials involved mounting a Klemm Kl 35 primary trainer on top of a DFS 230 assault glider. The composite aircraft was towed into the air by a Ju 52/3m. The concept proved workable, with the Kl 35 eventually being superseded by a Fw 56 Stösser and, later, a Bf 109E. Although the flight and handling characteristics were largely trouble-free, the separation phase saw the Bf 109 striking the DFS 230 on several occasions, including one where tail-wheel of the Bf 109 went straight through the canopy of the DFS 230, almost hitting the pilot. The strut framework was modified, with the Bf 109 mounted at different incidences in order to obtain the best possible flight characteristics.

The DFS 230 was eventually replaced with a Ju 88A-4, onto which a Bf 109F was mounted. The Ju 88 carried no crew, with the Bf 109F pilot controlling both aircraft. Upon reaching the intended target, the Bf 109 pilot would release the Ju 88, which was, in essence, a flying bomb, and then guide it by means of remote control. A report dated 17 June 1943 stated:

> The Mistel combination offers the possibility of using the Ju 88A-4 as an unmanned Grossbombe (Large Bomb) remotely controlled by the Bf 109F to a target of a predetermined glide path. With a range of 1,500 km, the Mistel can deliver a 3.5-ton payload of high explosives. Such aircraft can be stripped of all unnecessary equipment and can therefore carry substantial amounts of explosives. This method has the advantage that the fighter can remain outside the range of the anti-aircraft guns of a sea target since it can disengage its payload from out of range of said anti-aircraft fire and escape due to its superior speed from any pursuing fighter cover. Another advantage is that such a mission requires only one pilot.[23]

A Bf 109E, seen as a carrier for the DFS 230 assault glider. (*NMUSAF*)

Another view of the Bf 109E-DFS 230 combination. (*NMUSAF*)

In the event, the Mistel S1, consisting of an obsolete Bf 109F and a war-weary Ju 88, became operational in mid-1944. The combined maximum take-off weight of the Mistel S1 was 16,000 kg, including a warload of 3,156 kg. On 14 June, the invasion fleet was unsuccessfully attacked by a single Mistel. The Bf 109/Ju 88 combination was slow and cumbersome, with the Bf 109 being unarmed and lacking a radio (these had been removed to reduce weight). The Mistel S1 was shot down by a 410 Squadron Mosquito. During subsequent sorties, the Bf 109F carried an armament consisting of a pair of MG 17s. The Mistel S1 was rarely used on operations, with fewer than 100 conversions completed. The Mistel S1 was eventually replaced by the Mistel S2 and the improved Mistel S3. Both the Mistel S2 and S3 consisted of a Fw 190A-8 and a Ju 88. The BMW 801 engine of the Fw 190 was more powerful than the DB 601 of the Bf 109F, and also offered a slightly increased range. The Mistel S2 and S3s were used on operations on both the Western and Eastern Fronts, with largely unsuccessful results. Late in the war, it was planned to attack Scapa Flow using Mistel S2 and S3s. This did not take place.

Last-ditch Defence

With USAAF heavy bombers raiding the Reich on an almost daily basis, various methods of bringing the bombers down were considered. In late 1944, a radical and truly desperate idea was brought forward by Ob Hajo Hermann.

The previous year, Hermann had devised the *Wilde Sau* (Wild Boar) night-fighter tactics. Hermann suggested the formation of special Luftwaffe units, consisting of volunteer pilots, who would bring down the USAAF B-17s and B-24s by means of intentionally ramming the bombers. The Luftwaffe pilots would fly specially modified Bf 109Gs and Ks. These fighters were to have their self-protective armour removed, with the armament being limited to one 13-mm MG 131 cannon containing sixty rounds. The reduction in overall weight meant an increase of speed and manoeuvrability. The tactics devised by Hermann were that the ramming Bf 109s would climb to an altitude of around 10,000 metres and then dive vertically towards the USAAF bombers. If hundreds of bombers could be brought down during one raid by means of ramming, the USAAF would require weeks or even months to recover from such a disastrous loss of so many aircrew and aircraft. It was thought that the USAAF daylight raids over Germany would, if not cease completely, be considerably reduced. It was expected that the Luftwaffe pilots committed to ramming tactics would suffer 50 per cent losses. With complete Allied air superiority over Germany and with conventional fighter tactics being largely ineffectual, Hermann's plan became the subject of much discussion within the Luftwaffe High Command. To make the greatest possible impact, Hermann envisaged committing 650 pilots or more in one single sortie.

Göring supported the ramming tactics, but would not consider committing any experienced fighter pilots. Instead, trainee pilots would have to suffice.

In February 1945, the various Luftwaffe fighter training schools received a secret order of the day asking for volunteer pilots for an unspecified mission. Large number of pilots did volunteer for a special ramming unit named *Sonderkommando*

Elbe formed of 135 pilots, with some 150 Bf 109s having been modified. Codenamed Operation Wehrwolf (Werewolf), the Bf 109s of *Sonderkommando Elbe* were thrown into action on 7 April 1945 against 1,300 USAAF bombers. Only 120 Bf 109s got airborne, far less than deemed necessary by Hermann. Instead of annihilating the USAAF bomber formation, only eight were brought down by ramming. Nearly sixty Luftwaffe fighters were lost—the majority from *Sonderkommando Elbe*. As it turned out, this was the only dedicated Luftwaffe ramming sortie during the war. Of the USAAF aircraft lost, it would appear that only eight went down as a result of intentional ramming.[24]

No further ramming operations were attempted. Nevertheless, an even more desperate operation saw one confirmed suicide sortie taking place. When, on 16 April, Soviet forces crossed the Oder and Neisse Rivers, ten Bf 109 pilots of *Schlachtgeschwader* 104 volunteered to fly their aircraft into the bridges that had been abandoned undamaged, in a fashion similar to the *Kamikaze* tactics employed by Japanese pilots. There was no chance for the pilots to escape from their Bf 109s. Suicide operations had been contemplated previously, but the Luftwaffe High Command remained undecided regarding such highly controversial tactics. Several Mistels were also part of the operation, with escort being provided by III./JG 4. In the end, little was accomplished in this desperate attempt to stop the Soviet march towards Berlin.

The End

By April 1945, it was clear that the war would soon be over. Although many units had ample supplies of aircraft, the lack of fuel resulted in few operations being conducted.

Luftwaffe Bf 109 units, 9 April 1945

Unit	*Luftflotte*	Total No. of aircraft	Serviceable aircraft	Remarks
III./JG 4	Reich	61	56	
I./JG 27	Reich	29	13	
II./JG 27	Reich	48	27	
III./JG 27	Reich	19	15	
1./NJG 11	Reich	16	15	Night fighter unit
4./NJG 11	Reich	14	9	Night fighter unit
7./NJG 11	Reich	21	19	Night fighter unit
NAGr. 1	Reich	16	9	Tactical reconnaissance unit

II./JG 51	4	7	5	
II./JG 52	4	43	29	
I./JG 53	4	27	27	
Stab JG 76	4	1	1	
NAGr. 12	4	30	26	Tactical reconnaissance unit, including some Hs 126s
NAGr. 14	4	42	19	Tactical reconnaissance unit, including some Bf 110s
NA Staffel Kroatien	4	17	16	Tactical reconnaissance unit, including some Hs 126s.
II./JG 3	6	51	49	
III./JG 3	6	47	46	
Stab JG 6	6	4	4	Including a few Fw 190s
III./JG 6	6	21	17	
Stab JG 52	6	8	7	
I./JG 52	6	40	37	
III./JG 52	6	32	30	
Stab JG 77	6	1	1	
I./JG 77	6	30	26	
II./JG 77	6	36	30	
III./JG 77	6	34	25	
JG 1	6	109	97	*Ergänzung* (attrition replacement unit)
NAGr. 2	6	30	20	Tactical reconnaissance unit
NAGr. 3	6	37	22	Tactical reconnaissance unit
NAGr. 4	6	2	2	Tactical reconnaissance unit
NAGr. 8	6	35	21	Tactical reconnaissance unit
NAGr. 15	6	31	26	Tactical reconnaissance unit
Stab JG 53	Ladko West	1	1	
II./JG 53	Ladko West	39	24	
III./JG 53	Ladko West	40	24	
IV./JG 53	Ladko West	54	27	

NAGr. 13		39	26	Tactical reconnaissance unit
I./JG 51	Ladko East Prussia	10	8	
III./JG 51	Ladko East Prussia	23	7	
NAGr. 4	Ladko East Prussia	26	17	Including some Fw 189s
Stab JG 5	General Norwegen	?	?	
III./JG 5	General Norwegen	?	?	
IV./JG 5	General Norwegen	?	?	Including some Fw 190s
Aufkl. Gr. 32	General Norwegen	?	?	Tactical reconnaissance unit, including some Fw 190s
NAGr. 5	Ladko Courland	25	18	Tactical reconnaissance unit, including some Fw 190s
NAGr. 11	General Italien	24	14	Tactical reconnaissance unit

In April and May 1945, some Luftwaffe pilots sought refuge in neutral Sweden. On 12 April, two Bf 109G-10/R2s of 2.(F)/122 landed at Rinkaby. The pilots had been planning to defect for some time. However, before this could be achieved, their respective families had to be rescued from the inevitable vengeance of the Gestapo. The opportunity arose when the unit was ordered to fly to Cirava in Latvia, but, having heard a BBC radio transmission reporting the successful defection of a Fw 189 crew to Sweden, they opted to fly to Sweden instead. Both pilots were allowed to stay in Sweden.

Other arriving Luftwaffe pilots were not so fortunate. According to an agreement between Sweden and the USSR, all German troops arriving in Sweden on 1 May or thereafter were to be handed over to Soviet authorities. Additional Bf 109s did arrive, with two of them landing at Rinkaby on 8 May. Apart from the pilots, both Bf 109s also carried a passenger crammed into the rear fuselage. Both crews and aircraft were eventually handed over to Soviet authorities.

On 4 May, Field Marshal Montgomery and Admiral Friedenburg signed a document demanding the unconditional surrender of all German forces in north-east Germany, Denmark, and the Netherlands. All fighting was to cease at 8 a.m., British Double Summer Time, the following day. However, the Luftwaffe prepared to fight on other fronts, most particularly against the Soviet forces. A General Order, issued during the final hours of 4 May, ordered Luftwaffe units to relocate

The two Bf 109G-10/R2s that arrived at Rinkaby, Sweden, on 12 April 1945. *(Bengt Hermansson/Forced Landing Collection)*

to Norway and Prague, with the final take-off being at 6.30 a.m. In all, 114 aircraft, including nine Bf 109Gs arrived at Norwegian airfields in the morning of 5 May.

Two of the Bf 109s to land at Kristiansand-Kjevik on the southernmost tip of Norway were Oblt Fritz E. Krause and Uffz Willi Buder of 7./NJG 11.

> My (Oblt Krause) Bf 109G, marked with double blue chevrons, showed her best side, all systems working perfectly. Buder seemed to be having problems with his machine. He was flying too close to me, wing to wing. As we had no radio communication he was giving me hand signals through his side screen which I couldn't understand. I was preoccupied with the question of what to do if visual flight across the Skagerrak proved impossible, or if I failed to find the lighthouse (near Kristianstad). Once we reached the Norwegian coast we would have insufficient fuel to return to Denmark ... The closer we got to Norway, the worse the weather became. Out to sea a storm raged, with cloud down to the surface in places. I flew against all the rules, just above the wave crests. Meanwhile I had worked out what Buder was trying to tell me. His instruments had packed up, possibly owing to flak damage overlooked in the hurried pre-departure checks. My aircraft offered him the only chance of staying the right way up, and he dared not lose sight of me ... Luckily, the decision to turn back did not arise. After half an hour the storm abated, the clouds lightened, and soon the rocks of the south coast of Norway were recognisable. But from so low an altitude I couldn't make out the contours of the coastline. Were we east or west of Kristiansand? I remember instinctively turning east and following the coastline. We were overjoyed to see the lighthouse with its two red bands. On landing, Willi Buder ground looped and skidded, writing his aircraft off. The flight had obviously used up all his strength.[25]

Another Bf 109G unit, 2./NAGr 1, based at Hohn, also attempted to reach Norway. Although the unit's personnel resisted the order to relocate, its commanding officer,

Hptm Erzberger, nevertheless ordered his pilots to take-off in the prevailing poor weather. Although maps had been issued, these were to 1:1,000,000 scale. However, the engine of Erzberger's Bf 109 did not start. Only minutes before the 8 a.m. ceasefire deadline, another pilot, Hptm Büchel, managed to take-off, narrowly avoiding hitting a fire truck that the commander of Hohn airfield had ordered to block the runway. No other pilots followed Büchel into the air. After performing a few circuits, Büchel landed. The war was over.

Of the 4,810 Luftwaffe aircraft surrendered in the British Zone alone, 897 were Bf 109s. Out of these, twenty-three Bf 109s were found at *Fliegerhorst* Schleswig-Land (*Jagel*), Germany, and 206 in Denmark. Somewhat surprisingly, in November 1945, the Danish government requested a number of former Luftwaffe aircraft to be handed over for use in training aircraft mechanics. This included two Bf 109s. The identities and ultimate fate of these aircraft is unknown.

The majority of the Bf 109s surrendered to the Allies were scrapped, with a few selected for evaluation and preservation. However, as the primary single-seat fighter of the Luftwaffe, no requirement existed to retain large numbers of Bf 109s. Compared with transport and training aircraft, the Bf 109s had no civilian applications whatsoever. Instead, along with other former Luftwaffe combat aircraft, they were quickly scrapped and smelted down, with the materials being re-used for civilian purposes. A somewhat different approach was seen in Eastern Europe, with several Bf 109s surrendered in Austria being transferred to Bulgaria—most of which were ceded to Yugoslavia soon afterwards.

A destroyed Bf 109G sits on a dump following the end of the war. (*NMUSAF*)

4
Beyond Germany

Foreign Operators

Inevitably, foreign interest in the Bf 109 was great. However, it was not cleared for export until 1938, and only then because of desperately needed raw materials offered as barter by Switzerland and Yugoslavia. Nevertheless, as the premier Luftwaffe single-seat fighter, it was inevitable that large numbers would be operated by other European air arms. All of Germany's Allies, including Bulgaria, Croatia, Finland, Hungary, Italy (both the *Regia Aeronautica* and the post-September 1943 ANR), Japan (evaluation only), Romania, and Slovakia received Bf 109s, with licence production taking place in Hungary and Romania. Out of these countries, Bulgaria, Hungary, Romania, and Slovakia would during the latter stages of the war also use their Bf 109s against the Luftwaffe. Interestingly, Bf 109Gs were also transferred to the anti-communist Russian Liberation Army in 1944 and 1945. Incredibly, a few Bf 109s were used operationally by the USSR against the Luftwaffe. Others were thoroughly tested, as described separately. Two neutral nations, Spain and Switzerland, also operated Bf 109s, while the USSR obtained a batch of Bf 109Es for evaluation. Finally, Yugoslavia purchased Bf 109Es in 1939, as well as operating captured Bf 109Gs post-war. Lithuania ordered fourteen Bf 109Cs in 1939 and 1940, but none were delivered. Fascinatingly, a Brazilian delegation visiting Germany in 1939 declared an interest in acquiring Bf 109's. Sweden attempted to obtain a manufacturing licence for the Bf 109, however the DB 605 engine was built under licence in Sweden and used to power the Saab J 21A fighter and Saab B 18B bomber. During the war, several Bf 109s were captured and subjected to thorough evaluation in France, the UK, the USSR, and the USA.

Bulgaria

Although Bulgaria remained neutral during the initial stages of the Second World War, the country was firmly within the German sphere of interest. On 23 January

1941, Bulgaria unofficially joined the Axis Alliance, eventually signing an agreement with Germany and Italy on 1 March. In the build-up to the invasion of Greece and Yugoslavia, 680,000 German troops entered Bulgaria, with units of the Luftwaffe's VIII. *Fliegerkorps* deployed to four Bulgarian airfields. However, it is worth noting that both *Czar* Boris III, as well as a large percentage of the Bulgarian population, retained strong pro-Russian opinions.

The *Vazdushni na Negovo Velichestvo Voyski* (His Majesty's Air Force, VVNV) showed great interest in the Bf 109, although Germany was initially reluctant to deliver any Bf 109s to Bulgaria, instead selling large quantities of obsolete former Czech aircraft. Nevertheless, an initial batch of ten Bf 109E-4s arrived in June 1940. Four Bf 108s were also delivered for use as conversion trainers by the 6 *Polk* (6th Fighter Regiment) pilots. In VNVV service, the Bf 109E was named *Strela* (Arrow), with the numeric type designator 7047 assigned. An additional nine Bf 109E-7s arrived in 1941. On 1 October 1941, the Black Sea Air Defence Command was established with one fighter *orlyak* (group), named *Galata*, based at Varna. The *Galata Orlyak* consisted of three fighter *yatos* (squadrons)—including 682 *yato* based at Balchik, and 692 *yato* based at Saraphovo—with about half-a-dozen Bf 109Es each. A third *yato* operated Avia B.534s.

In 1941, an aircraft repair facility was inaugurated at Karlovo that specialised in combat aircraft, including Bf 109s. Following the Japanese attack against Pearl Harbor, Bulgaria joined Germany in declaring war against the USA and Great Britain on 13 December 1941. However, Bulgaria remained neutral against the USSR.

In March 1942, all fighter and bomber units were organised into the *Vazdushna Escadra* (Air Group). Until the summer of 1942, Bulgaria had been spared war. However, on 12 June 1942, a small number of USAAF B-24 Liberators raided Romanian oil installations at Ploesti with the bombers flying unhindered across Bulgarian airspace. As a result, the VVNV fighter squadrons were to receive more modern aircraft under a modernisation programme called the Barbara Plan. The Luftwaffe also established the *Jägdfliegerführer* Balkan in order to co-ordinate air defence operations in the area. The supply of sixteen Bf 109s was approved by the RLM in December 1942, with the first twenty-seven Bf 109G-2s destined for the VVNV arriving in March the following year. The name 'Strela' was retained for the Bf 109G, with the numeric type designator 7097 being assigned. In all, an eventual total of 145 Bf 109Gs (including eighty-four G-2 and G-4s) were supplied to the VVNV. The first VVNV unit to receive *Gustavs* was the 3/6. *Orlyak*, based at Karlovo, which initially received twenty-three Bf 109G-2s. The 3/6. *Orlyak* was part of the 6th *Polk*, and consisted of three squadrons and a staff flight. Following conversion training, the 3/6. *Orlyak* was declared operational in July 1943. Apart from the Bf 109s, the VVNV also took delivery of ninety-six Dewoitine D.520s.[1]

On 1 August 1943, the USAAF initiated Operation Tidal Wave—a low-level raid against the oil fields at Ploesti. With radar stations picking up the B-24 Liberators as they headed north across Greece, it was initially believed that the target was the Bulgarian capital, Sofia. However, the VVNV fighters were unable to intercept any of the USAAF bombers until their return flight. Over Ploesti, the B-24s had taken a severe beating from Luftwaffe and Romanian Bf 109s, which meant that the Liberators turned south piecemeal. Two Bf 109E pilots, *Poruchiks* (Lieutenants) Petr Bochev and Stoyan Stoyanov, intercepted the B-24s, with Bochev claiming three shot down (two were eventually confirmed), while Stoyanov claimed to have forced down one Liberator. *Poruchik* Stoyanov would become the highest-scoring VVNV fighter pilot with six confirmed victories—three B-24s and three P-38s.

The Ploesti raid had direct and immediate implications for the VVNV. On 12 August 1943, the 3/6. *Orlyak*, equipped with sixteen Bf 109G-2s, deployed to Bojourishte airfield to defend Sofia. *Reichsmarschall* Hermann Göring also offered forty-eight additional Bf 109s as a gift to the VVNV; twenty-three Bf 109G-2/4s arrived in late 1943. The surrender of Italy on 8 September meant that Bulgaria was within range of USAAF and RAF bombers based in southern Italy. After a USAAF raid against the Skopje marshalling yard in early October, four Bf 109s were deployed to Skopje. The intention was to use the *Gustavs* for airborne early warning and ambush tactics during any forthcoming raids against Sofia. Two days after arriving at Skopje on 19 October, a USAAF P-38 was shot down.

On 14 November 1943, the first of a total of ten USAAF raids against Sofia took place. No less than ninety-one B-25s and forty-nine P-38s of 12 AF attacked the marshalling yards, as well as Vrajdebna airfield. Only fifteen Bf 109s of the 3/6. *Orlyak* were able to intercept, scoring one confirmed kill, a P-38, while losing one Bf 109 shot down with its pilot killed, as well as two more *Gustavs* damaged in forced landings. Ten days later, USAAF B-24s of the 15 AF raided the marshalling yards in Sofia in poor weather. Four B-24s were claimed shot down. One Bf 109 was lost.

During four USAAF raids between 14 November and 20 December, four VVNV Bf 109Gs were lost. During the fourth USAAF raid against Sofia on 20 December, *Poruchik* Dimitar Spissarevsky was killed when he intentionally rammed a B-24 Liberator. In all, seven P-38 Lightnings and three B-24 Liberators were brought down by VVNV fighters during this raid. Two Bf 109Gs were lost, with both pilots killed. Several more Bf 109s were damaged. The VVNV fighter units usually received insufficient advanced warnings of impending raids, with the firepower of both the Bf 109G and the D.520 considered insufficient.

On 2 January 1944, an additional twenty-eight Bf 109Gs were donated by Germany, with twenty-five *Gustavs* arriving on 11 and 12 January. Due to poor weather, a further forty Bf 109G-6s were stuck at airfields in Austria and southern Germany. By 25 February, nineteen of these aircraft had reached Bulgaria. Thirteen more were stranded at Aspern, with half-a-dozen more at Semlin and Straubling. The remaining two Bf 109G-6s intended for the VVNV had been lost in crashes. A USAAF raids against Sofia on 10 January resulted in claims for twelve aircraft destroyed. During this raid, Luftwaffe fighters joined the VVNV Bf 109s and D.520s in the defence of the Bulgarian capital for the first time. However, five Luftwaffe pilots were killed, with several more baling out. The accumulated VVNV and Luftwaffe fighter losses on this day reached thirty-one, with many experienced pilots killed or injured. The RAF visited Sofia during the night of 10–11 January. In early 1944, the 2/6. *Orlyak* had begun to re-equip with Bf 109Gs.

The RAF returned to Sofia on the night of 29 March with a force of fifty Mosquitoes, inflicting heavy damage. The following day, the USAAF performed its heaviest raid on Sofia; no less than 367 B-17s and B-24s, escorted by 150 P-38s, were met by seventy-one VVNV fighters, including thirty-nine Bf 109s of the 2/6. and 3/6. *Orlyaks*. Four B-24s and three P-38s were shot down, with the 3/6. *Orlyak* losing one pilot killed and two Bf 109s. The final USAAF raid on Sofia took place on 17 April; nine Bf 109s were shot down, with six pilots killed. Another three Bf 109s suffered severe damage in forced landings. One Bf 109 pilot, *Poruchik* Bonchev, rammed a USAAF B-17. Remarkably, he survived, and was thrown clear when the Fortress exploded. Bonchev was eventually executed by the Germans after being shot down over Macedonia in November 1944.

In June 1944, Karlovo airfield was hit twice by Allied aircraft. On 12 June, RAF bombers destroyed eighteen fighters and training aircraft, killing twenty airmen. The second raid on 26 June by USAAF aircraft was even more destructive; no less than seventy VVNV aircraft were destroyed, although only two of these were Bf 109s, and twenty-five airmen were killed. The final two combat sorties against the USAAF occurred on 17 August, when the 3/6. *Orlyak* claimed four B-17s and one B-17 probably shot down during a raid against Nish, and on 26 August, when one fighter and one bomber were brought down.

Between 1 August 1943 and 9 September 1944, VVNV fighter pilots scored fifty-three confirmed victories, among them thirty-seven four-engine bombers (mostly USAAF B-17s and B-24s, but also including one RAF Stirling) and sixteen P-38s and P-51s. Another seventy Allied aircraft, including forty-eight bombers and twenty-two fighters, were claimed as probables. The majority of these victories were scored by Bf 109 pilots. The VVNV fighter pilots of the 6 *Polk* had flown 970 sorties, including 550 by the 3/6. *Orlyak* and 275 by the 2/6. *Orlyak*. Twenty-three pilots were killed and twenty-seven fighters were lost in combat, with about thirty fighters suffering battle damage.

During the summer of 1944, Bulgaria attempted to seek an armistice with the Allies. However, peace talks in Istanbul failed, with the government reiterating the country's neutral stance towards the USSR, as well as declaring an end to operations against Britain and the USA. The Russians exhibited little understanding in the Bulgarian stance, demanding an immediate declaration of war against Germany. When this did not happen, the USSR declared war against Bulgaria on 5 September. A ceasefire was immediately sought, with a socialist-led *coup d'état* taking place. On 9 September, after Soviet troops had entered the country, Bulgaria changed sides. Following a brief reorganisation, fighting resumed, this time against German forces. VVNV units were involved in operations over southern Serbia and Macedonia.

In early September, the 2nd *Orlyak* had fifty-two Bf 109Gs, with the 3rd *Orlyak* having forty-nine Bf 109Gs.

Between 9 September and 8 October, the VNVV lost eleven aircraft, including five Bf 109s, to flak. On 12 November, a dozen Bf 109Gs of 3/6. *Orlyak* strafed the airfield at Pristina, Kosovo. Having completed the strafing runs, the commanding officer of the 3/6. *Orlyak*, Captain Atanasov, was spotted by a number of USAAF P-51 Mustangs. The P-51 pilots apparently mistook the Bf 109 for a Luftwaffe aircraft, making several firing passes. However, Atanasov managed to escape without being hit.

On 1 January 1945, sixty-two Bf 109s were operational and evenly divided between the 2nd and 3rd *Orlyaks*. A total of nine Bf 109Gs and seven D.520s of the 6 *Polk* were lost between September 1944 and May 1945 during 650 sorties. Seven pilots were killed.

In July 1945, 100 Bf 109Gs and 'Ks located in Austria and southern Germany arrived in Bulgaria. Although Yak-9s had already entered service, the Bf 109s were operated by the 6 *Polk* until gradually withdrawn from late 1946. In that year, fifty-nine (or up to 100, depending on the source) Bf 109s began to be transferred to Yugoslavia as war reparations. Some Bf 109s continued in service as advanced trainers with the 3rd *Escadrila* at Telish. However, by 1949, all Bf 109s had been retired.

Croatia

The Independent State of Croatia was proclaimed on 10 April 1941, a mere four days after German-Italian invasion of Yugoslavia. Since the formation of Yugoslavia following the end of the First World War in 1918, Croatian antipathy to Serbian domination—based on cultural, religious, and political matters—saw the emergence of the Croatian nationalist movement *Ustasa*. Most Croats were devout Catholics, while the Serbs belonged to the Christian-Orthodox Church. Led by the Ustasa nationalist Ante Pavelic, the Independent State of Croatia was pro-Axis, supporting the German invasion of the USSR with ground and air forces. The Croatian Legion (*Hrvatska Legija*) was formed on 27 June 1941, with an air group, known as the *Hrvatska Zrakoplovna Legija* (HZL) formed on 12 July for the express purpose of fighting on the Eastern Front. The Croat air arm was named *Zrakoplovstvo Nezavisne Drzave Hrvatske* (Air Force of the Independent State of Croatia, ZNDH). A request for twenty-two former VVKJ Bf 109Es remained unfulfilled. However, a number of obsolete former VVKJ aircraft were handed over.

Subsequently, a number of Croatian pilots received flight training in Germany before being posted to the HZL. Initially, the HZL consisted of two air units (one fighter and one bomber), which were directly subordinated to the RLM. In the event, two fighter squadrons were formed—the 10. and 11. *Zrakoplovno Lovacko Jato* (ZLJ).

On 28 September, eleven HZL pilots left Fürth, flying ten Bf 109Es and one Bf 109F to the Eastern Front. One of the pilots was Lt Mato Dukovac, who was to become the highest-scoring Croatian pilot with forty-four confirmed victories and one unconfirmed victory to his credit. Two Bf 109s crashed during the ferry flight, with a third seriously damaged at Lvov. Upon arrival at Poltava in eastern Ukraine, the 10.ZLJ was redesignated as 15(*Kroat*)./JG 52 attached to III./JG 52. Maj. Franjo Dzal was commander of the 15(*Kroat*)./JG 52. The first combat operation was flown on 9 October, with a Kharkov R-10 claimed as shot down by Lt Ewald Baumgarten, the unit's liaison officer, although the victory was not confirmed. The unit then transferred to Taganrog, arriving on 12 November, before moving to Mariopol three weeks later, on 1 December. The first confirmed aerial victories occurred on 2 November, when two Polikarpov I-16s were downed near Rostov by Hptm Vladimir Ferencia and Lt Ewald Baumgarten. Five confirmed and six probable air-to-air victories were claimed during fifty combat sorties in 1941. The harsh conditions on the Eastern Front meant that unit strength by the end of the year had been reduced to seven Bf 109Es, only three of which were serviceable.

The first weeks of 1942 saw little aerial activity, mostly due to the prevailing cold weather. On 9 February, Maj. Culinovic claimed a pair of Polikarpov I-16s. The first confirmed victory occurred on 2 March, when Cvitan Galic shot down an R-10. Further victories were claimed, with the Croatian pilots holding their own against the (mainly) obsolete Soviet aircraft. On 24 April, a Bf 109E was destroyed at Mariupol in a Soviet air raid. Three days later, Hptm Berislav Supek landed his Bf 109E near Rostov behind Soviet lines. It was thought that Supek had become lost. However, after returning to Yugoslavia after the end of the war, he claimed to have defected. The first confirmed defection occurred on 4 May, with Oblt Nikola Vucina landing his Bf 109E on the Soviet side of the front line.

By now, the *Emils* were becoming increasingly difficult to maintain due to wear and tear, with three lost in accidents during May 1942. A small number of attrition-replacement Bf 109Es eventually reached 15.(*Kroatische*)/JG 52. Some of these had previously been operated by JG 27 in North Africa. However, unit strength was never more than eight serviceable Bf 109Es. Dissatisfaction with the Bf 109E, which was now obsolete, resulted in demands for more modern Bf 109s. On 1 July, the first Bf 109G-2 arrived, with fourteen in service by the end of the month. In all, the pilots of 15.(*Kroat*)/JG 52 had flown 1,115 sorties in Bf 109Es, scoring between sixty and sixty-six victories. Most of the Russian pilots were inexperienced, as recalled by Josip Helebrandt:

> Russian fighters were no match for us. The hardest thing was to find an enemy aircraft to shoot down, and we were not the only ones searching. Once you had found one, the only thing to do was to approach, aim, fire a short burst and break. It was the same whether it was an SB, a *Rata* or a MiG. Real dogfights, with twisting and turning where you could show what you really knew, were quite rare. It seemed as if the only thing these poor lads (had) learned was how to take off, fly straight and land. I felt real pity for them. But it was war, and war is always an unfair game.[2]

During the summer and autumn of 1942, the Croatian pilots continued to fly different kinds of sorties, e.g. *Freie Jägd*, bomber escort, airfield defence, ground attack and *Jabo* sorties. Eight new pilots, all of whom had previously served with the VVKJ, arrived in October 1942. On 15 November 1942, the Bf 109G-2s were transferred to II./JG 52, with the 15(*Kroat*)./JG 52 pilots and ground crew returning to Croatia for rest and recuperation. Since 9 October 1941, the unit had flown a total of 3,698 sorties, claiming 164 Soviet aircraft shot down and nearly fifty probables. Four pilots had been killed, with a further two missing. Five ground crew had also been killed.

The unit returned to the Eastern Front in mid-February 1943. However, out of the eleven pilots taking off in poor weather conditions from Krakow, Poland, only eight arrived at Lvov. Two pilots, Lt Zlatko Stipcic and Lt Nicola Vice, force-landed near Lvov, while Obfw Josip Stipic crashed fatally 40 km north of Lvov. On 31 March, the first sortie was flown from Kertch, in which Lt Andjelko Antic was shot down following a skirmish with eight LAGG-3s. Operations continued, with many *Freie Jägd* and escort sorties flown. However, on 14 May, two pilots defected, landing their Bf 109G-2s near Krasnodar. Little more than a month later, on 15 June, another pilot defected. The German High Command immediately grounded 15(*Kroat*)./JG 52, launching an investigation to determine the cause of the defections. The unit Commander, Oblt Franjo Dzal, was replaced by Oblt Pavao Sic. Two further members of 15(*Kroat*)./JG 52 defected to Turkey on 20 July, flying across the Black Sea in a Klemm Kl 35 liaison aircraft. This made the Germans even more sensitive about the loyalty (or lack thereof) of the Croatian pilots. Nevertheless, the unit remained at the front, eventually receiving an infusion of newly-trained pilots.

Operations resumed on 29 October. Two days later, on 1 November, no less than eleven Soviet aircraft were shot down. The following day, Franjo Dzal returned to command the HZL as *Geschwaderkommodore* upon the direct orders of Hermann Göring. However, losses continued to mount, and the decision was taken to remove 15(*Kroat*)./JG 52 from operations. On 15 March 1944, pilots and ground crew began to travel back to Croatia. Shortly after their return to Zagreb, 15(*Kroat*)./JG 52 was reformed as 1./JGr *Kroatien*. With a cadre of highly experienced pilots and a number of pilots fresh from flight training, it was decided to deploy 1./JGr *Kroatien* to the Eastern Front.

However, the HZL was disbanded on 21 July 1944. In its place, the Hvratska Zrakoplovna Izobrazbena Skupina (Croatian Air Force Training Group, HZIS) was formed. The pilots of 1./JGr *Kroatien* eventually arrived at Libau near the Baltic Sea. While here, Mato Dukovac and another pilot, Vladimir Spoljar, defected to the USSR on 20 September. The remaining pilots were grounded, and ordered to serve as infantry men. During three combat tours, the Croat pilots claimed 299 confirmed aerial victories with between forty-two and forty-six probables. More than 5,000 sorties were flown. Twenty-one pilots scored five or more victories.

By mid-1944, insurgent forces resisting the Ustasa nationalists and German occupation had been gathering strength since the summer of 1941. The ZNDH was heavily engaged in anti-partisan operations.

An order for thirty Bf 109s was placed, with the aircraft to be divided evenly between the Bf 109G-6, G-10, and G-14. On 24 November, an initial batch of Bf 109G-14AS's arrived. The Bf 109s were assigned to the 2 *Lovacko Jato* (fighter squadron) and the 14.LJ. On 1 January 1945, seventeen Bf 109s (twelve serviceable) were on ZHDH charge. Ten Bf 109K-4s were ordered, along with four Bf 109G-12 conversion trainers. It was hoped that sufficient numbers of Bf 109K-4s would make it possible to replace the older G-variants. However, several Bf 109s were

A Croatian Bf 109G-10 at Lucko in May 1945. (*Boris Ciglic*)

lost to RAF fighters and through defections; three Bf 109s were destroyed in a strafing attack at Lucko on 24 March by Mustangs of 213 and 249 Squadrons. On 16 April, two Bf 109Gs flown by Vladimir Sandter and Josip Cetkovic, arrived at RAF airfields in Italy. Four days later, another pair of Bf 109 pilots, Vinko Tatarevic and eleven-victory ace Josip Helebrandt defected to Communist forces at Mostar. Some success occurred on 23 April when Ljudevit Bencetic and Mihajlo Jelac shot down two 213 Squadron Mustangs near Zagreb, scoring the final victories of Croatian pilots during the war. However, Jelak's *Gustav* was hit, forcing the Croat pilot to make a crash landing.

In all, the pilots of 2.LJ had flown about 150 sorties and 450 training flights in Bf 109s. By early May, some of the remaining ZNDH personnel had surrendered to British or US forces, with others surrendering to Yugoslav Communist forces. Despite the war in Europe officially coming to an end on 8 May, pockets of Ustasa forces continued to fight until 28 May.

Finland

Finland had expressed an interest in acquiring Bf 109s as early as 1940 and 1941. However, it was not until December 1942 that an agreement was reached for the delivery of thirty Bf 109G-2s. On 1 February 1943, a contract for sixteen new and fourteen refurbished Bf 109G-2s was signed. It was said that all aircraft lost in combat would be replaced on a one-for-one basis. Ten days later, on 10 February,

Maj. Ernrooth of *Lentolaivue* (aircraft squadron, LeLv) 34, travelled with seventeen pilots to Germany for conversion training. The Bf 109s were picked up at Wiener Neustadt, with the first sixteen (serials MT-201 to MT-216) handed over on 9 March, arriving at Helsinki-Malmi airfield four days later. The Bf 109s were delivered to *Lentolaivue* 34, which had been formed on 23 January 1943. The first Bf 109 combat success occurred on 24 March 1943 when a Pe-2 was shot down near Tallinn by WO Ilmari Juutilainen. Continuous patrols over the Gulf of Finland were flown to stop Soviet attempts in breaking the naval blockade, resulting in a number of victories. The remaining fourteen Bf 109s (serials MT-217 to MT-230) were handed over at Erdingen on 10 May, arriving at Helsinki-Malmi two days later. One Bf 109, MT-226 (W Nr 13592), was damaged during the ferry flight, and replaced by W Nr 14827 on 21 February 1944. However, non-operational accidents meant that less than twenty Bf 109s were available at any one time. By early 1944, only thirteen Bf 109s were operational.

On 20 May, four Soviet fighters were shot down over Lavasaari, with one Bf 109 being downed by anti-aircraft artillery. Apart from Yak-1 and LaGG-3 fighters, Polikarpov I-153 biplane fighters were met on several occasions. Although slower than the Bf 109, the I-153 pilots were often able to avoid combat through the superior manoeuvrability of their aircraft. A 'P-38 Lightning' was claimed on 10 July, which was probably misidentified with a captured Fw 189. The only Lend-Lease combat aircraft used by the Soviet air arm in the area was the Douglas A-20 Havoc, with one shot down over Seiskari on 20 August. The 100th victory for Lentolaivue 34 occurred on 4 October when Plt Off. Yrjö Pallasvuo shot down a LaGG-3. Five Bf 109s had been lost, including four in aerial combat.

The first Finnish Bf 109G-2, serial MT-201. This particular aircraft served with LeLv 34, 24, and 28, and was flown by, among others, aces E. Luukkanen and Hasse Wind, A total of 32.5 victories were claimed in this Bf 109. It was consigned to storage on 12 December 1944 having accumulated 232 hours and twenty minutes in the air. (*Arlanda Civil Aviation Collection*)

An additional eighteen Bf 109G-2s were delivered between 9 August 1943 and 1 June 1944. A follow-on contract for thirty Bf 109G-6s was signed on 15 March 1944, with deliveries beginning the following day.

On 18 February 1944, HeLv 34 was officially renamed *Hävittäjälentolaivue* 34 (34 Fighter Squadron—HLeLv 34). In early March, No. 2 Flight was transferred to HLeLv 30, which was responsible for the air defence of the Finnish capital, Helsinki. With the arrival of the improved Bf 109G-6, HLeLv 34 began to transfer its Bf 109G-2s to HLeLv 24. By the end of April, HLeLv 24 had received fifteen Bf 109G-2s, with the units Brewster B-239s being transferred soon afterwards to LeLv 26.

On 9 June, Soviet artillery began to shell Finnish army positions along the Mannerheim Line on the Karelian Isthmus. Soviet forces had nearly 1,600 combat aircraft available, which flew 1,150 sorties despite poor weather which kept most Finnish aircraft grounded. The odds were overwhelming. Only three Finnish fighter squadrons were available, HLeLv 24 (fourteen Bf 109s) based Suulajärvi, HLeLv 34 (sixteen Bf 109s) based at Kymi and HLeLv 26 (sixteen Brewster B-239s).

The largest number of air sorties during the Soviet offensive occurred on 20. In all, thirty-one Soviet aircraft were shot down, with no Bf 109s being lost. Between 7.10 a.m. and 8 a.m., WO Juutilainen managed a score of four:

> Flying in formation, we met the Ruskies below us between Ristiniemi and Ruonti. We made a formation attack on the enemy, I managed to shoot at one Yak-9, and it went into the sea smoking. At this point, I saw ten or eleven DB-3F's coming from Ristiniemi in Virolahti, and there were Il-2s below and closer to Ristiniemi. In a steep dive I shot down the leading plane of a five plane formation. There was another formation behind it (five or six planes) and I shot into flames the right engine of one DB-3F on the right side. Someone came up from behind me, and put the other engine on fire. The plane went in 8 km south of Ristiniemi. After this I had to fight two Yak-9s. I shot one down, Another MT appeared and between us we tried for a long time to get the other Yak. We stopped that between Narvi and Seiskari and broke off, when we saw more planes coming in. Battle altitude 2,000–100 metres. My plane was MT-426.

During an afternoon sortie, Juutilainen downed a P-39 Airacobra. This huge loss of aircraft did not prevent the Soviets from capturing the city of Viipuri in the evening of 20 June.

The Soviet offensive lasted for thirty-eight days, during which the Bf 109 squadrons claimed no less than 425 aircraft, with a further seventy-eight damaged. The Soviet forces had suffered huge losses. Nevertheless, it was obvious that the Finns in the long run stood little chance against the numerical superiority of the Soviets. Peace negotiations had been going on for some time.

The final Bf 109G destined for *Ilmavoimat* arrived on 30 August 1944. In all, 159 Bf 109Gs were delivered (forty-eight Bf 109G-2s, 109 Bf 109G-6s and two Bf 109G-8s) with another three lost *en route* to Finland. The Bf 109G-6s were a mix of different sub-variants—fourteen G-6/R6s fitted with the two underwing 20-mm MG 151s, and fifty-seven G-6/U2s fitted with an enlarged wooden stabiliser, fin and rudder. Most of the Bf 109G-6s were fitted with the Erla *Haube*.

The final victory was on 3 September 1944 when WO Ilmari Juutilainen shot down a Lisunov Li-2. With ninety-four victories, of which fifty-eight were scored while flying Bf 109s, Juutilainen was the highest-scoring Finnish ace. A total of 663 victories were claimed, with HeLLv 34 and 24 scoring the lion's share with 345 and 300 victories respectively. LLv 30 and 28 scored three and fifteen victories. Fifty-six Bf 109s were lost to all causes, including twenty-seven in air combat, with twenty-two pilots killed and a further two taken PoW.

On 4 September 1944, Finland signed a truce with the USSR. One of the terms of the truce involved expelling all remaining German forces – consisting of more than 200,000 soldiers and some 200 aircraft - out of Finland by 15 September. This was compounded by the fact that the Russian-led Allied Control Commission grounded all Finnish military aircraft. In the event, the ban was lifted, with operations against German units in northern Finland beginning in earnest on 1 October. Only a single Bf 109 sortie was flown—on 26 October by Maj. Eino Luukanen of HeLv 34. With the front having moved beyond the nominal range of the Bf 109, the fighting was left to other units. By early 1945, 102 Bf 109s remained in service.

According to the 1947 Peace Treaty, only sixty fighters were allowed, which meant that a large number of Bf 109s were consigned to storage. Post-war, an additional forty-one Bf 109s were written off in accidents, with three pilots losing their lives.

By 1950, three squadrons were still operating Bf 109s. The total number of hours flown on Messerschmitts during this year was 1,885. This dropped to 1,100 hours in 1951.

A state funeral was organised following the death of Carl Gustav Mannerheim in Switzerland on 23 January 1951. On 2 February, Mannerheim's funeral procession in Helsinki included several flypasts by eight Bf 109s. In all, twelve Bf 109s were airborne, including reserves.

On 13 March 1954, Lt Col Erkki Heinilä performed the final flight of the Bf 109G in *Ilmavoimat* service, which brought to an end eleven years of service. This particular Bf 109, serial MT-507, has been preserved. The last Bf 109Gs were withdrawn from use on 23 November 1954. In Finnish service, the Bf 109Gs had accumulated some 23,000 flying hours; only three of the 162 delivered Bf 109Gs were lost during the delivery flights. The Bf 109G remained in Finnish service until late 1954. Two aircraft have been preserved.

Hungary

Although quasi-military aviation had existed since the 1920s, the MKHL was not openly acknowledged until September 1938. Interestingly, a number of Bf 109s had participated in an air show in Budapest in June 1937. The fighter element of the

MKHL was flying Fiat CR.32 biplanes, with an order for forty Bf 109s placed. However, due to concerns over a possible armed conflict with Romania over Transylvania, Germany declined the order. Instead, the MKHL turned to Italy, which sold Fiat CR 42s and Reggiane Re 2000s, with the latter eventually being built under licence in Hungary. An interesting comparison between the Italian fighters and the Bf 109 was later made by Lt Daniel Holeczy:

> At that time I considered myself an experienced pilot, with some 300 hours in the Fiat CR.32, Fiat CR 42 and the (Re 2000). The controls of the 109 were not as light as those of the Italian machines. An Italian fighter moved like a pencil—you had an immediate reaction. In the 109 you had to use some force—the reaction was there but it was heavy. The German aircraft were hard, heavy, coarse, more difficult to fly, but they were much faster. The 109 had a very narrow track and during take-off and landing you had to work hard to keep straight. Suddenly we jumped from around 800 to 1,200 hp—that was a lot of horsepower in those days.

Nevertheless, the MKHL retained an interest in the Bf 109, with negotiations for the production under licence of Bf 109Fs initiated in 1941. The company MAVAG was to build the fuselages; the intention was that half of the Hungarian-produced Bf 109s were to be supplied to the Luftwaffe. In the event, three Bf 109D-1s were delivered by rail on 19 September 1942 to allow MAVAG to acquaint themselves with German manufacturing techniques. The trio of Messerschmitts were in poor condition, and only two were restored to airworthiness. The first, serial V.601, was assigned to the MHKL for evaluation, with the second one, V.602, being used by the *Repülö Kisérleti Intérzet* (Flight Research Institute, RKI) for various tests—the prefix letter 'V' indicated *Vadász* (fighter). The third Bf 109D-1 was used as a ground instructional airframe. One Bf 109D, possibly one of those delivered in 1942, was captured by the Red Army near Sárvär, Hungary, in 1945.

A Bf 109E was supplied to MAVAG in 1943. It reportedly received the serial number V.604, although this cannot be confirmed. In the same year, the first of about forty *Emils* began to arrive in Hungary. These aircraft were not destined for the MHKL, remaining on Luftwaffe charge. The Bf 109Es were used as advanced trainers for both Luftwaffe and MHKL pilots by the *Ausbildungskommando Jägd* and the *Vadászkiképzö-százdad* (literally, 'fighter training squadron'), based at Börgönd. Other Hungarian-operated Bf 109Es were based at Szombathely and Tapolca. Additionally, *Emils* also saw service with the 101/6 Fighter Squadron, albeit only as trainers. Interestingly, two Bf 109Es starred in the 1944 movie '*Magyar Sasok*' ('Hungarian Eagles') and were painted in MHKL insignia.

The first Bf 109 variant to see combat with the MHKL was the Bf 109F. However, instead of being sold to Hungary, the fighters were transferred on loan from Luftwaffe stocks according to an agreement signed in October 1942. That month, eight pilots from 1/1. Fighter Squadron began conversion training at Stariy Oskol, USSR, with aircraft and instructors from JG 52. Two more Hungarian pilots arrived in November 1942. A dozen Luftwaffe Bf 109F-4s located at a *Luftflotte* 4 storage depot at Rostov were initially loaned, not fully handed over until 30 November. The MHKL pilots began flying combat sorties already on 15 November. The Hungarian unit was designated as 1. *Ungarische Jabostaffel* by the Luftwaffe. Although formally part of 1/1. Fighter Squadron, it was known as the *Bánlaky-csoport* (Banlaky-Grouping). Initially, ground-attack sorties dominated. On 16 December, a pair of Il-2 Shturmoviks were shot down in separate sorties. By the end of 1942, the Hungarian pilots flew some 140 sorties. On 31 December, eight Bf 109F-4/Bs were transferred from Luftwaffe stocks.

The first fatality occurred on 11 January when the six-victory ace *Hadnagy* (Lieutenant) Imre Pánczél crashed near Kadubez. The unit had to hurriedly abandon Stariy Oskol on 22 January due to a Soviet offensive. Five damaged or unserviceable Bf 109s, as well as two Ar 96s, had to be left behind.

In March 1943, 1/1. Squadron was based at Poltava in eastern Ukraine, later moving to Kharkov-Osnava. Initially, many ground-support sorties were flown, with the emphasis later changing to escort and interdiction sorties. Twenty-three Bf 109s, including a few *Gustavs*, arrived in May. During the preceding month, an Il-2 Shturmovik and an La-5 were claimed, but remained unconfirmed. The first confirmed victory of 1943 was a Douglas A-20 on 29 April. Soon afterwards, the 5/2. Fighter Squadron began to receive Bf 109s. According to Luftwaffe records, thirty-one Bf 109F-4s had been handed over to the Hungarians by the spring of 1943. Most of these F-4s had been modified from the earlier Bf 109F-2. In all, at least fifty, or as many as sixty-nine, Bf 109F-4s were used by MHKL squadrons. The MHKL serials V.01 to V.69 (later amended to V.001 to V.069) were assigned to the Bf 109Fs, although the highest confirmed serial was V.041. Surviving aircraft were returned to the Luftwaffe. It seems that the Bf 109F was planned for series production by MAVAG, but nothing came of this. Interestingly, Hungary also showed interest in the Me 209, although as this did not enter production none were delivered.

A number of Bf 109G-2s were delivered in 1943, equipping the 5/1 Fighter Group. Operating on the Eastern Front, the two squadrons of 5/1 Fighter Group accumulated sixty-seven air-to-air victories by October 1943, after which the pilots and ground crews were rotated back to Hungary for rest and recuperation. Simultaneously, the Bf 109G-2 entered production at the MAVAG works at Györ. After only a few Bf 109G-2s had been built, production switched to the improved Bf 109G-4. Initially, much equipment had to be supplied from Germany, including DB 605 engines, VDM propellers, flight instruments (including radios), and the armament. However, by the end of 1943, the only parts imported from Germany were the cockpit canopies and the flight instruments. In all, eighty aircraft were produced in 1943.

The upgraded Bf 109G-10, and later the G-14, was introduced in 1944, with considerable numbers being built by MAVAG. By 13 April 1944, no less than 367 Bf 109s had been delivered. The MKHL would eventually become the second biggest operator of the Bf 109. On this day, the MAVAG factory at Györ was severely damaged in a USAAF bomb raid. Dispersal of Bf 109 production began immediately and was spread to thirty-four different locations, with final assembly taking place at Györ. However, when USAAF raided the MAVAG factory in

July 1944, machinery and jigs were moved to an underground rock quarry near Budapest. Production quickly restarted, with an average of one Bf 109G completed each day. When Russian forces arrived in late 1944, about 800 Bf 109s had been built by MAVAG.

By early 1944, three MKHL squadrons, the 1/1, 2/1, and 5/3 *Vadászszázad* (fighter squadron) began to receive MAVAG-built Bf 109Gs. The country was now within reach of Italian-based USAAF bombers, with the first raid occurring on 17 March. The RAF had, incidentally, made their presence known over Hungary since mid-1942. Additionally, Soviet long-range bombers had targeted Budapest on 4 and 9 September 1942, which had come as a particular shock to the Hungarian population.

Two Bf 109Gs were lost during the 17 March raid, with no USAAF aircraft losses. The USAAF and subsequent RAF raids influenced the German decision to occupy Hungary on 19 March. Budapest was hit on 3 April, with USAAF fighters shooting down two Bf 109Gs. During two raids on 12 and 13 April, MKHL air defences brought down fifteen USAAF aircraft, including seven B-24 Liberators and eight escort fighters. During the month of April, two Bf 109 squadrons, 1/1 and the recently-formed 2/1, flew 114 intercept sorties. Six USAAF aircraft were shot down, with six Bf 109 pilots being killed.

On 1 May, a reorganisation saw 1/1, 2/1, and 5/3 Squadrons renumbered 101/1, 101/2, and 101/3 Squadrons, all becoming part of the 101 (Puma) *Vadaszosztály* (Fighter Group), based at Veszprém and commanded by *Örnagy* (*Major*) Aladár Heppes. A brief lull in the raids meant that the Puma Fighter Group had time to rest and also further train air combat tactics. This was especially important to the 101/2 and 101/3 Fighter Squadrons as their pilots were relatively inexperienced. However, it proved to be the calm before the storm, with 101/1 Squadron first seeing action on 24 May and claiming one B-17 Fortress, three B-24s, and one P-51 Mustang. However, one Hungarian pilot was killed, with eight out of 13 Bf 109Gs suffering damage. A USAAF 15 AF shuttle bomb raid on 2 June involving 600 bombers saw military and railway installations around Hungary severely damaged. On 21 June, a force of some 950 USAAF bombers and escort fighters was intercepted by twenty-eight MKHL Bf 109Gs, which, along with several Luftwaffe fighters brought down five P-38 Lightnings and a P-47 Thunderbolt. MKHL losses were far greater, with thirteen Bf 109s and five pilots killed. On 2 July, the USAAF lost approximately fifty aircraft to combined MHKL and Luftwaffe interceptors and anti-aircraft artillery. However, out of the eighteen Bf 109Gs of the 101/1 Squadron committed to battle, three were lost, along with their pilots.

Further USAAF raids against Hungarian targets continued throughout the summer, with 101/1 Squadron achieving 100 air-to-air victories by 22 August. Apart from losses of pilots and aircraft in combat, several Bf 109Gs were also lost to strafing USAAF fighters.

In September 1944, it was decided to add a further three Bf 109G squadrons to the 101 Fighter Group, which was thus redesignated as a Fighter Regiment. The three additional squadrons, Nos. 101/4, 101/5, and 101/6 (training only), formed the 101/II Fighter Group, which was based at Kenyeri. Operations officially began on 19 September. The following month, the MHKL Bf 109 squadrons were placed under the command of Luftwaffe's 8. *Jägddivision*. This was made to utilise the meagre fighter resources for joint MKHL and Luftwaffe operations.

With Soviet forces approaching Hungary, it was decided to cease operations against USAAF and RAF aircraft from 7 November and to instead concentrate on fighting against Soviet air and land forces. With Budapest the target of Soviet forces, many sorties were flown in support of the Hungarian troops within and around the city. From 6 January 1945, all MKHL fighter squadrons were controlled by a Luftwaffe unit *Stab* JG 76, through which all fighter operations over Hungary were organised. An additional two Bf 109G squadrons, Nos. 102/1 and 102/2, were formed as part of the 102 Fighter Group, but the loss of experienced pilots and aircraft continued to mount. In January 1945, thirty-three German-built Bf 109G-10s were received as attrition replacements. However, on 16 April, Hungary was wholly occupied by Soviet forces. The remaining MKHL units withdrew to Austria in late March, with the 101 Fighter Group moved to Tulln and, finally, to Grosspetersdorf. The final sortie was flown on 17 April, resulting in one Yak-9 shot down, albeit for the loss of three Bf 109s.

During 1944 and 1945, the 101 Fighter Group had shot down 322 Allied aircraft (including seventy-two four-engine bombers and 144 Soviet aircraft), while losing forty-six pilots in action. The 102 Fighter Group had accounted for eighty-five Soviet aircraft destroyed. Nine 102 Fighter Group pilots had been killed on operations.

MKHL Messerschmitt Bf 109s			
Variant	**Quantity**	**MKHL serial**	**Remarks**
Bf 109D-1	3	V.601, V.602	The third aircraft did not receive a serial
Bf 109E	Approximately 40	–	Used for training. Retained Luftwaffe insignia
Bf 109F-4	41–69	V.001-V.069	On loan from Luftwaffe
Bf 109G-2/G-4	84	V.310-V.394	German-built
Bf 109G-2/G-4/G-6	150	V.751-V.899	MAVAG-built
Bf 109G-10/G-14	205	W.001-W.225	MAVAG-built
Bf 109G-10/G-14	33	–	Retained Luftwaffe insignia

Italy

The first close encounter with the Bf 109 occurred at the 1937 Zurich Air Meeting. Ernst Udet secretly arranged for an Italian pilot to fly a Bf 109. The pilot, Major Aldo Remondino, later recalled: 'The flight lasted one hour, and I could form a clear opinion of the features of the monoplane. It was undoubtedly more advanced as far as speed and climb were concerned than our Fiat CR.32, but had remarkably inferior manoeuvrability.'

At the time, the standard *Regia Aeronautica* (Royal Air Force, RA) fighter was the Fiat CR.32 biplane. Italian pilots were also able to observe first-hand the exploits of the Bf 109 during the Spanish Civil War. Nevertheless, many Italian fighter pilots preferred the open-cockpit biplane over the technically more advanced and higher performance monoplane—manoeuvrability was seen as the primary requirement of any fighter aircraft. Interestingly, the Fiat G.50 and Macchi C.200 monoplane fighters both had open cockpits.

In August 1939, four Bf 109Es lent by the Luftwaffe were evaluated at Guidonia. The DB 601 engine in particular aroused much interest, with the Alfa Romeo Company subsequently negotiating for the licence manufacture of the DB 601. In March 1940, Alfa Romeo even put forward a suggestion to build the Bf 109 under licence at Pomigliano d'Arco near Naples. Instead, the Fiat G.50 entered large-scale production, and following the outbreak of war, all of the Bf 109s were returned to Germany.

The next opportunity to sample the Bf 109 arrived during the autumn of 1940 when, during the latter stages of the Battle of Britain, an Italian expeditionary force consisting of Fiat BR.20 bombers, Fiat CR.42 and Fiat G.50 fighters deployed to Belgium. The difference in performance characteristics between the Luftwaffe and Italian fighters resulted in difficulties in joint operations. In the event, the two Fiat G.50 squadrons of 20 *Gruppo* received one Bf 109 each for conversion training. However, when the Italian contingent left Belgium in April 1941, conversion training had not been completed.

Italian forces actively supported the German invasion of Yugoslavia in April 1941. A large number of former VVKJ aircraft were captured, with some being evaluated. One former Yugoslav Bf 109E-3 was rebuilt at Tirana by 150 *Gruppo* personnel. The Bf 109 was s/n 2502 (code L-2), which had previously been operated by the Independent Fighter Flight at Mostar. Parts from another VVKJ Bf 109, code L-13, were also used in the rebuild. However, although painted in RA insignia, the Bf 109E most likely never flew in Italy.

It was not until 1943 that Bf 109s entered service with the RA. On 27 February 1943, the RA requested the supply of 300 fighters and 200 bombers, and within little more than two months, on 5 May the RA requirement had been amended to include 300 Bf 109s as well as a large number of other combat aircraft. By then, the first batch of Bf 109s had already entered service, having been delivered on 19 April. Prior to the armistice in September 1943, the RA received at least 122 Bf 109s (including fifteen Bf 109F-4s, six Bf 109G-2s, ten Bf 109G-4s, and ninety-one Bf 109G-6s). Two Bf 109s were received by 4 *Stormo* on 18 May 1943. Based at Ciampino near Rome, conversion training was initiated at Vicenza, but soon afterwards, on 20 June, orders were received to hand over the Bf 109s to the 23 *Gruppo*, 3 *Stormo*.

Initially, few flights were made in the Bf 109s, with the unit's Macchi C.202s retained in the meantime. One Italian pilot, Giulio Reiner, later recalled that, 'compared to Italian fighters, [the Bf 109s] appeared finished and built with far less attention to detail, but nonetheless they looked solid, effective and easily maintained, in other words perfect for war...'

The 3rd and 150th *Gruppi Autonomi* became the major RA Bf 109 operators. Based at Comiso in Sicily, 150 *Gruppo* performed its first sortie on 25 April, although conversion training proceeded with some difficulty due to a certain lack of co-operation from the Luftwaffe, as well as a lack of spares. The first combat sortie took place over a month later on 28 May.

On 9 June, Lt Drago of 150 *Gruppo* shot down a USAAF Spitfire flown by 1Lt McMann of the 31 FG/308 FS. Later the same day, a large number of USAAF fighters, searching for McMann intercepted a number of Italian fighters, downing two Macchi C.202s and one Bf 109—the latter flown by Lt Drago, who managed to reach the island of Pantelleria before eventually returning to Sicily on the last evacuation flight. By 13 June, the two *Gruppi Autonomi* had flown 323 sorties, claiming twenty-three Allied aircraft shot down. Thirteen Bf 109s had been lost. Further clashes with Allied fighters and bombers ensued, but results were limited due to the overwhelming Allied aerial superiority. On 9 July, the 3rd and 150th *Gruppi Autonomi* had twenty-one Bf 109s each, albeit only six of the latter unit's aircraft were operational. On this day, 150 *Gruppo* flew its last sortie—3 *Gruppo* having flown its final sortie three days earlier on 6 July.

With the invasion of Sicily, pilots and ground crews were evacuated to the mainland. No less than forty-five Bf 109s were found at Comiso by the RAF.

It would appear that Bf 109s were also operated by 22 *Gruppo*, with one aircraft lost near Salerno on 23 July. Additionally, twelve Bf 109s were transferred

BF 109s of 150 *Gruppo*. (*Gregory Alegi*)

A 363 *Squadriglia* Bf 109F. (*Gregory Alegi*)

to 70 *Squadriglia* in July. Based at Cerveti, the unit participated in the defence of Rome. However, only a single Bf 109 remained operational by early September.

On 8 September 1943, Italy surrendered. Many Italian airmen chose to fight on the Allied side in the Co-belligerent Air Force, while others eventually joined the *Aeronautica Nazionale Repubblicana* (ANR), fighting for the Fascist puppet-state *Rebubblica Sociale Italiana*.

ANR Use

Following the armistice, German forces occupied central and northern Italy. A Fascist-led republic, the *Repubblica Sociale Italiana* (RSI), was subsequently established.

An air arm, the *Aeronautica Nazionale Repubblicana* (ANR) was formed. Beginning in mid-1944, about 200 Bf 109s (G-6, G-10, G-12, G-14, G-14AS, and K-4 variants) were delivered to the ANR. Two *Gruppo Caccia* (literally, 'fighter group'), each consisting of the *Squadriglie*, were equipped with Bf 109s, with a third *Gruppo* not becoming operational. On 29 May 1944, the II° *Gruppo Caccia*, based at Cascina Vaga, began to receive Bf 109G-6s transferred from I./JG 4. Conversion training included gunnery practice, as well as tactical formation flying (such as the *Rotte* and *Schwarm* formations employed by the Luftwaffe). To ease conversion training, a pair of Bf 109G-12s arrived at Cascina Vaga.

The ANR units were wholly integrated into the Luftwaffe air defence system. Operations began on 22 June, with the II° *Gruppo Caccia* intercepting Allied bombing raids against northern Italian cities. During take-off on 24 June, the Bf 109G flown by *Sottotenente* Gino Gamberini veered off the runway and overturned, catching fire and killing Gamberini during recovery; the accident was due to sabotage. The remaining ten Bf 109s intercepted a group of P-47s of the French GC II/5 *Lafayette*, with two Thunderbolts claimed shot down—although in reality no Thunderbolts were lost. The following day, another II° *Gruppo* pilot, *Sottotenente* Luziani, was killed in an accident.

The first success occurred on 29 June, when Capt. Bellagambi damaged a Martin 187 Baltimore of 21 Squadron (SAAF). The 3 *Squadriglia* had begun to receive Bf 109s in mid-June. On 2 July, II° *Gruppo Caccia* had twenty-six Bf 109s, sixteen of which were operational. The month of July saw intense operations, with Allied efforts to destroy all bridges over the river Po. By 31 July, II° *Gruppo Caccia* had lost twelve pilots killed (including two lost in take-off accidents), with another two pilots baling out, resulting in II° *Gruppo* being temporarily withdrawn from combat. The I° *Gruppo di Caccia* was still flying Fiat G.55 and Macchi C.205 fighters, although it was intended that Bf 109s would replace the Italian-built fighters.

In the event, no Messerschmitts arrived. On 25 August, German units initiated a blockade of fuel supplies to the ANR units, seizing control of ANR Bf 109s. Firmly opposed by the ANR crews, the blockade caused severe disruption to air operations and increased mistrust of the Germans. It must be said that relations between the ANR and Luftwaffe had been marked by a severe lack of co-operation and co-ordination of operational activities. However, in late September, the

An ANR Bf 109G undergoing engine and undercarriage checks. (*Gregory Alegi*)

decision was rescinded, with II° *Gruppo Caccia* resuming operations a couple of weeks later. The month-long blockade had caused irreversible damage, with both sides treating the other with a certain degree of suspicion. On 11 October, six ANR Bf 109s were greeted with a hail of flak prior to landing at Villafranca. None of the Bf 109s were hit, but this incident only worked to fuel Italian lack of faith in their German allies. On 19 October, three B-26 Marauders were shot down, for the loss of one Bf 109. In the eyes of the Germans, the ANR fighter pilots had redeemed themselves. When II./JG 77 was transferred from Italy, a few Bf 109Gs were handed over to II° *Gruppo Caccia*, with the first Bf 109G-14s arriving the following month. On 2 November, the ANR had forty-two (twenty-six serviceable) Bf 109s. The personnel of II° *Gruppo Caccia* moved frequently between Aviano, Lonate, Orio al Serio, and Osoppo to reduce losses to Allied strafing raids.

In late 1944, the personnel of I° *Gruppo Caccia* left for Germany for training on the Messerschmitt Me 163 rocket fighter. Initially the pilots flew gliders at Rangsdorf, later moving to Holzkirchen for additional training. In the end, the ANR did not receive any Me 163s. Instead, I° *Gruppo Caccia* returned to Italy to fly Bf 109Gs.

In Italy, the II° *Gruppo Caccia* continued to intercept Allied formations. However, Allied air superiority and poorly trained and inexperienced ANR pilots, meant few successes. A MAAF briefing stated that the ANR:

> … again proved to be a poor investment for its German backers, paying little or no dividend for the effort—the Me-109s and the even more precious fuel expended. On only one day, 10 December, did the Italian pilots engage our

An ANR I° *Gruppo Caccia* Bf 109G. The mechanic is still standing on the right wing having hand-cranked the engine, still holding the handle in his hands. (*Gregory Alegi*)

> aircraft, and their results must have been disappointing. One B-25 was shot down for the loss of four Me-109s destroyed, one probably destroyed and four damaged. Fascist propaganda gave credit to the fighters for two additional B-25s (actually lost to flak) plus one fictional victory.[3]

In the last days of 1944, a batch of Bf 109G-10/ASs began to arrive. On 12 January, the personnel of III° *Gruppo Caccia* left for Holzkirchen for conversion training, joining the personnel of I° *Gruppo Caccia*. Due to poor weather, some of the training had to be transferred to Fürth. On 7 February, fifty-seven pilots of I° *Gruppo Caccia* had completed flight training. The unit had a strength of twenty-two Bf 109s, including two Bf 109G-12s. By the end of February, I° *Gruppo Caccia* had arrived in Italy, and was declared operational. On 1 March, the ANR had sixty-five Bf 109Gs and K-4s available. Simultaneously, eighty pilots of III° *Gruppo Caccia* were still undergoing training at Holzkichen and Fürth.

However, lack of fuel and an increased level of partisan activity reduced the effectiveness of the ANR fighters. On 24 April, the pilots of II° *Gruppo Caccia* were ordered to fly to Orio del Sero, where the Bf 109s would be handed over to the Luftwaffe. In two days, twenty-six ANR Bf 109s reached Orio del Sero. One ANR pilot later reminisced:

> [Following landing] I taxied up to a corner of the airfield following the signals of an old German officer, completely drunk, who kept saying '*Deutschland kaputt*' and ordered me to take my parachute away from the plane, then bathed it with petrol and set it afire, repeating his refrain and weeping...[4]

In the summer of 1945, eleven Bf 109G-10s and G-14s in varying conditions were offered to the post-war Italian Air Force by the aircraft manufacturer Agusta. The aircraft were located at Casorate and at various airfields. The offer was rejected in November 1945. In their place, the Italian Air Force soon received large numbers of Supermarine Spitfires, P-47 Thunderbolts, and P-51 Mustangs.

Japan

The RLM had given the approval of the export of the Bf 109, to be powered by the DB 600 G, to Japan on 10 August 1938. A month earlier, the aircraft manufacturer Kawasaki had forwarded a request, on behalf of the Imperial Japanese Army Air Force (IJAAF), for Bf 109s. The possibility of producing the Bf 109 under licence in Japan was also discussed, for which the Japanese would pay a fee of 700,000 *Reichmarks*. However, it was not until 7 June 1939 that a formal contract for ten Bf 109E's was signed. With the outbreak of war, delivery of aircraft, engines and other materials from Germany to Japan proved a major headache due to the omnipresence of the Royal Navy. At this juncture, the representative of the company Fokkes and Koch, located at Mukden in Japanese-controlled Manchuria, contacted the Commander of the Manchurian Air Force, Major Maruyakama, regarding the Messerschmitt fighters—Messerschmitts were nothing new in Manchuria, with a number of Bf 108 Taifuns operated by the state airline. Apparently, Major Maruyakama was most anxious to receive the Bf 109's following the end of their evaluation by the IJAAF, although nothing came of this. The contract was eventually reduced to a mere two aircraft.

Two WNF-built Bf 109E-7s (W Nr 6524 and 6525) arrived in Japan on 28 April 1941 via the Spanish port of Bilbao. A small technical team, including test pilot Willi Stör, arrived a couple of days later, having travelled east on the Trans-Siberian Railway. The Bf 109s were brought to Kagamigahara, where Kawasaki was to be responsible for assembly and test flying before formal transfer to the IJAAF. As it turned out, the DB 601 A engines had suffered from the sea journey. They were transferred to the Kawasaki engine works at Kobe for reconditioning, delaying the first Bf 109 flight in Japan until 14 July (W Nr 6524), with the second one taking to the air on 23 July. It would appear that engine problems plagued the test flights of the second Bf 109. Both Bf 109s were transferred to Tachikawa on 1 August, where formal IJAAF commenced.

Ultimately, the Bf 109 was not considered for front-line service by the IJAAF, although the codename 'Mike' was nevertheless assigned to it by the Allies. During the early stages of the war, numerous Allied pilots reported to have met and fought against Japanese-operated Bf 109s. One example of this occurred on 25 December 1941, when an American Volunteer Group (AVG) claimed to have encountered a Bf 109 during a dogfight over Burma. Japan also evinced interest in the Bf 109F and Bf 109G. On 18 September 1943, two Bf 109F-4s were set aside for export to Japan. Although unlikely, one of these could possibly have reached Japan in 1942 or 1943 courtesy of the submarine *U-234*. Incidentally, in 1944, US forces found a Bf 109F-4 at Bordeaux, which, apparently, was one of the aircraft originally destined for Japan.

Although no Bf 109s entered operational service with the IJAAF, or even licensed production begin, Kawasaki did however proceed with the manufacture of DB 601 A engines, for which the licence rights had been acquired in April 1940. A few DB 601 As were imported and used to power the Kawasaki Ki-60 heavy interceptor, which was not selected for production. The Kawasaki-built DB 601 A were designated Ha-40 (later redesignated as the Ha-60 in a common Imperial Army-Navy system) and fitted to the Ki-61 fighter. When Allied fighter pilots first encountered Ki-61s in 1943, this new fighter appeared so un-Japanese with its inline engine that it was initially believed to be of German or Italian design. As a result, the Ki-61 was assigned the codename 'Tony'.

Romania

The Romanian air arm, the *Aeronautica Regală Română* (Royal Romanian Aeronautics, ARR) was a major operator of the Bf 109. By 1939, an attempt had already been made and failed to secure a licence for the Bf 109E, although Germany promised to deliver a number of fighters. Beginning in 1940, the first of sixty-nine Bf 109E-3/E-4/E-7s arrived—in this year, eleven factory-fresh Bf 109E-3s were delivered, with thirty-nine refurbished Bf 109E-3s following in 1941.

The Bf 109s were assigned to *Grupul 7 vânătore* (7 Fighter Group), which consisted of three squadrons: Nos. 56, 57, and 58. The delivery of Bf 109s was a necessity for Germany in order to secure the supply of oil from Romania. A staunch ally of Germany, Romanian forces took part in Operation Barbarossa, the invasion of the USSR. The initial goal was to capture the provinces of Bessarabia and Trans-Dnestra, which contained a large percentage of ethnic Romanians. On 8 July 1941, fifty Bf 109Es were in service.

The Bf 109s were primarily used as fighter-bombers, although clashes with Soviet aircraft did occur. One such incident took place on 21 August, when a dozen Bf 109s engaged a large formation of Il-2 Shturmoviks with a strong fighter escort. One Polikarpov I-16 was shot down for the loss of two Bf 109s, including the one flown by the 7 FG's commanding officer, Major Popisteanu. By early August 1941, German and Romanian forces had reached Odessa, with the Soviet garrison finally surrendering on 16 October.

Between 22 June and 16 October 1941, ARR fighter pilots had flown 4,739 sorties, claiming 322 Soviet aircraft shot down and another seventy-one destroyed on the ground. ARR losses by the end of the year included some forty pilots killed and fifty-nine fighters lost to all causes, including nine Bf 109s. One Bf 109 pilot, Nicolae Polizu, had scored eight aerial victories.

Following the capture of Odessa, ARR aerial activity was considerably reduced, with only 1,021 sorties flown between 17 October 1941 and 1 August 1942. Few Soviet aircraft were met in the air, with only seven aerial victories claimed. During this period, fifteen former Luftwaffe Bf 109E-7s were received. On 31 August 1942, fifty-three Bf 109Es were operational.

By the late summer of 1942, German forces were closing in on Stalingrad. For the final push towards Stalingrad, Romania contributed the Third and Fourth Armies and about 100 aircraft, with the latter organised within the *Comandamontul Aviatei de Luptă* (Combat Air Command, CAL)—7 FG was among the CAL units. By early September, 7 FG was based at Tuzow flying escort, airfield protection, and *Freie Jägd* (free hunt) sorties. Soviet aircraft continuously attacked Tuzow, which only added to the operational difficulties. A week later, 7 FG was transferred to Karpovka. In early October, the CAL was renamed *Gruparea Aeriană de Luptă* (Combat Air Group, CAG). On 19 November, the Soviet counter-offensive began, with Karpovka airfield retaken only a few days later. A dozen Bf 109s had to be abandoned during the retreat. In early January 1943, 7 FG was merged with the 5 Bomb Group. Named *Grupul mixt Locotenent comandor Iosefscu*, the unit had ten Bf 109Es and six He 111s. By then, all other CAG units had been withdrawn from the Stalingrad area. The reason why the Bf 109s and He 111s were retained was simply due to the fact that the Luftwaffe was able to support these aircraft with spares and maintenance. However, by late February 1943, the *Grupul mixt Locotenent comandor Iosefescu* was returning to Romania. On 1 February 1944, only twenty-six Bf 109Es remained in service. Nine Bf 109Es had been lost between June and December 1941, twenty in 1942, and one in the first six months of 1943.

More modern Bf 109Gs were due to be delivered to ARR, with conversion training beginning at Tiraspol on 8 April 1943 using two Bf 109F-4s and four Bf 109G-2s. In all, some forty Bf 109GG-2s and G-4s were handed over to the ARR. Although the aircraft remained Luftwaffe property, they were finished in ARR colours. Furthermore, a number of ARR pilots were attached to JG 3 for operational training, including Luftwaffe tactics, with a combined ARR-Luftwaffe unit created, the *Deutsch-Königlich Rumänischen Jägdverband* (German-Royal Romanian Fighter Unit). Led by Lt Eberhard von Borewski, the unit flew its first sortie on 29 March. By early June, the unit was dissolved. The Romanian pilots had flown a total of 583 sorties, scoring twenty-eight victories for the loss of three pilots killed.

By June 1943, 7 FG was based at Mariupol in Crimea. Although several Soviet aircraft were claimed shot down, the unit faced increasingly heavy opposition, both from V-VS fighter units and flak. In October 1943, 7 FG returned to Romania to be replaced by 9 FG.

The Romanian oil fields at Ploesti provided a large share of the oil required by the German armed forces. Already in 1942, USAAF bombers had struck Ploesti with little success. A large-scale USAAF raid on 1 August 1943, code-named Operation Tidal Wave, met with fierce resistance from ARR fighters and flak. An ARR unit, the *Escadrila 53 vânătoare*, attached to I./JG 4, was dedicated to protecting the Ploesti oil fields. ARR fighters claimed ten B-24 Liberators shot down.

With the Soviet offensive continuing westwards, Crimea was evacuated in April 1944, with 9 FG arriving back at Tiraspol on 6 April. With USAAF bombers initiating a campaign against Bucharest and other Romanian cities, strengthening the air defences of Romania became a matter of urgency. Although outnumbered by USAAF fighters and bombers, there were some notable successes. On 10 June 1944, nearly 100 P-38 Lightnings of 12 AF arrived over Romania. ARR fighters and flak, in conjunction with Bf 109s of I./JG 53 and III./JG 77, brought down twenty-three of the Lightnings. However, the omnipresence of the USAAF and Soviet forces approaching Romania resulted in the ARR losing many experienced pilots in combat. During one shuttle mission between Italy and the USSR, seventeen Bf 109s of 9 FG intercepted the USAAF formation with disastrous results, losing seven of their number.

The final sortie against USAAF aircraft took place on 18 August, with twenty-seven ARR Bf 109s clashing with USAAF P-51 Mustangs. Not a single Mustang was downed by ARR pilots, with four Bf 109s being lost, along with at least three Luftwaffe fighters. One of the Romanian pilots shot down was Alexandru Serbãnescu, a fifty-five-victory ace. At the time, the ARR fighter strength consisted of Bf 109Gs and IAR 80/81s, with a few Bf 109Es based at the coastal town of Mamaia with 2 FS.

On 19 August, the ARR received orders to cease attacking USAAF aircraft. The following day, a large Soviet offensive against north-eastern Romania was launched. As a result, a *coup d'état*, supported by the Romanian King and government, took place on 23 August, resulting in Romania changing sides in the war. Initially, confusion reigned between the former allies. Nevertheless, some 200 Luftwaffe aircraft were seized, including a few Bf 109Fs and at least one Bf 109G-12 (the latter located at Arad). On 26 August, two Luftwaffe Bf 109s were shot down, with one ARR Bf 109 brought down by ground fire.

The Soviets immediately began to pressure the ARR High Command into supporting its operations. Following a brief re-organisation, the ARR were able to commit the newly-formed *Corpul 1 Aerian Român* (1 Romanian Air Corps) to operations starting on 7 September. Four fighter squadrons, with a total of thirty-three Bf 109s were available. Several ARR aircraft were shot down by Soviet ground fire. Soviet mistrust in their new allies remained high throughout the remainder of the war, with ARR pilots prohibited from landing at any Soviet airfield under any circumstances.

On 15 September, a strafing attack by six ARR Bf 109s against Szamosfalva destroyed several Hungarian and Luftwaffe aircraft. An offensive against Hungary began in late October, officially ending on 19 December. December saw poor weather, which restricted operations, with 9 FG transferring to Miskolc on 20 December. By the end of the year, nine Bf 109s had been lost, including four shot down by enemy fighters, another two by flak, with others written off in accidents. In all, 551 sorties had been flown.

At the time, 9 FG was the only ARR Bf 109 unit. Soon afterwards, the re-established 1 FG received a number of former Luftwaffe aircraft, as well as a few refurbished Bf 109G-2s and G-4s. However, less than a dozen Bf 109s could be mustered by 1 FG, with the unit flying its first combat sortie on 20 February.

The final ARR aerial victory of the war occurred on 25 February, when Adjutant Aviator Constantin Nicoarã shot down a Luftwaffe Bf 109K-4. Apart from a few aerial combats, most missions were ground support for Romanian and Soviet troops. On 26 March, two 1 FG pilots defected, landing at Trencin in western Slovakia. Their reasoning was that only Germany was able to stop the Communist onslaught against Romania. Both ARR Bf 109 units moved to Badin on 7 April, moving to Piestany later in the month. The last sortie took place on 11 May, with four ARR pilots attacking General Vlassov's troops near Prague.

On 1 June 1945, a few ARR Bf 109 pilots participated in a huge airshow held at Wiener-Neustadt. Among the aircraft was the first IAR-built Bf 109Ga-6, serial 316. Upon returning to Romania a few days later, the Bf 109s were bounced by USAAF P-51 Mustangs, with the USAAF pilots merely waggling their wings in salute to the AAR pilots. Moments later, Soviet Yak fighters bounced the ARR Bf 109s. Both sides appeared to have been trigger happy, as one Bf 109 and one Yak were reported to have been shot down.

In 1946, the few remaining Bf 109Es were withdrawn from use. However, the Bf 109G continued in use until the early 1950s, when they were largely supplanted and eventually replaced by Soviet-designed aircraft.

Romanian Licence Production

Beginning in 1944, Messerschmitt supplied major assemblies for forty-eight Bf 109G-2s to be assembled by IAR. These aircraft were used as advanced trainers. Initial plans called for the assembly of seventy-five Bf 109Gs from components supplied by Messerschmitt. Total production was to include 465 fuselages and

530 DB 605 engines. Similar to Bf 109 production in Germany, IAR-Brasov planned to disperse production, with engine manufacture to be handled by facilities at Ucea, Cugir, Satul Lung, and Colibasi; fuselages at Caranbeses, Barlova, and Herculane; propellers to be built at Campulung; and final assembly at Caransebes. Two other aircraft manufacturers, SET and ICAR, would also become involved in Bf 109 manufacture at Copsa-Mica-Cugir and Blaj. Apparently, tools and heavy machinery were ordered from Sweden, but did not arrive in time.

On 26 November 1942, fifteen Bf 109Ga-4s were ordered from IAR for delivery from May–August 1944. A heavy USAAF bomb raid meant that only six (serial numbers 301, 304, 305, 307, 311, and 312) had been delivered by August 1944. A second order for sixty Bf 109G-6as was placed on 11 August 1943, with deliveries to take place from November 1944 to May 1945 (serial numbers 302, 303, 306, 308–310, 313–315, 318, and 319) and June 1945 to November 1947 (serials 316, 317, and 320 to 375).

An additional order for 175 Bf 109Gs was placed on 24 September 1943. In the event, none had been delivered by war's end, with the order eventually being cancelled. In all, IAR built a total of seventy-five Bf 109Ga4/Ga-6, serials 301–375, with the first aircraft reaching operational squadrons in April 1945. Production ended post-war. The Romanian-built Bf 109Gs differed externally by having an elongated *Beule* on the upper front fuselage.

Slovakia

Following the German occupation of Czechoslovakia, Slovakia declared its independence on 14 March 1939. Led by Jozef Tiso, Slovakia inherited a mixed bunch of aircraft, and an independent air arm, the *Slovenské Vzdusné Zbrane* (SVZ), was formed in late 1939.

A territorial dispute with Hungary led to brief conflict between March and April. When Germany invaded Poland on 1 September, Slovak forces took part. Following the German invasion of USSR on 22 June 1941, a Slovak expeditionary force was formed. Operating a mix of Avia B-534 fighters and two-seat Letov S-328s, the Slovak units were withdrawn in late 1941—although they would however return to the Eastern front the following year. On 25 February 1942, eighteen pilots and eighty-eight mechanics were sent to Karup-Grove in Denmark to initiate training on the Bf 109E, commanded by Captain Ondrej Dumbala. After returning to Slovakia on 6 July, the majority of the Slovak airmen were transferred to the 13th Fighter Flight based at Maikop until early 1943, when the unit began a nomadic existence on the Eastern Front.

By end of 1942, twenty-seven Bf 109Es had arrived. The 13th Fighter Flight was organised as part of JG 52 and designated 13 (*Slowakei*) *Staffel*—13.(Slow)/JG 52. On 28 November 1942, 1Lt Vladimir Krisko and Sgt Jozef Jancovic claimed three Polikarpov I-16s shot down. However, it was obvious that the *Emils* could not match the more modern Russian fighters.

On 5 January 1943, a batch of Bf 109F-3s arrived, followed on 1 March by Bf 109G-2s and, shortly afterwards, Bf 109G-4s. These fighters were not formally transferred to the SVZ but on loan. As such, they retained the Luftwaffe insignia with the propeller spinners painted in Slovak colours.

On 11 September 1943, the Commander of 13th Flight requested the unit be withdrawn from operations 'because of deteriorated morale'; in late October 1943, 13.(Slow)/JG 52 was removed from operations and returned to Slovakia. During one year of heavy fighting, 210 Soviet aircraft were claimed shot down, with the most successful Slovak pilot being Major Ján Reznák and his thirty-two victories. However, these claims were most likely inflated for propaganda purposes and the exact number remains very difficult to ascertain. Several Slovak pilots who entered service with the post-war Czechoslovak Air Force claimed that most of the victories were made-up. Following the battle of Stalingrad, some of the Slovak airmen deserted. Due to this reason, the Germans occasionally referred to the Slovaks as, '*Partizanen nummer zwei*'.

Five surviving *Emils* were ferried to Slovakia in mid-1943. Upon their return to Slovakia, the 13th Fighter Flight was based at Vajnory. Commanded by 1Lt Vladimir Krisko, the unit was unofficially renamed in February 1944 as the Emergency Flight. Eleven Bf 109Es of different sub-types and three thoroughly obsolete Avia B-534s represented the entire strength of the Emergency Flight. The unit was transferred to Piestany to serve in the defence of the Slovak capital, Bratislava. On 13 March, a Luftwaffe Bf 110 opened fire against two SVZ *Emils*—apparently the Luftwaffe crew had mistaken the Slovak fighters for USAAF Mustangs. Staff Sergeant Rudolf Bozík promptly shot the Bf 110 down and subsequently claimed it to have been a USAAF four-engine bomber.

In the event, fourteen factory-fresh Bf 109G-4s arrived, and the unit was placed under the command of the Luftwaffe's 8th *Jägddivision*. Many sorties were flown against USAAF bombers, yet the pilots had been issued with secret instructions to, if possible, avoid combat with the Americans. In response to increasing German criticism regarding the effectiveness of the Slovak fighter pilots, the deputy commander of the Emergency Flight, 1Lt Juraj Puskár, found a chance to respond during a raid against Bratislava on 26 June. Led by Puskár, eight Bf 109Gs rose against the American raiders. One B-24 Liberator was shot down and two B-17 Flying Fortresses damaged by the SVZ Bf 109Gs. However, USAAF fighters quickly shot down five of the Slovak Messerschmitts, seriously damaging a further two. Four of the pilots, Juraj Puskár, Gustav Lang, Stefan Jambor, and Pavol Zelenák, were killed. The remaining four Bf 109Gs were handed over to the 12th Fighter Flight.

By August 1944, Soviet forces were fast approaching Slovakia. The Germans began to disarm. Slovak forces, believing their fighting spirit to be dubious, but the Slovak units based at *Tri Duby* (Three Oaks) fought back. German numerical air superiority meant that twenty-six of the surviving aircraft, including two Bf 109G-6s flown by R. Božik and F. Hanovec, sought refuge behind Soviet lines, landing near Lvov. The Slovak pilots were immediately organised into a Combined Flight before being incorporated into the 1st Czechoslovak Fighter Regiment. Between 2 September and 18 October 1944, nineteen Luftwaffe aircraft were claimed destroyed, with another eight damaged. On 25 October, S/Sgt Gustav Kubovič was shot down and killed by German flak over Dukla in Bf 109G-6 W Nr 161742.

In all, forty-three Bf 109s were supplied to Slovakia, including one Bf 109B, one Bf 109D-1, two Bf 109E-1/Bs, two Bf 109E-2s, two Bf 109E-3s, seventeen Bf 109E-4s, two Bf 109E-7s, two Bf 109E-7/Trops, and fourteen Bf 109G-6s.

Spain

As recounted earlier, a large number of Bf 109s were operated by the *Legion Condor*. In June 1938, the Spanish Nationalist fighter pilot Juaquín García Murato was allowed to fly a Bf 109C at La Cenia. Murato was hugely impressed with the Bf 109 and recommended the acquisition of a number of Messerschmitts. The RLM and the Spanish nationalists soon reached an agreement that Bf 109s would be delivered. In October 1938, three Spanish fighter were seconded to 3./J88 to obtain operational experience with the Bf 109.

With the end of the Spanish Civil War on 29 March 1939, the remaining *Legion Condor* Bf 109's were transferred to the *Ejército del Aire* (EdA). On 12 May 1939, 450 aircraft were assembled at Barajas for a victory parade, with thirty-four Bf 109s included in this number. Of the more-than fifty Bf 109s transferred, a number were consigned to storage at Logroño, where the *Maestranza Aérea de Logroño* (MAL) overhaul and repair centre was located. Bf 109Bs were the first to arrive, which were eventually replaced in *Legion Condor* service by Bf 109Es. The Jumo 210-powered

A Legion Condor Bf 109B provides suitable backdrop for two Guardia Civil personnel. (*NMUSAF*)

Bf 109Bs were assigned to *Grupo* 5-G-5. Fourteen Bf 109Bs have been identified as serving with the EdA.

In May 1939, forty-four Bf 109Es, which had arrived in Spain only weeks prior to the end of the Civil War, were formally handed over at León to the Spanish air arm. The Bf 109B subsequently received the nickname '*Bipala*', with the Bf 109E becoming known as the '*Tripala*'. This was a reflection their respective two- and three-bladed propellers.

In Spanish service, the *Legion Condor* numeric system was retained. The Bf 109s were coded in the 6-1 to 6-131 range. The Grupo 5-G-5 was reorganised as the 25 *Grupo*, and based at Recajo. A few Bf 109Bs were apparently assigned to the *Escuela de Caza* (Fighter School), based at Reus. Following outbreak of war, most of the Bf 109s were concentrated at Reus, turning away belligerent aircraft from Spanish airspace. In late 1940, eight Bf 109s were temporarily transferred to 28 *Grupo*, supplementing its Fiat CR.32 biplane fighters. The Bf 109s remained on Mallorca until early 1941, with one (6-109) lost in a mid-air collision. During the last months of 1940, 23 *Regimento de Caza* (23 Fighter Regiment) was formed. Of the two *Grupos*, Nos. 24 and 25, the latter was based at Recajo and equipped with some thirty-five Bf 109s—24 *Grupo* flew Polikarpov I-15bis biplane fighters. The 23 *Regimento* was transferred to Reus in August 1941.

Following the German invasion of the USSR, a Spanish volunteer unit, known as *Escuadra Azul* (Blue Legion), was sent to fight on the Eastern Front. Becoming operational on 1 June 1942, the unit was part of JG 51 and known as 15.(Span)/JG 51. Led by *Comandante* Angel Salas Larrazabel (who had scored seventeen victories during the Spanish Civil War), the Spanish pilots achieved 154 victories, with *Capitán* Hevia's eight victories the top score, while losing four pilots. The *Escuadra Azul* flew its final sortie on 23 November 1943 and returned to Spain shortly afterwards.

In late 1942, a few Bf 109s were transferred to Alcalá de Henares, near Madrid, where they were used as conversion trainers for pilots destined for the *Escuadrilla Azules* (Blue Squadrons) operating on the Eastern Front.

On 30 May 1942, MAL reported being responsible for maintaining forty 'BFW 109s', thirty-seven Jumo 210 engines, and forty-five Bf 109Es. These quantities included a fair number of aircraft used for spares and recovery.

Fifteen former Luftwaffe Bf 109F-4s were acquired in 1943. The aircraft were handed over at Paris-Villacoublay on 17 May and ferried to Spain by EdA pilots two days later. One of the Bf 109F-4s was lost in a crash near Tours prior to arriving in Spain.

The Bf 109F-4 became known as the '*Zacuta*' (literally, 'knapsack') and was intended as a conversion trainer for the Spanish pilots serving with the Blue Legion on the Eastern Front. However, with the withdrawal of the Blue Legion from operations following Franco's orders, the Bf 109F-4s were divided between the *Escuela de Caza* and 23 *Regimento*.

Severe fuel shortages beginning in 1943 reduced the number of flying hours—a situation that was to continue into the immediate post-war years. Spain was ruled by the dictator *Generalissimo* Franco, with the country having been isolated both politically and economically; on 27 February 1946, France closed its land, sea, and air borders with Spain. As a result, Spain closed its airspace to unauthorised foreign aircraft. French military aircraft, in particular, crossed into Spanish airspace, where they were intercepted by Bf 109s and Polikarpov I-15bis fighters based at Bañolas near the Franco-Spanish border.

In late 1946, two EdA Bf 109Es intercepted a French Air Force AAC.1 Toucan flying sedately over the Mediterranean. The leader made several passes against the AAC.1, but did not fire. The wingman followed suit, but upon returning to base, the leader sharply asked why the wingman had not fired on the AAC.1. The wingman's response was that he had not seen his leader fire, and, with the lack of radios, was unable to receive such an order. It turned out that the leader had indeed fired on the transport, but that the guns had jammed! In retrospect, the shooting down of a French Air Force transport aircraft would have surely created an international incident. On another occasion, EdA Bf 109s were scrambled to intercept what was believed to be an RAF Spitfire, although no Spitfire was observed. In February 1948, France finally opened its borders with Spain, and the Bf 109s were transferred back to Reus as a result.

In late 1945, the EdA adopted a new aircraft designation system. Fighter aircraft were assigned the prefix letter 'C', indicating *caza* (fighter) and a sequential code. The Bf 109B was assigned the designation 'C4', the Bf 109E 'C5' and the Bf 109F-4 'C10'.

The Bf 109s had a secondary role as ground-attack aircraft. However, they were unable to carry rockets or bombs, instead having to rely on the machine gun and cannon armament, which reduced their effectiveness. Aside from the constant lack of fuel, the Bf 109s also suffered from a shortage of spares. Indigenous manufacturers, such as CASA and Hispano, were able to supply spares, but it was obvious that the Bf 109s could not be kept airworthy for much longer. Nevertheless, the MAL personnel did their utmost to keep the Bf 109s in the air. By the late 1940s, twelve Bf 109s—on average, depending on engine and airframe hours, and other availability issues—were serviceable. In 1950, three Bf 109Bs, six Bf 109Es, and three Bf 109Fs remained in 23 *Regimento* service. Other Bf 109s were attached to the *Escuela de Caza*.

Interestingly, a small number of aircraft were modified as target tugs. In 1951, the Bf 109 designations were amended to C4B (Bf 109B), C4E (Bf 109E), and C4F (Bf 109F). However, by the early 1950s the Bf 109 had virtually disappeared, with one remaining on 23 *Regimento* charge until 1955.

For information on the Spanish-built Bf 109 derivatives, please refer to the section on Spanish developments.

Switzerland

Following the international debut for the Bf 109 at the Dübendorf International Air Meet in 1937, the Swiss *Flugwaffe* showed a strong interest in the Messerschmitt fighter. However, the Bf 109 was not yet under consideration for foreign export—the He 112 was offered in its place. Nonetheless, the Swiss persisted in their request for

Bf 109s. The RLM finally relented because the Swiss industry could offer high-grade cutting machinery in exchange for the fighters. In late 1938, an initial batch of five Bf 109D-1s were ordered by the *Kriegstechnische Abteilung* (KTA), with a follow-up order for five more being placed soon afterwards. These Bf 109D-1s were all built by Arado and issued with the serial numbers J-301 to J-310.

Although the Bf 109D-1 was, at the time, one of the most advanced fighters in the world, their primary use was to familiarise Swiss pilots and ground crews with the new Messerschmitt fighter. Additionally, fifteen Bf 108B Taifuns were also purchased for use as conversion trainers. The arrival of the first Swiss Bf 109D-1 (J-303) was inauspicious, with the undercarriage collapsing upon landing at Dübendorf on 17 December 1938. The pilot, Oblt Mooser, survived without injuries. The Bf 109 was returned to Germany for repairs. The second Bf 109D-1 to arrive (J-305) on 5 January was damaged in a belly landing and also returned to Messerschmitt for repairs. Both J-303 and J-305 were returned to Switzerland in May 1939. The other eight Bf 109D's had all arrived by 19 January 1939.

All aircraft arrived unarmed, with a pair of 7.45-mm MG 29s fitted in the front fuselage. This armament was considered too weak for aerial combat. The Bf 109Ds were assigned to *Fliegerkompanie* 15 (FlK 15), based at Payerne. On 1 September, FlK 15 had six operational Bf 109Ds. When the first Bf 109Es arrived, the Bf 109D-1s were relegated to second-line units. They were operated for conversion training, including gunnery training. The final Bf 109D-1s were withdrawn from use in 1949, all of which were scrapped.

Initially, a batch of thirty Bf 109E-3as were ordered on 7 May 1939, with an additional order for fifty placed on 27 April 1940. All of the *Emils* were built by Messerschmitt at Regensburg, and were assigned the *Flugwaffe* serial numbers

A *Flugwaffe* Bf 109D-1. (*ETH Archives*)

J-311 to J-390. Together with the Morane-Saulnier M.S. 406 (built under licence as the Dewoitine D-3801), the Bf 109E equipped the fighter squadrons of the *Flugwaffe*. With Switzerland being neutral, combat aircraft of all nationalities were to be turned away upon entering Swiss airspace. On 4 June 1940, several Luftwaffe Bf 110s of II./ZG 1 and Heinkel He 111s of kg 55 violated Swiss airspace. One Bf 110 was shot down by *Flugwaffe* Bf 109Es, crashing north of Morteau in France and killing the crew.

From 1943, many USAAF heavy bombers sought refuge in Switzerland. One serious incident occurred on 5 September 1944, when USAAF P-51 Mustangs shot down one Bf 109E, damaging another. The Mustangs, flown by 1Lt Earl Erickson and 2Lt Nathan Ostrow of the 339 FG, were escorting a battle-damaged B-17G, and were not aware that they had crossed into Swiss airspace. When a pair of *Flugwaffe* Bf 109Es appeared, Erickson and Ostrow shot down Bf 109E serial J-378. The pilot, Oblt Paul Treu, was killed. The second Bf 109, serial J-324 flown by Oblt Robert Heiniger, was then attacked. Heiniger managed to force-land his damaged fighter near Dübendorf—the Bf 109s belonged to *Fliegerkompanie* 7. A revision of neutrality colour schemes resulted from this incident.

Following the end of the war, one additional Bf 109E-3, serial J-392, was assembled from spares. Amazingly, another eight Bf 109Es were subsequently built by Doflug at Altenrhein. These aircraft incorporated a number of modifications, including a Saurer fuel pump and injection nozzles, Hasler twin-ignition gear, PEM spark plugs, and Escher Wyss EW-V6 controllable pitch propellers. The Bf 109Es

Two *Flugwaffe* Bf 109Es. The aircraft closest to the camera, serial J-313, was the third Bf 109E delivered. The second aircraft, serial J-393, was built in Switzerland after the end of the war. (*ETH Archives*)

An image of Swiss neutrality; a sentry is seen guarding two Bf 109Es. (*ETH Archives*)

were withdrawn from use in 1948. One, serial J-355, was set aside for preservation, with a number of DB601 engines transferred to vocational schools.

Between 1940 and 1945, fifty-nine Luftwaffe aircraft made unscheduled arrivals in Switzerland. This number included two Bf 109F-4/Zs, which landed at Belp on 25 July 1942 due to poor weather and fuel exhaustion. Both were retained in Switzerland, eventually being obtained post-war by the *Flugwaffe*. The serials J-715 and J-716 were assigned in 1946. Both of the Bf 109Fs were test-flown once. With no spare parts available, the Bf 109Fs were subsequently handed over to the aircraft manufacturer Eidg. Flugzeugwerk and ferried to Emmen. Of special interest was the DB601E engine, which was fitted with a special 'cold start' mechanism that made it possible to perform scrambles without warming up the engine. Apparently, although investigated, nothing was gained from the engine experiments. Both Bf 109Fs were scrapped in 1947.

Following the internment at Dübendorf of a Bf 110G-4 night fighter fitted with the latest SN-2 radar gear on 28 April 1944, the Germans offered the immediate delivery of twelve Bf 109G-6s, but only if the Bf 110 was destroyed by the Swiss authorities. This was to avoid the radar and its secrets from falling into Allied hands. Apparently, a commando raid led by Otto Skorzeny, who the year before had managed to snatch Benito Mussolini from underneath the noses of the Allies, was considered. Nevertheless, upon inspection, it became obvious that the Swiss had made a thorough inspection of the radar. After tense negotiations, the Bf 110 was blown up with the German air attaché in attendance.[5]

One of the dozen Bf 109Gs supplied to Switzerland. (*Arlanda Civil Aviation Collection*)

The first six Bf 109Gs arrived at Dübendorf on 20 May 1944, with the remaining six arriving two days later on 22 May. The Bf 109G-6s (all built by Messerschmitt at Oberpfaffenhofen) replaced one squadron's older and less capable Bf 109E-3s. However, it was soon discovered that the Bf 109Gs suffered from serious defects, with the manufacturing quality considered sub-standard. The DB 605 engines were in need of complete overhauls, resulting in the *Flugwaffe* demanding economic compensation from Daimler-Benz. In the event, the matter was settled post-war. As a result, the Bf 109Gs —or, as they were commonly referred to, '*Daimlers*'—were rarely flown and eventually withdrawn from use in 1947. Two additional Bf 109Gs, which had been interned during the war, were taken over and given the serials J-713 and J-714. On 29 May 1946, J-713 went missing on a training flight. The wreck, along with the body of 1Lt Zweiacker was not found until 4 September 1953. One Bf 109E is preserved at Dübendorf.

USSR

Captured former Luftwaffe Bf 109s were occasionally used by the VVS for specific purposes. The first such confirmed instance was in the spring of 1942 when a Bf 109E was attached to a special task group led by Major Fyodor Telegin. Apparently, the Bf 109 had been flown across the front line by a defecting 15.(*Kroat*) JG 52 pilot. Painted in VVS insignia, the Bf 109 was test-flown by the fighter ace

Aleksandr Pokryshkin. He managed to scare the crews of two Soviet aircraft, who elected to perform rapid forced landings. A reconnaissance flight over Taganrog was also made, with the express purpose being: 'to check how a Messerschmitt with Red stars is received'. During the sortie, the engine of the Bf 109 began to struggle, forcing the unnamed pilot to land. He was nearly lynched by Soviet troops, eventually rescued by Pokryshkin and the Deputy Commander of the southern front Air Force, General Nikolai Naumenko. Pokryshkin later wrote:

> The [Bf 109] was equipped with a high-performance radio, had a reinforced windscreen front window and a headlight, the cover of which could be ejected. These were features we could only dream about ... But the Bf 109 also had serious deficiencies: the diving characteristics were worse than those of the MiG-3. This was already known to me from combat experience, when I had to escape from Messerschmitts on a recce flight. The German aircraft recovered slower from a steep dive followed by vertical manoeuvres. These deficiencies I put in my mind and planned to utilise them when planning air combat manoeuvres...[6]

Either in late 1941 or the summer of 1942, two Bf 109s were forced to land at Kotelnikovo by Sergei Luganskiy and I. F. Kuzmichev of 270 IAP. According to Luganskiy's memoirs, the Commanding Officer of 270 IAP, Major Fyodor Telegin, was involved in this incident rather than Kuzmichev. Following a cursory combat evaluation, the Bf 109s were used to make a low-level fighter bomb attack on a German army vehicle pool at Taganrog. On this occasion, the Bf 109s were flown by Luganskiy and Kuzmichev. A few reconnaissance sorties were also made, with the Bf 109s retaining Luftwaffe insignia. On one such sortie, Major Telegin's Bf 109 was hit by German anti-aircraft fire, forcing Telegin to land on the Soviet side of the front line. Intriguingly, a Luftwaffe intelligence report dated 27 September 1943 stated that 813 IAP Fighter Squadron were operating nine Bf 109s. The Soviet Naval Air Force Military Aviation School at Yejsk also operated Bf 109s.

When Soviet forces advanced on the Crimean peninsula, a captured Bf 109 was used by the Commander of the 3rd IAK, General Yevgeni Savitskiy, to fly a reconnaissance sortie over Khersones. Savitskiy completed the sortie, observing eighty Luftwaffe aircraft on the ground, however he was sternly reprimanded upon his return by General Khruykin: 'If you fly once more without permission, I will raise the question of your dismissal of the command of 3 IAK.' Apparently, Savitskiy made a few more flights over the German lines in the Bf 109.[7]

Following the defeat of the German 6th Army at Stalingrad, the *Nationalkommittee Freies Deutschland* (National Committee for a Free Germany, NFD) was formed. The NFD would recruit German prisoners of war to form infantry units to fight alongside the Russians. Commonly referred to as the Seydlitz *Armee* after its commanding officer, Walther von Seydlitz-Kurzbach, an aerial unit was also established. During the final stages of the war, the Seydlitz aerial unit of the NFD operated in the Baltic and eastern Poland areas. In early April 1945, one Bf 109s marked with the black-white-red stripes of the pre-Nazi German flag dropped leaflets over Königsberg (present-day Kaliningrad); the lower surface of the wings were inscribed: '*Freies Deutschland*'. Further details of the operations by the Seydlitz aerial unit are unclear, with some aircraft, including at least one Fw 190, apparently marked with a red *Balkenkreuz*.

See Appendix III for further details of the Soviet evaluation of the Bf 109.

Yugoslavia

During a visit to Germany in January 1938 by Yugoslav Prime Minister Milan Stojadinović, negotiations for the supply of Bf 109s were initiated. When visiting Jüterbog on 18 January, Stojadinović was greeted with the sight of Bf 109D-1s of I. and II./JG 132. The Yugoslav military attaché in Berlin was well aware of the qualities of the high-performance Bf 109, and urged that this fighter had to be obtained by the *Vazduhoplovstvo Vojske Kraljeve Jugoslavije* (VVKJ, Royal Yugoslav Air Force). Herman Göring did his utmost to dissuade the VVKJ from ordering the Bf 109E, stating that the fighter was simply too advanced.

> I would dissuade you from the Bf 109. There is too much with which your brave pilots are unfamiliar in this new aircraft. They should convert by degrees to such fast warplanes or they will suffer many casualties, particularly during landings, and will develop a fear of really advanced fighters.[8]

Nevertheless, a contract for fifty Bf 109Es and twenty-five spare DB 601A engines was signed on 5 April 1939. An order for an additional fifty Bf 109Es was placed on 23 June. In the end, only seventy-three Bf 109E-3as were delivered, with forty arriving in 1939. Two (serial numbers L-28 and L-55) were written off in accidents before delivery. In April 1940, deliveries were halted, with the Luftwaffe taking precedence. However, twelve former Luftwaffe Bf 109E-3s were received in March 1941. The Bf 109s were assigned the serial numbers 2501 to 2583 and the codes L-1 to L-73 and L-89 to L-100.

The delivery of Bf 109s to Yugoslavia was controversial, but with the Yugoslav government able to supply large quantities of iron, chrome, and copper ores, which in exchange were of vital importance to the German arms industry, it was deemed important to fulfil the order.

The unit chosen to receive the Bf 109s was the 6. *Vazduhoplovni lovački puk* (6 Fighter Regiment), based at Belgrade-Zemun, which at the time was equipped with Hawker Fury biplanes. An embarrassing incident occurred during the arrival of the first three Bf 109s on 14 August. The first two landed safely, with the ferry pilot of the third Bf 109 forced to perform a belly landing in front of senior VVKJ officers, the German air attaché, and several Messerschmitt representatives. In the end, the latter managed to turn the unfortunate event into a slight propaganda victory, claiming that the Bf 109 'could be landed on its belly with impunity!'

Yugoslav Bf 109Es at Zemun in April 1940. (*Boris Ciglic*)

The VVKJ pilots did indeed find it difficult to master the Bf 109. Many aircraft suffered damage in belly landings, while others were grounded due to the inadequate supply of spares. In order to convert Hawker Fury pilots onto the Bf 109, a flight training programme was implemented, which included ten hours on Hawker Hurricanes followed by twenty hours on the Bf 108 Taifun. However, by early 1941, the pilots of 6 Fighter Regiment had, on average, less than fifty flying hours on the Bf 109. This was of course totally inadequate to cover all aspects of fighter operations, or indeed to build up basic flight experience. Although the overall handling characteristics of the Bf 109 were judged as being better than those of the Hawker Hurricane, the narrow-track undercarriage and the VDM propeller variable-pitch mechanism in particular caused quite a few accidents.

In early 1941, sixty-four Bf 109s were in service. A number of Bf 109s were transferred to 2 Fighter Regiment. The political situation during the first months of 1941 saw Yugoslavia put under intense pressure from Germany. On 25 March, Yugoslavia signed a treaty with Germany and Italy. However, anti-German elements staged a *coup d'état* two days later, rejecting the Axis alliance. This provoked a strong reaction from Germany. On 6 April, German and Italian forces invaded Yugoslavia.

On the eve of the invasion, the VVKJ had sixty-one Bf 109E-3as and E-3s available.

VVKJ Bf 109E units, 6 April 1941				
Unit	**Base**	**Commander**	**Quantity**	**Remarks**
Independent Fighter *Eskadrila*	Mostar-Kosor	Kp Mihajlo Grbic	3	This unit also had three Hawker Hurricanes and two Avia BH-33Es.

702 *Eskadrila* VZ	Belgrade-Zemun	Pk Dragutin Rupcic	2	Liaison unit. Also operated Bf 108s and Fi 156s.
2 (Fighter) *puk*	Kraljevo	Ppk Franjo Pirc		
31 *Grupa*	Knic		19	
101 *Eskadrila*	Suslicko Polje	Kp Kosta Lekic		
141 *Eskadrila*	Suslicko Polje	Kp Franc Berginc		
6 (Fighter) *puk*	Belgrade-Zemun	Ppk Bozidar Kostic		
32 *Grupa*	Prnjavor	Mj Danilo Djordjevic	27	
103 *Eskadrila*	Prnjavor	Kp Ilija Vlajic		
104 *Eskadrila*	Prnjavor	Kp Bora Markovic		
51 *Grupa*	Belgrade-Zemun	Mj Adum Romeo		
102 *Eskadrila*	Belgrade-Zemun	Kp Milos Zunjic	10	

(Adapted from Shores, C., Cull, B., and Malizia, N. *Air War for Yugoslavia, Greece and Crete, 1940–1941*, p. 187–188)

Sgt Stojanovic standing in front of Bf 109E serial L-44. (*Boris Ciglic*)

The initial Luftwaffe raid against Belgrade on the morning of 6 April was met by thirty-four VVKJ fighters, including twenty-nine Bf 109s. Sgt Stojanovic of 102 *Eskadrila* was shot down by a twin-engine bomber. Stojanovic had to force-land his Messerschmitt, but sustained severe injuries. In all, four Luftwaffe bombers were claimed by VVKJ Bf 109 pilots. On the debit side, 32 *Grupa* was reduced to five airworthy Bf 109s, with 51 *Grupa* losing two Bf 109s. Apart from fighting against the Luftwaffe, the VVKJ Bf 109 pilots also ran the risk of being shot down by its own flak units, as the latter fired at every Bf 109 within sight. The Luftwaffe Bf 109s all had yellow-painted noses, and orders were issued to fire on all Messerschmitt fighters painted in this manner. There was little respite, with a second wave of Luftwaffe aircraft, consisting of fifty-seven Ju 87 dive bombers and thirty Bf 109s arriving over Belgrade at 1,000 hours. Nine Bf 109s of 32 *Grupa* as well as a few 51 *Grupa* Bf 109s intercepted the Luftwaffe formation, claiming two Ju 87s and one Bf 109 shot down. The Luftwaffe conducted two further raids against Belgrade during the day, inflicting heavy damage. In all, Luftwaffe pilots claimed to have destroyed 19 VVKJ Bf 109Es. Actual losses were somewhat lower, with 6 (Fighter) *puk* losing eight aircraft destroyed and fifteen damaged. Five pilots were killed and another seven wounded. Two Bf 109s of 2 (Fighter) *puk* were also lost. Additionally, Bf 110s of III./ZG 26 claimed two Bf 109s shot down in the vicinity of Sarajevo. The VVKJ Bf 109 pilots claimed the destruction of twenty-two Luftwaffe aircraft. However, it would appear that actual Luftwaffe losses consisted of two Do 17s, one JG 54 Bf 109, four Bf 110s, and four Ju 87s.

The following day saw further air raids against Yugoslav targets. The Bf 109s of 32 and 51 *Grupa* were scrambled on numerous occasions, claiming three Luftwaffe bombers. Several VVKJ Bf 109s were shot down or damaged by Bf 109Es of 4./JG 54, with five Yugoslav pilots killed and another three either baling out or forced to land. An order was issued to transfer all surviving 32 *Grupa* Bf 109s to Veliki Radinci—only four Bf 109s were left at Prnjavor. However, one Bf 109 was destroyed on landing at Veliki Radinci, severely injuring Captain Grozdano. In the early hours of 8 April, three 51 *Grupa* Bf 109s also arrived at Veliki Radinci. The 31 *Grupa* Bf 109s were stuck at Kragujevac due to the airfield being muddy and waterlogged—it was planned to burn the fighters if they could not take off.

Two of the 31 *Grupa* Bf 109s at Veliki Radinci were destroyed in a strafing attack on 11 April. During the morning of 12 April, the last eleven Bf 109s of the 6 (Fighter) *puk* were intentionally burned at Veliki Radinci. On the same day, the Independent Fighter *Eskadrila* sent off one Hurricane and one Bf 109. The latter returned safely, but was destroyed in a strafing attack at Mostar the following day. Although isolated VVKJ crews would continue to fight until 17 April, no serviceable Bf 109s remained. During the brief war, twenty-seven VVKJ fighter pilots had been killed. A small number of VVKJ pilots subsequently joined the Croatian Air Force. Reportedly, German forces captured seven complete Bf 109s as well as five fuselages. Italian forces also captured a few VVKJ Bf 109s—for further details, see the Italian chapter.

Partisan and Post-1945 Service

In October 1944, about ten Bf 109Gs were found at Kovin airfield near Banat by NOVJ units. The fighters were split evenly between the NOVJ and the Soviet forces. Along with other captured Luftwaffe aircraft, the Bf 109s were incorporated into *the Eskadrila za vezu* and used for liaison flights. Two additional *Gustavs* arrived when two Croatian pilots, Josip Helebrant and Vinko Tatarevic, defected on 20 April 1945, landing at Mostar. In early May 1945, the Independent Headquarters Squadron flew several sorties against the remaining German forces. The final operation of the war occurred on 28 May when a Ju 87 *Stuka*, escorted by Bf 109Gs, attacked enemy enclaves.

In all, seventeen Bf 109Gs captured during the closing stages of the war were available to the JRV. These aircraft were concentrated at Zagreb and Belgrade, but remained unused until 1947. In this year, fifty-nine Bf 109Gs were received from Bulgaria as part of war reparations. These Bf 109s were transported to Zagreb for refurbishment. The German radios were removed and replaced by Soviet ARS-10 radios. A small number of Bf 109Gs had a K-24 camera fitted. Additionally, a G-24 gun camera was fitted to some *Gustavs* to aid air combat training. The first aid kit was moved closer to the cockpit. The six two-seat G-12 conversion trainers (designated UMe 109) had the Erla *Haube* fitted over the rear cockpit—presumably, this modification had been carried out in Bulgaria. An additional two Bf 109Gs were reportedly converted as G-12s.

A JRV Bf 109G-10 seen following a landing mishap in the immediate post-war era. (*Boris Ciglic*)

A JRV Bf 109G-12 perched precariously on its nose following a landing accident. Note that an Erla *Haube* has been fitted over the instructor's rear seat. (*Boris Ciglić*)

No. 83 Wing, based at Cerkilje, received Bf 109s, along with 172 Fighter Wing, also based at Cerkilje. Conversion training included a number of flights in the three available two-seat Bf 109G-12s. On 16 November 1950, 172 Fighter Wing deployed to Zemunik, near Zadar. During the confrontation with Italy over the city of Trieste, both 83 and 172 Fighter Wings flew a number of sorties along the Yugoslav-Italian border. Fifty hours daily were flown, with some aircraft damaged in accidents. In August 1954, the *Gustavs* began to be replaced by more modern aircraft.

Czech 109s

With large-scale dispersal of combat aircraft production, a Bf 109G assembly line was set up in 1944 at Čakovice near Prague where the company Avia began to build Bf 109G-14s, as well as converting older 'G' models into G-12 two-seat conversion trainers. With the end of the war, it was found that the assembly line at Čakovice had survived largely intact. Large numbers of former Luftwaffe Bf 109s remained in the re-unified Czechoslovakia after the end of the war. Apart from complete aircraft, many components as well as DB 605 engines were available. Quite a number of Bf 109s became part of victory monuments celebrating the defeat of Nazi Germany.

The first Czech Bf 109G fighter, redesignated as the C-10 ('C' denoting *Cvičná letadla*—'training aircraft'), was flown for the first time on 22 February 1946. This particular aircraft had begun life as a Bf 109G-10 (W Nr 613156) built by WNF. The C-10 designation was amended soon afterwards to S-99, with 'S' standing for *Stihaci* (fighter). It was eventually decided to re-open the production line when the Czech government placed an order for a number of C-10/S-99s for the *Sbor národni bezpečnosti* (Security Air Force, SNB), which eventually received twenty-one S-99s. The aircraft were civilian registered OK-BYA to -BYU and operated on border patrol flights.

At the time, the reformed *Ceskoslovenske Vojenske Letectvo* (Czech Air Force, CVL) operated a mixed bag of Spitfire Mk. IXs (most were eventually sold to Israel) and Lavochkin La-5s and La-7s. Lacking funds, it was found that the simplest and easiest option was to initiate large-scale production of the Czech-built Messerschmitt as the CVL standard fighter. Although large numbers of DB 605A engines were available, it was found that these were prone to failure. In December 1945, the main DB 605A storage facility at Ústi nad Labem was destroyed in a fire. At the time, sabotage was suspected.

With an abundance of airframe components available and production gearing up, a new type of engine had to be selected. The only engine available in quantity was the 1,350 hp Junkers Jumo 211F and the 1,420 hp Jumo 211H, with the former eventually selected as the standard engine. Fitted with a VS 11 paddle-bladed propeller, the first Jumo-engine fighter, designated as the Avia S-199 flew for the first time on 25 January 1947, with test pilot Petr Siroky at the controls. Test flights showed the S-199 having poor flight and handling characteristics, being slower and less manoeuvrable than the Bf 109G. The CVL pilots usually referred to the S-199 as the Mezec (Mule). However, the initial S-199s were taken on charge by the Czech Air Force in February 1948. Apart from Avia, the S-199 was also built by Letov at its Letnany factory. A total of 543 S-199s were produced, including 414 by Avia and 129 by Letov. Interestingly, the victory monument Bf 109s around the country were subsequently robbed of any usable spares in order to assist S-199 production.

The two-seat Bf 109G-12 also entered small-scale production, with twenty-nine delivered in 1946 and 1947. Initially designated as the C-110, this was later changed to CS-99 to denote its advanced trainer status. Seventy-seven Jumo 211-powered CS-199s were delivered between 1948 and 1950, twenty-four of which were converted from CS-99s.

The first series S-199 was delivered on 2 February 1948. Six CVL Air Regiments operated S-199s, with the type remaining in front-line use until the early 1950s. In 1952, S-199s of 22 Squadron intercepted US Army Cessna L-19 Bird Dogs violating Czech airspace. Despite its poor reputation, the S-199 operational record in CVL service appears to not to have been worse than other comparable fighter aircraft operated by other air arms. Although it was undoubtedly demanding, one a pilot had managed to come to terms with the aircraft it was a different matter altogether. One CVL pilot, Flight Lieutenant Oldřich Prchal, later wrote:

> To this day I take my hat of [*sic*] to it because it was a plane that satisfied the desire for excitement. Every take-off and landing was a real experience for a young pilot. Anyone who mastered the Mule could handle any other plane with no problem. The only ones who cursed it were the ones who couldn't handle it. To this day I insist that the time when I was learning to fly the Mule and then flying in a fighter regiment, was the most beautiful time in my flying career.

Nevertheless, 124 aircraft were written off in crashes to all causes, with thirty-five pilots losing their lives. The last S-199 was finally retired in 1955.

Avia S-199 Technical Data and Performance Characteristics
Engine: One 1,340-hp Junkers Jumo 211 F
Wingspan: 9.92 metres
Length: 9.10 metres
Height: 2.60 metres
Track width: 2.10 metres
Wing area: 16.05 m^2
Weight, empty: 2,650 kg
Weight, maximum: 3,736 kg
Maximum speed: 590 kph at 6,000 metres
Range: 860 km (with external drop tank)
Service ceiling: 9,500 metres
Armament: 2 × 13-mm MG 131/13 Ns and 2 × 20-mm MG 151/20 N cannons. Capable of carrying 250 kg of bombs

Fighting for Israeli Independence

Following the end of the Second World War, the horrific crimes committed by the Nazis against the Jews were revealed. Survivors of the holocaust emigrated to Palestine, which was then a British Mandate. With hundreds of thousands of dispossessed Jews attempting to reach Palestine, the British authorities came under intense pressure from both Arab and Jewish insurgent groups.9 On 29 November 1947, the United Nations declared that two nations, one Jewish and one Palestinian, were to be established when the British Mandate ended on 14 May 1948.

A few light aircraft were already available to the *Sherut Avir* (literally, air service), and secretly operated on behalf of the Jewish resistance movement *Haganah*.

With war between the soon-to-be independent state of Israel and its Arab neighbours almost certain, a United Nations arms export embargo was imposed. Nevertheless, this resulted in a heterogeneous mix of aircraft being acquired through various cloak-and-dagger methods. However, most of these were trainers and transport aircraft unsuited for combat; what was needed were fighters and bombers. Having considered a number of options—including obtaining P-47 Thunderbolts from Mexico, purchasing a redundant US Navy aircraft carrier packed with arms and Grumman Hellcat fighters, or bribing RAF pilots to land their Spitfires at Israeli airfields—all failed. However, Czechoslovakia declared a willingness to sell ten Avia S-199s, with a contract signed on 23 April 1948. The cost for each aircraft was $44,600, with an additional $6,890 for ancillary equipment. The armament of each aircraft consisted of two 20-mm MG 151 cannons. Beginning on 6 May, Israeli pilots travelled to Czechoslovakia for conversion training. Some of the Israeli pilots had served in the RAF, US Navy, or USMC, while others had little flying experience apart from with light aircraft. Conversion training, which took place at Ceske Budejovice, was rather rudimentary, consisting of a few familiarisation flights in Avia C.2Bs (Czech-built Ar 96Bs) and one or two flights in the two-seat dual control CS-199 before getting to grips with the S-199. Even the experienced fighter pilots found the S-199 very tricky to handle. Lou Lenart, a former USMC F4U Corsair pilot, later stated:

> [The S-199 was] probably the worst airplane that I have ever had the misfortune to fly. It was a different engine, different propeller, fire through the propeller, the cannon never worked, the synchronisation often did not work, there were no self-sealing (fuel tanks), just one section of the seat was bullet proof and it was underpowered.
>
> I had no confidence in it whatsoever.[10]

As feared, war broke out on 15 May. The *Sherut Avir* had 675 personnel of all ranks, and thirty-five aircraft—none of which were fit for combat purposes. The S-199s were desperately needed to counter Egyptian Spitfires and Syrian Harvards.[11]

Instead of flying the S-199s to Israel, which was an especially daunting prospect, they were dismantled and loaded onto cargo aircraft. The first S-199 arrived in great secrecy at Tel Nof during the night of 20–21 May. Only the day before,

An IDF/AF S-199. Even though the S-199 had poor flight characteristics, it nevertheless provided Israel with the country's first fighter. (*Photograph via Arlanda Civil Aviation Collection*)

101 Squadron had been formed at Ekron. No. 101 Squadron would become the premier fighter squadron of the Israeli Defence Force/Air Force (IDF/AF). The S-199s were codenamed *Sakin* (knife). In service, the S-199 was usually referred to as 'Messerschmitt' or *Messer*. By 26 May, five S-199s had arrived, with one additional aircraft destroyed when the C-46 carrying it crashed. Aided by Czech mechanics, four S-199s had been assembled at Ekron by 29 May. The situation at the front was so desperate, that a quartet of S-199s were dispatched to attack a column of Egyptian troops and armour 16 kilometres away. The cannons of the S-199s had not been calibrated, with neither test flights nor even engine runs possible. The attack caused insignificant damage, with one S-199 shot down by flak. Its pilot, Eddie Cohen, was killed. Another S-199 was damaged in a landing accident. Nevertheless, the psychological impact was significant. Israel now had fighters. The fifth S-199 took to the air on 30 May. However, one S-199 was lost on the same day, with another one suffering damage. The net result was that on 31 May, only one S-199 remained serviceable.

On 3 June, Modi Allon shot down a pair of Royal Egyptian Air Force (REAF) Douglas C-47 bombers over Tel Aviv. Deliveries of S-199s continued, with a follow-up contract for 15 aircraft being signed. The Israeli S-199s that have been identified included (serial numbers) 30, 32, 33, 36, 37, 38, 42, 88, 89, 90, 91, 93, 94, 95, 96, 98, and 100, which were all built by Avia. One S-199 was impounded in Rome on 18 July, eventually being released in late November.

Operations continued, with 101 Squadron having ten serviceable S-199s on 9 July. On this day, fighting erupted following a brief truce. On 10 July, an S-199 flown by Lionel Morris Bloch was shot down by a Syrian Air Force Harvard, coming down near Qunaytra. The Avia S-199 pilots scored seven out of the eighteen aerial victories during the War of Independence, including three Royal Egyptian Air Force Spitfires. One S-199 had been converted as an *ad hoc* high speed reconnaissance aircraft.

On 5 November, no less than eighteen S-199s had been struck off charge, including twelve in accidents and four in combat. Four pilots had been killed, including three on operations. Nevertheless, it would appear that the purchase of an additional fifteen S-199s was discussed in late 1948. However, by late December, a large number of Spitfire Mk IXs began to arrive from Czechoslovakia, making the remaining S-199s redundant.

For a brief period, 101 Squadron operated Spitfires, Mustangs, and S-199s. Take-off procedures saw the S-199 getting off the ground after the Spitfires and Mustangs. This was due to the poor take-off characteristics of the S-199—if an accident occurred on take-off, the S-199 wreck would not block the runway for the other fighters. The final S-199 operational sortie took place on 26 December, when one S-199 provided escort for a photo reconnaissance Spitfire. However, five S-199s were still on charge in May 1949. The commander of 101 Squadron, Ezer Weizman, described the shortcomings of the S-199 in a report, recommending that the aircraft be retired. In IDF/AF service, the serials D-101 to D-124 were assigned to the S-199s.

After the final S-199s had been withdrawn, tentative plans to sell them to Yugoslavia remained unfulfilled. However, in October 1950, six 'Messerschmitts' (all unserviceable) were stored at Tel Nof. Interestingly, three Israeli P-51D Mustangs were fitted with Revi gunsights removed from the S-199s. One S-199 has been preserved.

Spanish Developments

The Messerschmitt Bf 109 had a long association with Spain, with the type having seen its baptism of fire during the Spanish Civil War. In 1943, the company Hispano Aviacion was formed by merging the Hispano-Suiza company (responsible for a number of successful inline aero engines) with several smaller companies. The year before, a licence to produce the Bf 109G-2 had been secured by Spain. Some 200 were ordered by the EdA. In order to ease production, twenty-five Bf 109G-2s were to be delivered as sub-assemblies, along with technical drawings and jigs. However, only the disassembled Bf 109G-2s arrived in Spain, with DB 605 engines and armament apparently having been requisitioned by the Luftwaffe. Additionally, only a few drawings were supplied, ensuring a protracted assembly of the aircraft. The only substitute engine available to the Spaniards was the 1,300-hp Hispano-Suiza

12Z-89. Installation and air tests were conducted in a Bf 109E-1 (serial 6-119). One problem was that the Hispano-Suiza engine rotated in the opposite direction (to the left) to the DB 605 (to the right). This necessitated modifications to the engine cowling and fin.

The modified fighter was given the designation Hispano HA-1109-J1L, the prototype making its maiden flight on 2 March 1945. Further *ad hoc* improvisations were necessary, as the intended Swiss-built Escher-Wyzz V71 L1 propeller had not yet arrived. Instead, a three-bladed Hamilton Standard propeller was fitted. Following the conclusion of the initial flight tests, the HA-1109-J1L prototype was transferred to the *Instituto Nacional de Técnica Aeronáutica* (National Institute for Aeronautical Research, INTA), in January 1946. The V71 L1 propeller was finally fitted, which required further testing to harmonise the new propeller with the engine. This took place at Alcalá de Henares airfield not far from Madrid.

Hispano had planned to build the HA-1109 in two batches, consisting of seventy and 105 aircraft respectively. However, neither materials nor engines had arrived in Spain prior to the unconditional surrender of Germany. Somewhat optimistically, Hispano stated its intention of delivering twenty-five aircraft in 1945, with final deliveries being scheduled for 1948. For several reasons, delivery fell way behind schedule. While 150 Hispano-Suiza 12Z-89 engines were ordered from Hispano's Paris facility, flight testing by INTA continued apace. In 1946 and 1947, the prototype was flown during fifty hours, with the engine receiving a further twenty-five hours of bench testing. A former Messerschmitt engineer, Frederick Prasyhofer, was hired to assist in the licence production of the Messerschmitt fighter. In the meantime, the EdA assigned the designation C.4J to the HA-1109-J1L.

Test flying came to a premature halt in 1947, when the HA-1109 prototype sustained damage in an emergency landing at Móron air base. The Hispano-Suiza 12Z-89 engines were to be supplied as knock-down kits, with final assembly taking place at Barcelona. The supply of engines turned out to be a major stumbling block. Until 1948, Hispano had completed eighty HA-1109s, but these were consigned to storage due to the non-delivery of engines. In the event, the Hispano-Suiza 12Z-89 turned out to be quite unsuitable for the HA-1109. In its place, the French-built Hispano-Suiza 12Z-17 was selected. By 1951, 150 HA-1109 airframes had been completed.

Protracted Testing

The initial half-dozen Hispano-Suiza 12Z-17 had arrived by this time. Three of the Bf 109G-2 pattern airframes (serials 1, 2, and 18 respectively), as well as three 1950-built HA-1109s (serials 81–83), were fitted with the new engines. One from each batch, Nos. 1 and 81, were fitted with de Havilland PD-63 propellers, which had the major drawback of precluding the fitting of a centrally-mounted cannon. Subsequent flight testing began during the spring of 1951. The factory designation was changed to HA-1109K1L, with the EdA designation remaining unchanged.

In May 1952, serials 18 and 82 were transferred to 11 *Regimento*, based at Tablada. It was initially intended to fit Breda-SAFAT machine guns to the aircraft. However, due to their obvious obsolescence as fighters, their role was changed to that of ground attack, and so two Hispano HS-404/-408 cannons and 80-mm Oerlikon rockets were carried. In all, nineteen C.4Js were delivered in 1952, with the majority allocated to the *Escuela de Caza* (Fighter School) based at Morón, with one delivered to 23 *Grupo* based at Reus and the final four remaining with INTA for continued flight testing. In the event, only twenty-one C.4Js were taken on charge by the EdA. Interestingly, at least six C.4Js were painted in Luftwaffe colours for the feature film '*Der Stern von Afrika*' ('The Star of Africa'). Released in 1957, the film depicts the career of Hans-Joachim Marseille, who scored an amazing 158 victories, mostly while serving with JG 27. In order to ease conversion training, a pair of two-seat aircraft, designated HA-1110K-1Ls were built in 1953. Seven of these were withdrawn from use in 1954–55, albeit temporarily, for the fitting of armament before being returned to service in 1957.

It had become clear to everyone involved that the C.4J was virtually useless as a combat aircraft, mostly due to the unsuitable Hispano-Suiza engine. As a result, contact was established with Rolls-Royce concerning the availability of the 1,600-hp Merlin 500-45 engine. Although relations between Britain and Fascist Spain had been cool since the end of the Second World War, the British government approved the sale in 1953. A Merlin engine was fitted in a mock-up fuselage, with the prototype of the new variant (serial number 197), designated HA-1112M-1L, flying its first flight on 30 December 1954 at San Pablo airfield. Due to the prominent placement of the radiator, the HA-1112M-1L soon received the nickname '*Buchón*' ('Pigeon'), with the EdA formally designating it as the C.4K.

Although inferior to the late-model Bf 109G and Ks with its shorter range and lower maximum speed, the C.4K was still a useful ground-attack aircraft. However, the Bf 109s traits of a weak undercarriage and insufficiently effective brakes had not been improved. This meant that numerous incidents and crashes occurred, with several aircraft written off. Nevertheless, 171 aircraft were retrofitted with Merlin engines, including the pair of two-seaters—the latter being redesignated as HA-1112M-4L—receiving the EdA serials C.4K-35 and -112 respectively.

Into Service

In November 1955, the C.4K entered service with the EdA, the first aircraft being assigned to 71 *Escuadrón de Caza-bombardeo*, a fighter-bomber unit based at Tablada. Little more than two years later, the squadron moved to nearby El Copero before finally being declared operational. In January 1958, the squadron deployed to Spanish Morocco, where guerrilla forces were fighting against Spanish troops—the conflict was known as the Ifni war. The HA-1112s were flown to Gando in the Canary Islands, escorted by CASA 2.111s, before arriving in Africa.

The C.4Ks flew a large number of convoy-escort, close-support, and armed reconnaissance sorties, with no aircraft being lost in combat. However, six C.4Ks were written off in accidents. Despite suffering from the highest accident rate of any EdA combat aircraft, the Buchón was quite well-liked by its pilots. In the event, more than 100 *Buchóns* were based in Spanish Africa, both with 71 and 72 Fighter Bomber Squadrons (both part of the *Ala* 7 Wing) as well as 364 *Escuadrón*. In spite of the number of sorties flown, the HA-1112 was not the ideal aircraft for the job. They were soon replaced by North American T-6 Texans. At the same time, one C.4K was assigned to the *Academia General del Aire* (EdA Air Academy) for personal use by the unit commander.

By 1963, about 100 *Buchóns* remained in service. The *Buchóns* had been retired from front line combat duties, being used instead as armament and advanced trainers. In this year, *Ala* 7 was transferred back from Africa to Tablada. In the summer of 1964, the unit was renumbered *Ala* 47, eventually being incorporated into the Tactical Air Command. The sole squadron of *Ala* 47, No. 471 Escuadron, could field no less than 55 C.4Ks. However, 471 *Escuadron* was disbanded in November 1965.

The protracted development of the Spanish Messerschmitt may be put down to several factors. Following the German surrender, support from Messerschmitt vanished. Also, during the immediate post-war years, the Franco regime was regarded with suspicion by the international community.

Incredible as it may seem, Lockheed F-104G Starfighters were taken on charge by the EdA at the same time as HA-1112s remained in service.

A formation of EdA Buchons. (*Arlanda Civil Aviation Collection*)

One of the two two-seat Hispano HA-1112M-4Ls. (*Arlanda Civil Aviation Collection*)

Hispano HA-1112 M1L Technical Data and Performance Characteristics
Engine: One 1,610-hp Rolls-Royce Merlin 500/45
Wingspan: 9.92 metres
Length: 9.13 metres
Height: 2.60 metres
Track width: 2.07 metres
Wing area: 16.05 m^2
Weight, empty: 2,445 kg
Weight, maximum: 3,180 kg
Maximum speed: 675 kph at 4,000 metres
Range: 770 km
Service ceiling: 10,200 metres
Armament: 2 × 20 mm-HS 404 or HS 808 cannons. 8 × 10 kg 80-mm rockets

Survivors

Several Bf 109s have survived, with a few still airworthy. Since the late 1980s, a growing number of Bf 109s have been recovered from remote wreck sites, particularly in Eastern Europe. According to the warbird magazine *Classic Wings* listing (originally compiled by Mikael Olrog), the total includes seventy-five Messerschmitt Bf 109s divided into eighteen Bf 109Es, sixteen Bf 109Fs, forty Bf 109Gs and one Bf 109K-4. Several of these are on display at aviation museums around the world, while others remain in storage or under restoration. A fairly large percentage of the latter consists of major (or minor) components recovered from wreck sites, particularly from Russia and northern Norway. Amazingly, parts of the Bf 109V10 (D-IAKO) were recovered in Germany some years ago. The fuselage of the Messerschmitt Me 209V1 is kept at Krakow. One Avia S-199 and a CS-199 are preserved in the Czech Republic, with one S-199 in Israel. Two HA-1109s, thirty-six HA-1112s, and one HA-1112 M4L two-seater still survive.

Since the late 1950s, *Buchons* have been seen in countless war movies and air displays, usually performing as Luftwaffe Bf 109s due to the lack of airworthy examples of the real thing. However, they have occasionally been called upon to depict North American P-51 Mustangs and Supermarine Spitfires in a few movies—depending upon the financial budget of the movie and the director's wishes. Several HA-1112s have been lost in crashes, attesting to the demanding handling characteristics of the Spanish Messerschmitt.

A Bf 109E preserved by the RAF Museum. (*Per Björkner*)

A Bf 109G-2 on display at the National Aviation Museum at Surčin, Belgrade. This aircraft belonged to the large batch of Bf 109Gs supplied to Yugoslavia from Bulgaria as war reparations. (*Author's Collection*)

A Bf 109G-10 kept by the National Museum of the United States Air Force. (*NMUSAF*)

Three *Buchons*, all painted in fake Luftwaffe colours, appeared at the 2011 Flying Legends airshow at Duxford, Cambridgeshire. (*Author's Collection*)

Appendix I

Pre-war Luftwaffe Bf 109 Fighter Units

With the pre-war expansion of the Luftwaffe, major reorganisation and renumbering took place before the war. This included the redesignation of the fighter units.

Date unit formed	Designation prior to 1Nov. 38	Designation after 1Nov. 38	Designation on 1May 39	Arrival of Bf 109s
15 Mar. 1937	I./(1)/JG 131	1./JG 130	I./JG 1	May 1938
1 Apr. 1936	*Stab*/JG 132	*Stab*/JG 131	*Stab*/JG 2	Feb. 1937
1 May 1934	I./(1)JG 132	I./JG 131	I./JG 2	May 1937
1 Apr. 1935	II.(s)/JG 132	I./ZG 141	I./ZG 1	Feb. 1937
1 July 1938	III.(1)/JG 132	II./ZG 141	I./ZG 76	Sep. 1938
1 July 1938	IV.(1)/JG 132	I./JG 331	I./JG 77	July 1938
1 Apr. 1936	*Stab*/JG 134	*Stab*/ZG 142	*Stab*/ZG 26	1937
15 Mar. 1936	I.(s)/JG 134	I./ZG 142	I./ZG 26	1937
15 Mar. 1936	II.(s)/JG 134	II./ZG 142	II./ZG 26	1937
1 Apr. 1937	III.(s)/JG 134	II.(s)/LG	I.(Z)/LG 1	1937

1 July 1938	IV.(1)/JG 134	III./ZG 142	III./ZG 26	Aug. 1938
1 Apr. 1937	I.(1)/JG 135	I./JG 233	I./JG 51	Nov. 1937
1 July 1935	II.(1)/JG 135	I./JG 333	I./JG 54	Sep. 1938 Redesignated II./ ZG 1 on 15 May 1939.
1 Oct. 1934	I.(1)/JG 136	II./JG 333	II./JG 77	May 1938
1 Apr. 1937	I.(1)/JG 137	I./JG 231	I./ZG 2	Apr. 1938
20 Apr. 1937	JG 232/ II.(1)/JG 137	II./JG 231	I./JG 3	Nov. 1938
1 Apr. 1938	I.(1)/JG 138	I./JG 134	I./JG 76	July 1938
1 Oct. 1937	I./JG 232/ I./(1)LG	I.(J)/LG 2	I.(J)/LG 2	Oct. 1937
1 Nov. 1938	*Stab*/JG 234	*Stab*/JG 132	*Stab*/JG 26	1 Nov. 1938
15 Mar. 1937	I.(1)/JG 234	I./JG 132	I./JG 26	May 1937
15 Mar. 1937	II.(1)/JG 234	II./JG 132	II./JG 26	Nov. 1937
1 July 1938	III.(1)/JG 234	I./ZG 143	I./ZG 52	July 1938
1 Apr. 1937	*Stab*/JG 334	*Stab*/JG 133	*Stab*/JG 53	1938
15 Mar. 1937	I.(1)/JG 334	I./JG 133	I./JG 53	1938
15 Mar. 1937	II.(1)/JG 334	II./JG 133	II./JG 53	1938
1 July 1938	III.(1)/JG 334	I./ZG 144	II./ZG 76	Aug. 1938
1 Nov. 1938		I./JG 433	I./JG 52	1 Nov. 38
1 Aug. 1938			I./Tr Gr 186	Aug. 1938. Disbanded 22 Oct. 1938

15 Nov. 1938			II./Tr Gr 186	Nov. 1938. Intended for service on aircraft carrier Graf Zeppelin.
15 July 1939			I./JG 20	Aug. 1939
15 July 1939			I./JG 21	15 July 1939
		II./JG 135	I./JG 70	15 May 1939
15 July 1939			I./JG 71	Aug. 1939

Appendix II

Bf 109 Production 1935–1945

Although exact numbers are unknown, the Bf 109 was the most-produced Luftwaffe combat aircraft, with some 33,000 being built between 1935 and 1945. The collapse of Germany in early 1945 and the destruction of many factory and Luftwaffe records all contribute to making a proper and accurate assessment of Bf 109 production quantities virtually impossible. Apart from production by BFW and Messerschmitt AG, the Bf 109 was also built by AGO, Arado, Erla, Fieseler, Focke-Wulf, and WNF. During the war, Bf 109 production lines were also established in Hungary and Romania.

A Bf 109E production line. (*Wolfgang Mühlbauer/DEHLA Archives*)

In 1939, Bf 109 production was transferred from Augsburg to Regensburg. A new factory was also established at WNF in Austria—later Ostmark following the *Anschluss* of March 1938. As the war progressed, it was intended to replace the Bf 109 with more advanced fighter aircraft, including the Me 309. However, the Bf 109 was to remain in large-scale production until the end of the war. By that time, it was outclassed by more modern Allied fighters.

There are several things to consider regarding aircraft production statistics. For one thing, following completion, an aircraft then has to be test-flown before being taken on charge. Only then is it transferred to an operational unit.

Production statistics for the pre-war era include nineteen Bf 109As, 341 Bf 109Bs, fifty-eight Bf 109Cs, 647 Bf 109Ds, and in excess of 500 Bf 109Es. Between September 1939 and April 1945, no less than 31,898 Bf 109s were built: 449 (Sep–Dec 1939); 1,719 (1940); 2,764 (1941); 2,673 (1942); 6,388 (1943); 14,765 (1944); and 3,140 (1945). This number includes 30,573 fighters, of which 28,103 (or 91.9 per cent) were formally accepted by the Luftwaffe. Additionally, 1,325 reconnaissance Bf 109s (the majority being Bf 109G-8 variants) were built. The highest output was reached in September 1944, when 1,605 Bf 109s (including ninety-four reconnaissance variants) were built, which equates to 53.5 aircraft per day. With the increasing number of Allied bomb raids against German aircraft factories, a programme of production dispersal was initiated in 1944, which lasted until the end of the war. Many aircraft were destroyed before delivery in crashes and Allied bomb raids. The handling characteristics of the Bf 109 also resulted in no less than 1,750 being written off in landing accidents.

The Bf 109G was produced in huge quantities between 1942 and 1945. (*NMUSAF*)

AGO

Originally formed in 1911 as Aeroplanbau G. Otto in Munich, the company changed its name the following year to Ago Flugzeugwerke GmbH. During the Great War, AGO produced a number of twin-seat reconnaissance aircraft, including those of its own design and those under licence from other manufacturers. Following the signing of the Treaty of Versailles in 1919, AGO stopped producing aircraft. In 1934, the company was reformed, with a new factory at Oscherleben established.

Both before and during the war, AGO mainly produced aircraft under licence, including Fw 190s, Ju 88s, and Bf 109s. In all, AGO built 715 early-model Bf 109s, ending with the Bf 109F-2.

Arado

Based at Warnemünde on the Baltic Sea coast, the Arado Flugzeugwerke was formed in 1933, having originally been known as the Arado Handelsgesellschaft. The same year, the company's chief designer, Walher Rethel, joined BFW, and was succeeded by Dipl. Ing. Walter Blume.

From the mid-1920s, Arado had built a number of biplane fighters, with the first monoplane fighter being the Ar 80. Following Luftwaffe rejection of the Ar 80, Arado went on to build more than 1,000 Bf 109s at its Warnemünde factory. Arado is today better known for the excellent Ar 96 basic trainer, the Ar 196 floatplane, and the world's first operational jet bomber, the Ar 234.

Bayerische Flugzeugwerke (BFW)

As related in the main text, BFW was responsible for the design and initial production of the Bf 109. Apart from prototypes, fewer than 400 Bf 109s (split between Bf 109As, Bs, Cs, Ds, and Es) were actually built at Augsburg-Haunstetten, with production transferred to Regensburg in 1939.

Erla

Formed at Leipzig in 1934 as the Erla-Maschinenwerk GmbH, the company initially built various ultra-light aircraft, including the Erla 5, some of which were used for long-distance flights. Both Arado Ar 68 and Heinkel He 51 biplane fighters were built under licence by Erla. Most major Bf 109 variants were subsequently built by Erla.

In 1944, the so-called Erla *Haube* (Erla 'hood') was introduced on late-model Bf 109Gs, becoming standard on the Bf 109K-4. Also known as the Galland hood, the Erla hood lacked the metal framing so prominent on the Bf 109 canopy. The one-piece Erla hood also bulged outwardly, thus increasing pilot vision out of the cockpit.

Fieseler

Formed by noted aerobatic pilot Gerhard Fieseler, the Fieseler Flugzeugbau company produced thousands of Bf 109s at Kassel-Bettenhausen. Among the Bf 109 variants built by Fieseler were the Bf 109T, intended for the aircraft carrier *Graf Zeppelin*. The best-known aircraft to emanate from Fieseler was the Fi 156, with the company also being responsible for the Fi 103 unmanned flying bomb.

Focke-Wulf

Formed at Bremen in 1924, the Focke-Wulf Flugzeugbau GmbH was responsible for a large number of highly successful aircraft, most notably the Fw 44 Stieglitz primary trainer, the Fw 56 Stösser, the Fw 58 Weihe twin-engine light transport, the Fw 190 fighter, and the Fw 200 Condor airliner and maritime reconnaissance aircraft. In 1934, Focke-Wulf unsuccessfully submitted the Fw 159 fighter for the Luftwaffe fighter competition. Both the Bf 109D and Bf 109E were eventually built under licence by Focke-Wulf at its Bremen factory.

Messerschmitt GmbH Regensburg

Messerschmitt GmbH Regensburg delivered its first Bf 109E-3 in January 1939. Of the 144 aircraft built in that year, the majority were released for export to Switzerland (seventy-nine E-3as) and Yugoslavia (forty E-3as), with only twenty-five delivered to Luftwaffe. Bf 109 variants built at Regensburg included the Bf 109E-3, E-3a (for Switzerland & Yugoslavia), E-4, E-4B, E-4BN, E-7, F-0, F-1, F-2, G-1, G-2, G-2/trop, G-3, G-4, G-4/trop, G-6, G-6/trop, G-6/AS, G-10, G-14, G-14/AS, K-2, K-4, with a total of 10,888 Bf 109's built by May 1945. In fact, about one-third of every Bf 109 produced during the war was built at Regensburg.

At Regensburg-Obertraubling in February 1944, two Soviet PoWs attempted to steal a Bf 109 and fly to Switzerland. Upon take-off, the Bf 109 hit a fence. The Russians, Lieutenants Dimitry Utevikov and Vassily Yaresh, were summarily tried and executed a few days later.

Two devastating USAAF raids, on 22 and 25 February 1944 resulted in major damage to the production facilities. The first raid destroyed or damaged about 200 recently-completed Bf 109Gs, as well as levelling two assembly halls and damaging others. The second raid saw a large quantity of tooling and aluminium sheeting destroyed in the intense heat created by numerous fires. Nevertheless, production resumed by early March, with five Bf 109Gs completed daily.

Wiener-Neustädter Flugzeugwerke GmbH (WNF)

Originally formed in 1933 in Austria as Wiener-Neustädter Flughafen Betriebs GmbH, the company was merged with another Austrian aircraft manufacturer, Hirtenberg, following the German annexation of Austria. Located south of Vienna, the new company was named Wiener-Neustädter Flugzeugwerke GmbH. Large-scale production of Bf 109s began in 1940, with some 8,500 aircraft in successive variants built by the end of the war.

Bf 109 Production by Manufacturer and Variant (Hungarian and Romanian Production Not Included)

	AGO	Arado	BFW	Erla	Fieseler	Fw	Me	WNF	Total
A	–	–	19	–	–	–	–	–	19
B	–	–	76	175	90	–	–	–	341
C-1	–	–	58	–	–	–	–	–	58
D-1	128	144	4	168	80	123	–	–	647
E	80	568	52	1,131	628	90	465	568	3,582
F-0							16		16
F-1	–	–	–	–	–	–	157	49	208
F-2	378	358	–	192	–	–	234	172	1,334 (1,380)
F-3	–	–	–	–	–	–	15 *	–	15 *
F-4	–	–	–	795	–	–	–	1,046	1,841
F-5	–	–	–	–	–	–	–	1	1
G-1	–	–	–	20	–	–	147	–	167
G-2	–	–	–	544	–	–	121	914	1,576

G-3	–	–	–	–	–	–	50	–	50
G-4	–	–	–	262	–	–	262	715	1,239
G-5	–	–	–	475	–	–	–	–	475
G-6	–	–	–	N/a	–	–	5,240	N/a	At least 12,000, including G–6 AS
G-6 AS	–	–	–	N/a	–	–	325	N/a	N/a
G-8	–	–	–	N/a	–	–	–	906	906
G-10	–	–	–	N/a	–	–	121	N/a	2,600
G-14	–	–	–	N/a	–	–	480	N/a	1,000 including G–14 AS
G-14 AS	–	–	–	N/a	–	–	1,584	N/a	N/a
K–4	–	–		N/a	–	–	1,194	N/a	1700
T	–	–	–	–	70	–	–	–	70
Total	715	1,070	361	11,051	799	326	10,888	8,500	33,170

* Indicates unconfirmed quantity

Appendix III

Allied Evaluation of the Bf 109

Australia

A few Bf 109s were captured and test-flown by 3 (RAAF) Squadron in North Africa in late 1942. Included among these Bf 109s was Bf 109G-2/trop W Nr 10639, which today can be seen at the RAF Museum, Hendon.

France

The first practical French experience with the Bf 109 occurred in early 1938, when a French team was allowed to test, albeit briefly, a Bf 109B-1 that had been captured in the Spanish Civil War before its transfer to the USSR. The team included the test pilot *Capitaine* Constantin Rozanoff of the *Centre d'Essais du Matériel Aériennes Militaires* (CEMA). Arriving at Sabadell north of Barcelona on 31 January, Rozanoff accumulated approximately thirty hours in the Bf 109 and a captured He 111B. The French test pilot was particularly impressed with the German fighter's level speed and dive characteristics, though he was critical of the strong engine torque in a climbing starboard turn. The French team returned home on 13 February. However, due to the heavy veil of secrecy in which the test flights had been performed, the test results were not made available to the various French aircraft manufacturers.

Following the outbreak of war, *Armée de l'Air* fighters clashed with Luftwaffe Bf 109s on several occasions, with both sides suffering losses. On 24 September 1939, three Bf 109D-1s of JGr.152 were shot down, with another two damaged. One of the Bf 109D-1s, flown by Gefr A. Hesselbach, was brought down by *Adjt Combette* of GC I/3, force-landing near Rimling. The Jumo 210-powered Bf 109D had only suffered minor damage and was repaired to flying condition. It was damaged at Nancy on 6 October, and is said to have been transferred into British hands on 22 December. The Bf 109D was ferried to Tangmere by Wg Cdr J. F. X. McKenna.

Bf 109E W Nr 1304 in French colours. (*Wolfgang Mühlbauer/DEHLA Archives*)

Two Bf 109Es arrived on French soil during the Phoney War. The first of these was a Bf 109E-1 of 2./JG 51 (W Nr 3326) flown by Uffz Georg Pavenziger, who was forced to land near Brumat on 28 September. The surprised but excited French dismantled the Bf 109, transporting it to Strasbourg. However, the Bf 109 was subsequently damaged in a belly landing at Nancy on 8 October. The fighter was reportedly handed over to the British and transferred to Boscombe Down for a thorough examination.

On 22 November 1939, a Bf 109E-1 (W Nr 1304) of I./JG 76 force-landed near Goesdorf following combat with French fighters. The pilot, Fw Karl Hier, became a prisoner of war. His Bf 109E, the first to fall into Allied hands intact, was subsequently transported to Orleans-Bricy for evaluation by CEMA.[1]

On 6 December, the Bf 109 arrived at CEMA. The first six days were spent on assembly and initial inspection of equipment. Taxiing tests were performed on 13 December, after which the fuel tanks were drained. Engine bench tests began on 15 December and French Air Force insignia was painted on the Bf 109. The first flight took place on 19 December, with further air tests being interrupted by poor weather. Two orientation flights took place on 22 December, with the pilot attempting to establish the optimal angle of climb of the German fighter. During one flight the following day, an altitude of 8,300 metres was reached before the DB 601 engine began to malfunction. The time taken to reach 8,000 metres was thirteen minutes and thirty-five seconds. Performance testing continued on 28 December. Pilot visibility forward and above was found to be 'very good', 'mediocre' sideways and to the rear, and 'non-existent' below. The Bf 109 was found to have excellent flight characteristics, although becoming longitudinally unstable during high-speed dives. Due to the strong engine torque, it was found that the pilot had to compensate by judicious application of both rudder and ailerons.

Following initial tests, a comparative evaluation against the Bloch 152, Dewoitine D.520, and Supermarine Spitfire Mk. I (one of which had been delivered to France) was performed by the *Centre d'Experiences Aériennes Militaires* (Military Aeronautics Test Centre, CEAM).[2] This included comparisons regarding 'combat aptitude', such as manoeuvrability and speed (in level flight, as well as in a climb or dive) of the Bf 109 and comparative performance with the French fighters. Interestingly, the following paragraph was included in the report: 'To avoid the combat trials degenerating into the chaos of individual mélées from which no conclusions could be drawn, [it] has been split in different phases where the attacks and the possible means of defence [have] been studied separately.'

It was found that the Bf 109 enjoyed a speed advantage over the D.520 and Bloch 152, possessing the ability to break off any combat by going into a dive. The stall characteristics of the D.520 were deemed considerably poorer (the report states 'brutal') than those of the Bf 109 due to the latter's wing leading edge slats. Additionally, the engine cooling of the D.520 in a climb was insufficient. However, the D.520 was declared more manoeuvrable, having less heavy stick force, particularly during pitch at high speeds. Regarding the Bloch 152, the German fighter had a superior rate of climb. Frustratingly, information regarding the Bf 109's performance against the Spitfire is missing from the evaluation report.

On 2 May, the Bf 109 was handed over to the RAF for further testing.

The third Bf 109 to make an unscheduled arrival in France belonged to 1./JG 76. While on a test flight, Uffz Karl Hager was forced to land his Bf 109E-1 (W Nr 3247) at Vitry-le-François. The French immediately replaced the Luftwaffe insignia with *Armee de l'Air* roundels and fin stripes, although the JG 76 code numeral '6' was retained. Unfortunately, the Bf 109 was destroyed soon afterwards in a mid-air collision with an M.S. 406.

Although many different German aircraft were extensively tested by the French after the end of the war, including the Do 335, He 162, and Me 262, it seems unlikely that any late-model Bf 109s were evaluated. Tellingly, no Bf 109s were included in the batch of more than 400 former Luftwaffe aircraft transferred to France from RAF stocks in 1947.

Great Britain

During the war, several Bf 109s were evaluated by different test establishments, including the Aeroplane and Armament Experimental Establishment (A&AEE) at Boscombe Down, the Air Fighting Development Unit (AFDU) at Northolt (later at Duxford), the Royal Aircraft Establishment (RAE) at Farnborough, 1426 (Enemy Aircraft) Flight at Duxford, and the Central Fighter Establishment (CFE) at Tangmere. Additionally, one Bf 109E was briefly on charge with Rolls-Royce—and later de Havilland—for engine and variable-pitch propeller tests. Other captured Bf 109s were briefly flown by various RAF and Commonwealth squadrons in North Africa. In several instances, individual Bf 109s were operated by several of the aforementioned test establishments, the aircraft being transferred according to requirements. Some of these Bf 109s and their use are briefly described below. Additional details can be found in Phil Butler's excellent book *War Prizes*.

The first Bf 109 to arrive relatively intact in Britain was Bf 109E-1 W Nr 3326, which was transferred from France to the A&AEE at Boscombe Down in early October 1939. Further details are lacking, although it seems unlikely that the Bf 109 was restored to airworthiness.

As related above, on 22 November 1939, a JG 76 Bf 109E-3 made an emergency landing at Woerth. The fighter was ferried to Orleans-Bricy, where it was painted in French Air Force insignia and evaluated by CEMA. A team from the RAE was allowed to inspect the Bf 109 in January 1940. On 2 May 1940, it was handed over to the RAF at Amiens, being flown to Tangmere by Fg Off. Hilly Brown of 1 Squadron the following day. It was then ferried to Boscombe Down for assessment by the A&AEE. On 14 May, the Bf 109 was flown to RAE Farnborough, where it was subsequently assigned the RAF serial AE479. Between May 1940 and July 1941, the Bf 109 accumulated a flight time of 47 hours and 50 minutes from seventy-eight flights while on charge with the RAE. The majority of the flights took place in May and June 1940 and involved handling, radio, and engine tests. The opportunity to evaluate a Bf 109E on the eve of the Battle of Britain was fortuitous, to say the least. Apparently, the Bf 109 was initially regarded as being on loan from the French government. Apart from the RAE, this particular Bf 109 was also tested by the Air Fighting Development Unit (AFDU).

Bf 109E RAF serial AE479 seen while undergoing flight trials in the UK. (*Wolfgang Mühlbauer/DEHLA Archives*)

A very comprehensive and detailed report regarding handling and manoeuvrability was written in September 1940, within which the directional stability of the Bf 109 was criticised:

> It is at high speeds that lack of a rudder trimmer most seriously inconveniences the pilot. At 215 mph the aircraft is trimmed directionally, no rudder being required. At higher speeds left rudder must be applied, and at 300 mph about 2 degrees of left rudder are needed. The rudder is very heavy at high speeds, and a large force is necessary to apply even such a small amount; this becomes very tiring, and affects the pilot's ability to assist a turn to the left. Consequently, at high speeds the Me 109 turns more readily to the right than to the left.

The advantages of the Bf 109 over the Merlin-powered Hurricane and Spitfire was the former's ability to climb steeply after pulling out of a dive, with the direct fuel-injection DB 601 engine continuing to function when negative *g* was applied, whereas the Merlin engine began to splutter due to the carburettor ceasing to deliver fuel. Hence, the Bf 109 pilot found that a useful manoeuvre when being chased was to push the stick forward suddenly and perform a semi-bunt—if the fighters followed then their engines cut, granting the Bf 109 a chance to escape.

It was also discovered that both the Hurricane and the Spitfire had a better turning radius than the German fighter: 'In a surprisingly large number of cases, however, the Me 109 succeeded in keeping on the tail of the Spitfire or Hurricane during these turning tests, merely because our pilots would not tighten up the turn sufficiently from fear of stalling and spinning.' In the report, the test pilot stated:

> From all this dog-fighting I am certain that if the pilot of a Hurricane or Spitfire finds himself attacked by a Me. 109 he can easily out-turn it, and can lose it straight away by doing any violent manoeuvre; the Me. 109 just cannot be made to do a really quick manoeuvre because at high speeds the controls are much too heavy, and at low speeds the slats come out, causing the ailerons to snatch, followed by the aircraft stalling if the manoeuvre is done more rapidly.

A Bf 109D-1 captured in France was flown from Coloummiers to Tangmere on 22 December by Wg Cdr J. F. X. McKenna. However, no further information can be found on this aircraft.

Hypothetically, as the Bf 109D was being replaced in Luftwaffe service with the improved Bf 109E, it may have been considered as being of less importance for evaluation, what with an airworthy Bf 109E already available.

A second Bf 109 fell into British hands on 27 November 1940. This particular Bf 109E-3 belonged to I./JG 51, with its pilot force-landing at Manston following a brush with the RAF. It was returned to flying condition using parts scrounged from other shot-down Bf 109s, which was eventually assigned the serial number DG200 and used by Rolls-Royce and de Havilland for engine performance and propeller variable-pitch trials. It is currently preserved by the RAF Museum.

On 24 July 1941, AE479 was transferred to the ADFU at Duxford. The Bf 109 had already been loaned to the ADFU for use in developing proper fighter tactics in September 1940. It was subsequently transferred to 1426 (Enemy Aircraft) Flight before ultimately being shipped to the USA in April 1942.

With the improved Bf 109F entering Luftwaffe service, one early-production Bf 109F-2 of I./JG 26 made an unscheduled arrival on British soil on 10 July 1941. During one sortie, Major Rolf Pingel (a *Legion Condor* veteran) was shot down by RAF Spitfires, belly landing his damaged fighter near St Margaret's Bay. Pingel later stated:

> I followed one of the *dicken Brummer* ['fat insects'—Short Stirlings] as it made its way back to England, and hoped to be able to carry out an attack. But then I was hit. Whether by one of its gunners or by an English fighter, I don't know. Perhaps both. My engine started to run unevenly, and oil and coolant temperatures began to climb. I tried to escape close to the ground, as I had done many times before. There were many English machines in the air around Dover. While still at low-level my engine came to an almost complete stop. Unable to bail out, I had no other choice but to belly-land.

Major Rolf Pingel's Bf 109F-2 seen soon after arriving on British shores. (*NMUSAF*)

Apart from a bent propeller, the Bf 109 was basically intact, quickly being restored to flying condition. The RAF serial number ES906 was assigned and the Bf 109F-2 flown at RAE Farnborough on 19 September. Comparative trials followed, but just over a month later, on 20 October, the Bf 109 was lost in a fatal crash when its Polish pilot was overcome by carbon monoxide poisoning.

In the wake of the Battle of El Alamein, a III./JG 77 Bf 109G-2/trop was captured in Libya. Initially tested by Sqn Ldr Bobby Gibbes of 3 (RAAF) Squadron, the Bf 109 was assigned the squadron code CV-V. It was then thoroughly evaluated by Wg Cdr Mungo Buxton, with detailed performance curves for the Luftwaffe fighter established. The RAF serial number RN228 was assigned on 1 November 1943, with the aircraft arriving at RAE Farnborough the following month. Subsequently acquired by 1426 (Enemy Aircraft) Flight in February 1944, the Bf 109 was selected for preservation. Under the leadership of Russ Snadden, the Bf 109 was restored to flying condition over a period of nearly thirty years, taking to the air once again on 17 March 1991. Unfortunately, it was damaged in a landing accident at Duxford soon afterwards. Today, the Bf 109 can be seen at the RAF Museum.

Formed at Duxford on 21 November 1941, the 1426 (Enemy Aircraft) Flight operated different Luftwaffe aircraft, touring RAF and USAAF airfields to provide pilots and aircrew with a closer look at the enemy. Six Bf 109s were operated by 1426 (Enemy Aircraft) Flight—serials AE479, DG200, NN644,

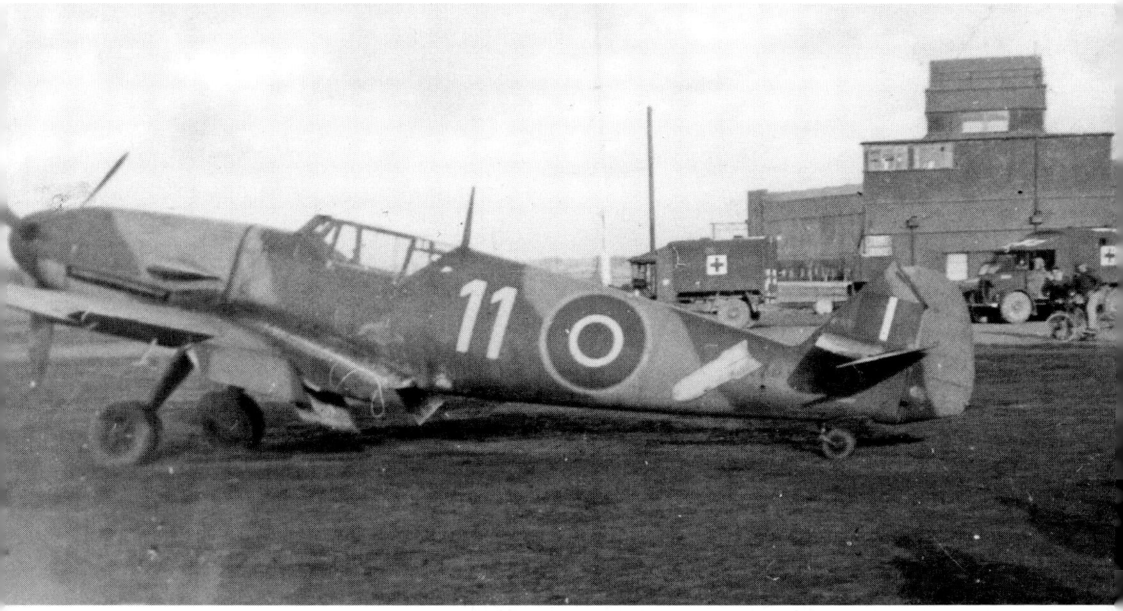

On 20 May 1942, Uffz Oswald Fischer of 10./JG 26 was hit by flak while attacking Brighton harbour. Fischer had no choice but to belly land his stricken Bf 109F-4. Apparently, Fischer attempted to destroy the aircraft, but failed, providing the RAF with a near-intact Bf 109F-4. Remarkably, the 10./JG 26 'falling bomb' insignia was retained after the Messerschmitt had been repainted in RAF colours as serial NN644. (*NMUSAF*)

Little is known about the pre-RAF history of this particular Bf 109G-6/trop. Assigned the serial VX 101, it lasted little more than one month with 1426. (Enemy Aircraft) Flight before being written off in a landing accident at RAF Thorney Island on 19 May 1944. (*NMUSAF*)

RN228, VD364, and VX101. The last of these was a Bf 109G-6/trop captured in North Africa or Italy. The aircraft arrived in the UK on 4 February 1944. As the fighter was damaged, it was initially seen as a source for spares. Nevertheless, the Bf 109 was put back into flying condition, taking to the air on 10 April 1944. Five weeks later, on 19 May, it was damaged beyond repair in a landing accident at Thorney Island. On 21 January 1945, 1426 (Enemy Aircraft) Flight was disbanded, with personnel and aircraft transferred to the newly formed Central Fighter Establishment at Tangmere.

On 21 July 1944, a Bf 109G-6/U2 (W Nr 412951) landed at Manston due to faulty navigation. Assigned the RAF serial number TP814, the Bf 109 was tested by the RAE and later the ADFU in comparative trials with the Spitfire IX, Spitfire XIV, and the Mustang III. It was found that the Bf 109 had a considerably higher diving speed than the Spitfire IX, although was inferior in most other respects. The Rolls-Royce Griffon-powered Spitfire XIV had superior speed, as did the Mustang III, with the latter also able to outturn the Messerschmitt fighter with ease. The famous test pilot Eric 'Winkle' Brown flew this Bf 109G-6/U2.

> I was particularly interested in the operation of the slats, the action of which gave rise to aileron snatching in any high-*g* manoeuvres such as loops or tight turns, so I did a series of stalls to check their functioning more accurately. The stall with the aircraft clean, with half fuel load and the engine throttled right back occurred at 105 mph (158 km/h). This was preceded by elevator buffet and opening of the slats about 20 mph (30 km/h) above the stall, these being accompanied by the unpleasant aileron snatching as the slats opened unevenly. The stall itself was fairly gentle with the nose dropping and the port wing simultaneously dropping about 10 degrees. In the landing configuration the stall occurred at 99 mph (160 km/h) with identical symptoms apart from heavier elevator buffeting.
>
> A number of dummy attacks on a co-operative Lancaster and a friendly skirmish with a Mustang flown by one of the RAE pilots revealed the fact that the slipstream of these aircraft caused the intermittent operation of the Bf 109G's slats so that accurate sighting became an impossibility. After an hour's flying I still had 26 Imp gal (120 litres) remaining of the 88 Imp (400 litres) with which I had taken-off, and as I came in to land at Farnborough I found that the approach was steeper than that of the Spitfire but the elevator feel was very positive and gave delightfully accurate control at 118 mph (190 kph). A substantial change of altitude was called for on the flare or round-out before touchdown, and even after ground contact the lift did not spill rapidly, and ballooning or bouncing could easily be experienced on rough ground. Once the tailwheel was firmly on the ground the brakes could be applied quite harshly, thus giving a short landing run, but care had to be taken to prevent any swing as the combination of narrow-track undercarriage and minimal forward view could easily result in directional problems.[3]

Brown later flew the two-seat Bf 109G-12 solo from the rear cockpit, which provided him with one of his 'rashest ventures'.

> [I was] interested to ascertain what sort of view the instructor had for landing. The answer was none! I had to make three very frightening attempts before regaining terra firma. The periscopic sight in the rear cockpit was of no use whatsoever in the vital final stage of flare, touch-down and landing run. One can only assumed [*sic*] that Luftwaffe instructors finding themselves in a Bf 109G-12 acquired a fatalistic acceptance of an inevitable reliance on their pupils for the finale of each training flight.

A few late-production Bf 109s were shipped to the UK. One of these was Bf 109G-14 W Nr 413601, which had been shot down by flak over northern France on 22 July 1944. Due to it being the first Bf 109G-14 to fall into British hands, it was shipped to Farnborough. The main point of interest was the MW-50 power boost system. Although not restored to flying condition, the Air Ministry serial AM229 was assigned, with the aircraft placed on static display (along with Bf 109G-14/U4 serial VD358) at the German Aircraft Exhibition, held at Farnborough between

29 October and 9 November 1945. It was then transferred to the Science Museum at South Kensington, London, for temporary display before being scrapped.

British Bf 109s						
W Nr	**Variant**	**Lw unit**	**Date captured**	**RAF serial**	**Operated by**	**Remarks**
3326	E-1	2./JG 51	Oct. 1939	N/a	A&AEE	Transferred from France
1304	E-3	1./JG 76	2 May 1940	AE479	A&AEE, AFDU, 1426 (Enemy Aircraft) Flight	Transferred from France. To USA in Apr. 1942
4101	E-3	IV./ JG 26	27 Nov. 1940	DG200	Rolls-Royce Ltd, de Havilland, A&AEE, 1426 /Enemy Aircraft) Flight	Preserved RAFM
12764	F-2	I/JG 26	10 Jul. 1941	ES906	RAE, AFDU	Written off 20 Oct 41 at Fowlmere, Cambs.
N/a	F	N/a	1941 or 1942	HK849	267 Squadron *	Presumed captured during Operation Crusader. RAF serial assigned 1 Apr. 1942. Fate unknown.
7232	F-4	IV./ JG 26	20 May 1942	NN644	RAE, 1426 (Enemy Aircraft) Flight, 47 MU	Presumed scrapped at 47 MU, Sealand
10639	G-2/ trop	III./ JG 77	13 Nov. 1942	RN228	3 (RAAF) Squadron, 1426 (Enemy Aircraft) Flight, EAF/ CFE	Preserved RAFM
N/a	G	N/a	Aug. 1943	N/a	72 Squadron	Written off 15 Aug. 43 near Pachino South, Sicily, when Fg Off. Hughes baled out due to engine glycol leak

N/a	G	N/a	Aug. 1943	N/a	185 Squadron	Coded GL.
	G-1		5 Sep. 1943	N/a	232 Wing	Captured at Gerbini, Sicily
8284	G-2	I./JG 27	5 Sep. 1943	N/a	N/a	Captured at Gerbini, Sicily
1810/4	G-2		Sep. 1943	N/a	1435 Squadron	Ferried to Safi, Malta. To 137 MU, Safi, 21 June 1945
N/a	G-6/ trop	JG 77	1943 or 1944	VX101	1426 (Enemy Aircraft) Flight	Arr UK from Middle East 4 Feb. 1944. Dbr 19 May 1944 at Thorney Island
412951	G-6/U2	I./JG 301	21 July 1944	TP814	RAE, AFDU	Written off 23 Nov. 1944 at Wittering
413601	G-14		22 Jul 1944	N/a	RAE, 6 MU, 23 Group	First G-14 captured. MW-50 engine boost evaluated. Not flown. Exhibited at German Aircraft Exhibition, RAE Farnborough, and later loaned to Science Museum for display Feb–May 1946. Scrapped
N/a	G-14/ U4	N/a	1944 or 1945	VD358	EAF/CFE, RAE, 6 MU	Coded EA-2. Exhibited at German Aircraft Exhibition, RAE Farnborough.
3114/2484 *	G-14/ U4	N/a	1944 or 1945	VD364	EAF/CFE	Dbr 17 May 1945 at Tangmere
N/a	G	N/a	1945		318 (Polish) Squadron	Noted at Treviso, Italy, Mar. 1946. Coded LW.
163824	G-14	N/a	1945	N/a		Shipped to Australia 1946. Preserved
464863	G-14	N/a	1945	N/a		Selected for preservation. Noted at Wittering in Feb. 1950, but most likely scrapped soon afterwards.

* Indicates unknown, or unconfirmed data

South Africa

One Bf 109E shot down over southern England in 1940 and despatched to South Africa for propaganda purposes and was preserved.

One III./JG 53 Bf 109F was captured at Martuba in November 1942 by 7 Squadron, SAAF. Only one flight in SAAF hands is recorded—on 27 November, when the CO 7 Squadron, Major Blaauw, ferried the Bf 109 to Shandur. The fate of this aircraft is unknown.

One Bf 109F-2/trop (W Nr 31010) was found at Marble Arch, Libya, by 7 Squadron SAAF. Subsequently shipped to South Africa, the Bf 109 was assigned with the SAAF serial 777. It was not flown by the SAAF but instead transferred to 62 Air School at Bloemfontein. The Bf 109 has survived and is on display at the National Museum of Military History, Saxonwold.

Another SAAF squadron based at Martuba, No. 4 Squadron, also had a Bf 109. It was subsequently coded KJ-?, with Major du Toit, the CO 4 Squadron, making one flight in the Messerschmitt on 6 January 1943. One tyre burst on landing, resulting in minor damage to the aircraft. In all likelihood, it was not repaired.

Sweden

Although neutral and unaligned, many Luftwaffe aircraft arrived in Sweden due to various causes, including navigational error, combat damage, and defection, with thirteen Bf 109s among them. Although no comparative evaluation between the Bf 109 and *Flygvapnet* (Swedish Air Force) fighters appear to have been made, several Bf 109Fs and Bf 109Gs were nevertheless test-flown. The primary interest concerned the Bf 109s armament and the DB 605 engines, the latter being built under licence in Sweden.

USA

Interestingly, the USAAF appear to have consistently referred to the Messerschmitt fighter as the Me 109 (or Me-109), rather than the Bf 109.

The first Bf 109 to make the journey across the Atlantic was a former II./JG 26 Bf 109E-3 (W Nr 1190). The fighter was not restored to airworthiness but instead used as a travelling exhibit first in Canada and later in the USA, for the purpose of raising funds for Britain. In August and September 1941, the Bf 109 was the subject of a detailed technical investigation. It has, amazingly, survived, and was displayed at Duxford, UK.

Bf 109E-3, W Nr 1190, undergoing detailed examination at Wright Field. The photo is dated 27 September 1941. (*NMUSAF*)

On 14 May 1942, Bf 109E W Nr 1304 arrived at Wright Field along with a second Bf 109 for spares. This Bf 109 had previously seen much use by both the French and the British before being despatched to the USA. It was eventually written off in a forced landing at Cambridge, Ohio, on 3 November 1942. However, it was soon replaced by a more modern Bf 109F.

During a visit to Moscow by the US Secretary of State Wendell Wilkie in November 1942, a Bf 109F-4 (W Nr 7640) was presented by the USSR government as a gift. Subsequently shipped to the USA, the Bf 109 was given the serial number EB-1 (most likely later amended to EB-101), and flown at both Wright Field and Eglin Field. It was used for general handling tests, as well as armament trials. By 21 March 1944, it had been flown for a total of thirteen hours by USAAF pilots.

Another photo of W Nr 1190 at Wright Field. (*NMUSAF*)

The fate of the Bf 109 is unclear, but it was most likely scrapped when it had outlived its usefulness.

On 14 March 1943, a Bf 109G-2/R2 of 2.(H)/14 was shot down by British forces near Zarzis, Tunisia. Subsequently handed over to 87 Fighter Squadron, USAAF, the Bf 109 was restored to airworthiness. Named *Irmgard*, the fighter was eventually shipped across the Atlantic, being tested to destruction at Wright Field during the spring of 1944.

A Bf 109G-6 trop (W Nr 16416) of 4./JG 77 captured at Soliman airfield in Tunisia on 8 May 1943 was shipped to the USA and evaluated by the Army Air Forces Material Command at Wright Field. The Bf 109 was assigned the serial EB-102 subsequently being test-flown by Major Frederic Borsodi, Chief of fighter aircraft testing. A report, dated 1 March 1944, states that upon arriving in the USA

The former Soviet Bf 109F-4 seen following its arrival in the USA. (*NMUSAF*)

This particular Bf 109G-2/trop. (W Nr 10605) was built by Erla and delivered to the Luftwaffe on 30 September 1942. While serving with the reconnaissance unit 2.(H)/14, it was shot down near Zarzis on 20 February 1943, with Lt Weinecke managing to perform a belly landing. Irmgard was the crew chief's girlfriend. (*NMUSAF*)

Above: Bf 109G-2/trop seen following restoration to airworthiness. (*NMUSAF*)

Left: The Bf 109G-2/trop Irmgard being tested to destruction in the USA. (*NMUSAF*)

the aircraft was assembled by North American, which removed the German radio and oxygen system, replacing it with US standard equipment. Additionally, the armour plating behind the pilot seat was removed as well. Having previously flown Curtiss P-40s, Borsodi stated that the cockpit was 'very small and cramped', which was a very common complaint from almost every Allied pilot who flew the Bf 109, with poor all-round visibility: 'This airplane is as blind as any fighter I have seen. Vision in all directions is restricted and no rear-view mirror is provided. In the air the visibility over the nose does not appear sufficient for deflection shooting.' At cruising speed, aileron and rudder control were deemed 'good'. At high speeds, elevator control forces were extremely high, with Borsodi calling this 'one of the most objectionable features of the airplane.' The report concluded:

> The ME-109G has a high rate of climb and good level flight performance. Its range is very limited as only 105 gallons can be carried internally and flights of over 300 miles leave little gasoline for reserve. It is very light on all controls below 400 kph but the turning radius is poor compared to our fighters. At high speed the controls become very heavy. The airplane is stable and should be a good gun platform but the vision is very poor under all conditions.

Regarding advantages and disadvantages over USAAF fighters, Borsodi said:

> The airplane has a higher rate of climb than most of our fighters. The automatic propeller control is good as it automatically gives the proper RPM for a given throttle setting thus relieving the pilot considerably. The gun sight is small, more compact than ours, and far easier to change a bulb.

Bf 109G, serial EB-102, was test flown in the USA. (*NMUSAF*)

> It is not as manoeuvrable, does not have the range, and has inferior visibility to practically all our first line fighters.

This particular Bf 109 suffered a landing accident at Wright Field on 1 September 1944, eventually being salvaged (scrapped) on 24 October 1944. It had been flown for twenty-nine hours in the USA.

During the final weeks of the war, a USAAF team initiated the task of locating and selecting Luftwaffe aircraft and equipment for evaluation. Although the formal name was Project Lusty, the team became known as 'Watson's Whizzers' after its commanding officer, Colonel Harold E. Watson. Although jet and rocket aircraft and technology received priority, three Bf 109s, possibly surrendered at Neubiberg, were selected for shipment to the USA. The aircraft were assigned the serials FE-122 to FE-124, but not restored to airworthiness due to their poor state. After being briefly put on static display at Freeman Field, they were disposed of.

The notoriously weak undercarriage resulted in EB-102 being written off following this accident. (*NMUSAF*)

This image provides a good view of the sand filter air intake. (*NMUSAF*)

Mention must also be made of an ARR Bf 109G-6 (W Nr 166133), which was flown to Foggia, Italy, on 25 August 1944 by sixty-four-victory ace Capt. Constantin Cantacuzino. The radio was removed before take-off, which made it possible for Lt Col. James A. Gunn to ride along as a passenger. Cantacuzino and Gunn were carrying a diplomatic message from the Romanian King, Michael. Exactly one month before, on 25 July, a Bf 109 flown by Lt René Darbois of I./JG 4 had landed at Santa Maria Capua Verde, Italy. Born in Metz, Darbois considered himself to be French. For some time, he had wanted to defect. The opportunity arose during a ferry flight, when Darbois managed to escape by feigning illness. Darbois eventually joined the Free French Air Force, flying Spitfire Mk IXs. He later flew helicopters during the first Indo-China war. His Bf 109 was shipped to the USA, and is now preserved by the NASM.

US airmen examining a captured Bf 109G following the end of the war. (*NMUSAF*)

One of the 'Watson's Whizzer's' Bf 109s that arrived in the USA. The fate of this Bf 109K-4 is unknown. (*NMUSAF*)

US Messerschmitt Bf 109s					
W Nr	**Variant**	**Lw unit**	**Date captured**	**Date arrived in USA**	**Remarks**
1190	E-3	II./JG 26	30 Sep. 1940	1941	From UK as static exhibit.
1304	E-3	JG 76	22 Nov. 1939	14 May 1941	Date shows arrival at Wright Field. Written off Cambridge, OH, 3 Nov. 1942
36313	E	N/a	Autumn 1940	May 1941	Used for spares
7640	F-4	N/a	Autumn 1942	Early 1943	Assigned serial EB-1, later EB-100
14329 or 14629	G-2/R2	2(H)./14	1 Mar. 1943	Oct 1943	Tested to destruction. Final test occurred on 13 May 1944
16416	G-6/ trop	JG 77?	14 July 1943	21 Mar. 1944	Date shows arrival at Wright Field. Assigned serial EB-102. Dbr 1Sep. 1944
160756	G-6	I./JG 4	25 July 1944	1944	Preserved NASM
166133	G-6	ARR	25 Aug. 1944	-	Written off at Foggia, Italy, 26 Aug 1944
N/a	G-10/ U4	N/a	May 1945	1945	Assigned serial FE-122, later T2-122. Preserved Planes of Fame, Chino, CA.
N/a	K-4	N/a	May 1945	1945	Assigned serial FE-123, later T2-123. Possibly loaned to University of Kansas, Lawrence, KS. Presumed scrapped.
610937	G-14	N/a	May 1945	1945	Assigned serial FE-124, later T2-124. Preserved.

USSR

The first Bf 109 to be tested by Soviet pilots was a Bf 109B-1 that had been captured in Spain. The German *Legion Condor* pilot had landed behind the front line in December 1937, serial 6.15. Before transfer to the USSR, the Bf 109 was test-flown by French pilots, as related above. Arriving at Odessa in early 1938, the fighter was soon despatched to the NII VVS for a thorough evaluation. When flown by the test pilot Stepan Suprun, one of the stabiliser struts failed. Suprun nevertheless managed to land safely, subsequently being strongly reprimanded by his commanding officer, Pyotr Stefanovskiy for not baling out of the damaged Messerschmitt. Suprun replied that he had discovered a weakness in the German fighter stating: 'the fascists were known to avoid dog-fights with the sharp-turning (Polikarpov) I-15s and I-16s in Spain.'[4]

In spite of this incident, the subsequent report of the evaluation, dated 14 April 1938, gave a clear indication that the performance characteristics, as well as construction techniques, were of great interest to Soviet aircraft designers.

The Molotov-Ribbentrop non-aggression pact between Germany and the USSR, signed on 23 August 1939, changed the European political and military balance at one stroke. A Russian delegation, including Stepan Suprun, arrived at Augsburg in October 1939. According to an 11 February 1940 agreement, it became possible to obtain state-of-the-art German aircraft. Among these were five Bf 109E-1s (including W Nr 2738), which arrived in May 1940. The Bf 109E-1s were thoroughly evaluated at the NII VVS and the LII. One of the fighters was subsequently dismantled for a detailed technical study. It was found that the Bf 109E-1 was superior in almost all respects to the main Soviet fighter, the Polikarpov I-16, particularly with regards to speed, rate of climb, and armament. Comparative trials were also made between the Bf 109E and the LaGG-3, MiG-1, and Yak-1. Following the beginning of Operation Barbarossa, the NII VVS was evacuated to Sverdlovsk. During the evacuation, one of the Bf 109E-1s crashed on 11 October 1941, killing the test pilot T. Chigarev.

Many Luftwaffe Bf 109s were captured and evaluated and evaluated during the war. The first of the Bf 109Fs to reach the NII VVS was a former JG 51 aircraft. Its pilot, Hptm Rolf Pingel, had to make a forced landing near Moscow in late 1941. A few months later, on 22 February 1942, Oblt A. Niss of 8./JG 51 made an emergency landing at Tushino. His Bf 109F-2 (W Nr 9209) was the subject of a thorough evaluation. Following repairs to the radiator and fuel tanks, the Bf 109 took to the air, only to be damaged on landing, with the right undercarriage and wing tip having to be replaced before it was handed over to the NII VVS.

Particular interest was paid to the armament of the Bf 109F and its centrally-mounted MG 151 cannon. The low-level characteristics of the Bf 109F—up to an altitude of 4,000 metres—proved superior to contemporary Soviet fighters. Engine accessibility also received praise from the Soviet evaluation team. Incidentally, in November 1942, a Bf 109F-4 (W Nr 7640) was presented to the USA.

During the advance against Stalingrad in late 1942, a Bf 109G-2/R6 of I./JG 3 (W Nr 13903) flown by Uffz Heinrich Blaut, was captured on 8 December near Proleika. Following quick repairs, the Bf 109G-2 was ferried to the NII VVS. Compared with the earlier Bf 109F, the Bf 109G-2 featured the more powerful

DB 605A engine, as well as being more heavily armed. The pilot armour protection was also significantly improved, and it was found that:

> The power plant on the German aircraft was more convenient to control, but the view from the cockpit, especially to the rear, turned out to be much worse than that of, let's say, the Yak-9. Engineer-Lieutenant Colonel A.N. Frolov, Chief of the Fighter Department, noted how painstakingly German designers and engineers sealed the construction elements. Slots on control surfaces were reduced to a minimum, motor cowlings fitted tightly against the fuselage, ant [*sic*]: the fuselage had rubber gaskets.
>
> Only the experimental I-185 fighter could compete with the Bf 109G-2 in rate of climb and only the MiG-3 could reach a service ceiling of 11,250 metres (the best series-produced examples could climb to 11,500 m). The Messerschmitt salvo weight was 4.67 kilograms per second.
>
> ... Underwing cannon considerabh [*sic*] reduced the horizontal manoeuvrability of the aircraft, which we called the 'five-pointer'.

When pitted against the Lavochkin La-5 in mock combat, it was determined that the Bf 109 had a somewhat higher diving speed. The Russian test pilot also noted that the control column was 'overbalanced', which increased the risk of entering a spin during sharp banking turns.

Additional Bf 109G-2s tested included a former II./JG 3 aircraft, captured on 19 March 1943. This Bf 109 (W Nr 14513) lacked the underwing cannon pods (thus being designated the 'three-pointer'), being nearly 20 kph faster.

On 10 September 1943, it was reported that fifty-four Bf 109s were on charge, eight of which were in flying condition. As the war progressed, Bf 109G-4 (including W Nr 14997 & 19968) and G-6s were captured and tested. The Soviet test pilots generally held a good opinion of the Messerschmitt fighters, calling it a 'soldier's aircraft', with the most common criticism directed against the poor visibility from the cockpit.

One of the Bf 109Fs captured and tested by the USSR. (*Carl-Fredrik Geust*)

Endnotes

Chapter 1

1. DLH took delivery of thirteen M 20bs, some of which were transferred to the Luftwaffe.
2. Nearly 1,000 Bf 108s were built until 1944, with production continuing in France until the late 1940s. Several Bf 108s and French-built Nord 1002s are still flying. A few Bf 108s were imported into Britain before the war—these were eventually requisitioned by the RAF. The Bf 108 named *Aldon* was in RAF service.
3. With the reorganization of BFW into Messerschmitt AG on 11 July 1938, the aircraft design prefix was changed from Bf to Me. The first aircraft to carry the Me design prefix was the Me 210 twin-engine heavy fighter, which was an utter disaster both for Messerschmitt and the Luftwaffe. Some claimed that the Me 210 was, in fact, more dangerous to its crews than to the enemy.
4. The Kestrel V engine was used to power the Hawker Hind light bomber then entering large-scale RAF service. The He 70 delivered to Rolls-Royce was ferried from Rostock to Hucknall on 27 March 1935. Registered as G-ADZF, the He 70 was used to test the Kestrel XVI and Peregrine engines. It accumulated 418 flying hours before being scrapped in 1944 or 1945.
5. Kosin, R. *The German Fighter since 1915* London, UK Putnam, 1988, p. 100.
6. The weak and narrow-track undercarriage was to plague the Bf 109 throughout its operational service. Murawski, M. J., and Atanasov, A., *Messerschmitt Bf 109 Early Versions*, Kagero 2015, p. 14.
7. Kosin, *op. cit.*, p. 105.
8. Murawski, M. J., and Atanasov, A., *Messerschmitt Bf 109 Early Versions*, Kagero, 2015, p. 18.
9. Gardner's average speed was 220 mph. Apparently, Francke subsequently handed over the trophy to Gardner in gratitude for having been allowed to participate in the race. *Flight International*, 29 July 1937 issue, p. 110.
10. van Ishoven, A., *Messerschmitt Bf 109 at War* (The Promotional Reprint, 1993), p. 198.
11. van Ishoven, *op. cit.*, p. 201.

12. Powered by a 240-hp Argus As 10C engine, the Fw 56 would become one of the Luftwaffe's standard advanced trainers with about 1,000 being built. A few were exported to Austria, Bolivia, Brazil, and Hungary.

Chapter 2

1. Jackson, R., *Messerschmitt Bf 109 A–D Series,* London, UK, Osprey Publishing, 2015, pp. 28, 30.

Chapter 3

1. 'Emil Über England', in *Air International,* October 1980, p. 199.
2. van Ishoven, *op. cit.*, p. 187.
3. Murawski and Atanasov, *op. cit.*, p. 63.
4. The rear gunner of the 38 Squadron Wellington, LAC John Copley, was awarded with the DFM. Specht survived and, despite losing one eye, re-joined his unit. He was eventually killed on 1 January 1945 during Operation Bodenplatte.
5. The Danish Army Air Force consisted of fewer than a dozen serviceable Fokker D.XXIs and some obsolete Gloster Gauntlets, while the Norwegian Army Air Force had a mere seven Gloster Gladiators. Apparently, German intelligence reported that a number of Hawker Fury biplanes were in Norwegian service. Only one Fury had actually been delivered—and struck off charge years before.
6. Ramsey, W. G., *The Battle of Britain: Then and Now* (London, UK, ATB Books, 1986), p. 292.
7. Cornwell, P. D., *The Battle of France: Then and Now* (London, UK, ATB Books, 1993), p. 428.
8. During the war, about 1,730 *Ritterkreutz* decorations were awarded to Luftwaffe aircrew. For higher achievements, a rising scale of embellishments were added to the basic *Ritterkreutz* decoration: with Oak Leaves (192 recipients); with Swords (41 recipients); with Oak Leaves, Swords, and Diamonds (12 recipients); with Golden Oak Leaves (only awarded to the Ju 87 *Stuka* pilot Hans-Ulrich Rudel); and the large *Ritterkreutz* (only awarded to *Reichsmarschall* Göring).
9. Über, 'England', in *Air International,* October 1980, p. 200. Oblt Neumann's Bf 109E came down outside Shanklin, the Isle of Wight.
10. Caldwell, D., *The JG 26 War Diary Volume One 1939–1942*, p. 61.
11. Ramsey, W. G., *op. cit.*, p. 602.
12. Murawski, M. J., *Messerschmitt Bf 109F: The Ace Maker* (Kagero, 2014), p. 30.
13. Shores, C., *Air War for Yugoslavia, Greece and Crete 1940–1941* (London, UK, Grub Street, 1998), p. 268.
14. *Ibid.*, p. 275.
15. Murawski, *Messerschmitt Bf 109F: The Ace Maker*, p. 77.
16. van Ishoven, *op. cit.*, p. 222.

17. Murawski, *Messerschmitt Bf 109F: The Ace Maker*, p. 58. Maj. Oesau had shot down Lancaster L7536 of 44 Squadron, one of seven Lancasters lost during this raid. Walther Oesau would eventually command JG 1, being shot down and killed on 11 May 1944. JG 1 subsequently became known as JG 1 Oesau.
18. Ethell, J. L., Price, A., *Target Berlin Mission 250: 6 March 1944*, p. 15.
19. This was most likely the last biplane fighter to be lost on operations during the Second World War.
20. Bernád, D., *Rumanian Air Force: The Prime Decade, 1938–1947* (Carrollton, USA, Squadron Signal, 1998), p. 40. The pair of ARR Bf 109's were flown by Traian Dârjan and Captain Cantacuzino, both of which had learned to handle the Messerschmitt fighter at Tiraspol under German aegis. Dârjan was shot by Lipfert, with Cantacuzino downed by another Luftwaffe pilot.
21. Andrei Vlassov was a former General-Lieutenant in the Red Army, and a Hero of the Soviet Union following his defensive actions during the siege of Leningrad. After being captured, Vlassov eventually joined forces with the Nazis in their war against Stalin's Communist regime. Following the end of the war, Vlassov was handed over to the USSR, tried, and hanged for high treason.
22. Other sources state that the ROA aviation component was not formed until 19 December 1944 at the orders of *Reichsmarschall* Hermann Göring. Interestingly, the reconnaissance squadron of the ROA included one Messerschmitt Me 262.
23. Forsyth, R., *Luftwaffe Mistel Composite Bomber Units* (Osprey, 2015), p. 17. In this context, mention must be made of the American use of war-weary B-17 Flying Fortresses and B-24 Liberators modified as flying bombs and used against German submarine bases and V-1 launching ramps. Such operations involved remote radio control from an escorting B-17 or B-24 during the final phase of the flight. However, the US bombers did not carry a piggy-back fighter.
24. See Alsdorf, D., *Auf den Spuren des 'Elbe-Kommandos' Rammjäger.* (Podzun-Pallas-Verlag, 2001); Price, A., *The Last Year of the Luftwaffe: May 1944 to May 1945*, p. 146.
25. Urbanke, A., 'The Luftwaffe's Last Throw of the Dice', *Aeroplane Monthly*, July 2008, p. 84.

Chapter 4

1. When Germany seized control of Vichy France on 11 November 1942, the spoils included 1,876 aircraft, including 242 Dewoitine D.520 fighters. This total included both operational D.520s as well as those being built by SNCASE at Toulouse, where the assembly line was surrendered intact. Apart from those supplied to Bulgaria, many D.520s served with the Luftwaffe and the *Regia Aeronautica.*
2. Savic, D., Ciglic, B., *Croatian Aces of World War 2*, p. 25.
3. Beale, N., D'Amico, F., Valentini, G., *Air War Italy 1944–45: The Axis Air Forces in Italy June 1994-May 1945* (London, Airlife Publishing), p. 131.

4. Beale, D'Amico, Valentini, *op. cit.*, p. 201.
5. The Bf 110G-4, W Nr 5547 of 6./NJG 6, was flown by Ofw Treynogga, who was subsequently repatriated. He was eventually killed on 5 June 1944 over Gracciano, Italy.
6. Geust, C.-F., Under the Red Star: Luftwaffe Aircraft in the Soviet Airforce (London, UK, Airlife), p. 87.
7. *Ibid.*, p. 97.
8. Jerin, Z., 'Emil Versus the Luftwaffe' in (publication date), p. 209.
9. British forces lost 223 killed and 478 wounded in Palestine between 1945 and 14 May 1948, with thousands of Arabs and Jews killed in the escalating fighting.
10. Aloni, S., *Year of the 'Mule': Avia S-199 Mezecs in Israeli service* (Air International, Issue 57), p. 7.
11. Former RAF airfields were scrounged for aircraft spares. At the time of Israeli independence, a few Spitfires were being rebuilt to airworthiness. Interestingly, shot down REAF Spitfires also contributed parts to these aircraft.

Appendix III

1. This particular Bf 109E was thoroughly evaluated by the French, British, and Americans, accumulating more flight hours at the hands of Allied pilots than those of the Luftwaffe.
2. Only one Armée de l'Air unit, GC I/3, had begun to receive Dewoitine D.520s by January 1940, with the first combat-capable D.520 only arriving on 17 April. Rather curiously, the comparative evaluation apparently did not include the M.S. 406—the most numerous French fighter—or the US-built Curtiss H-75 Hawk, large numbers of which had been ordered by the *Armée de l'Air*.
3. Brown, E., 'Best of the Breed—Messerschmitt's *Gustav*', in *Air Enthusiast June 1973* (Vol. 4 No. 6), p. 300.
4. Geust, *op. cit.*, p. 81.

Bibliography

Aloni, S., 'Year of the 'Mule' Avia S-199 Mezecs in Israeli Service'' *Air Enthusiast Issue* 57, p. 6–15.

Alsdorf, D., *Auf den Spuren des 'Elbe-Kommandos' Rammjäger*. Podzun-Pallas-Verlag GmbH, Berstadt, Germany 2001.

Avila Cruz, G., ''Bipalas', 'Tripalas' 'Knapsacks' Messerschmitt Bf 109s in Spanish Service.' *Air Enthusiast* 87, p. 62-71.

Axworthy, M., 'On Three Fronts Romania's Aircraft Industry During World War Two.' *Air Enthusiast Issue* 56, Winter 1994.

Bernád, D., *Romanian Air Force The Prime Decade, 1938-1947*, Squadron/Signal Publications, Inc., Carrollton, USA, 1999.

Bishop, E., *Their finest hour the story of the Battle of Britain 1940*, Ballantine Books Inc, New York, USA, 1968.

Blackah, P. & Lowe, M.V., *Messerschmitt Bf 109 Owner's Workshop Manual*, Haynes Publishing, Sparkford, Yeovil, UK, 2016.

Caldwell, D., *The JG 26 War Diary 1939-1945*, Grub Street, London, UK, 2007. Two vols.

Cornwell, P., *The Battle of France Then and Now*, 2007

de Zeng IV, H. L. & Stankey, D. G., *Dive-Bomber and Ground-Attack Units of the Luftwaffe 1933-1945*, Ian Allan Publishing, Hersham, UK, 2009.

Forsyth, R. *Luftwaffe Mistel Composite Bomber Units,* Osprey Publishing, 2015.

Geust, C.-F., *Under the Red Star Airlife*, London, UK, 1993.

Goyat, J.-M. 'Making the Messerschmitt', *Aeroplane Monthly*, July and August 1999.

Green, W. & Swanborough, G., 'Messerschmitt over Spain', *Air Enthusiast* 7, p. 182-194.

Green, W. & Swanborough, G., 'Balkan Interlude', *Air Enthusiast* 39, p. 58-74.

Green, W. & Swanborough, G., *The Great Book of Fighters*. MBI Publishing Company, Osceola, WI, USA, 2001.

Gunston, B., *World Encyclopedia of Aircraft Manufacturers*, Patrick Stephens Limited, Sparkford, UK, 1993.

Hitchcock, T. H., *Bf 109F Monogram Close-up* 9. Monogram Aviation Publications, Sturbridge, USA 1990

Irra, M., *'Mezek' Avia S/CS-199 Vol. 1*, Jakab Publishing, s.r.o, Nevojice 2010.

Jerin, Z. '*Emil* versus the Luftwaffe', *Air Enthusiast* September 1971, p. 209-211.

Mafé Huertas, S., 'Iberian 'Gustav' The Long-Serving Spanish Messerschmitts', *Air Enthusiast* 62, p. 49–55.

Kay, A. L., & Smith, J. R., *German Aircraft of the Second World War*, Putnam Aeronautical Books, London, 2002.

Kosin, R., *The German Fighter since 1915*, Conway Maritime Press, London, 1988.

Middlebrook, M., & Everitt, C., *The Bomber Command War Diaries An Operational Reference Book, 1939-1945,* Viking Penguin Books Ltd, Harmondsworth, UK, 1985.

Mladenov, A., 'A Decade of Air Power: Bulgaria 1940–1949', *Wings of Fame Vol.* 13, p. 92–111.

Mombeek, E., *Reichsverteidigung Die Geschichte des Jägdgeschwaders 1 'Oesau'*. Brussels, Belgium, 1993.

Murawski, M. J., *Messerschmitt Bf 109F The Ace Maker*, Kagero Publishing, Poland, 2012.

Murawski, M. J. & Wróbel, A., *JG 52 Aces on the Eastern Front*. Kagero Publishing, Poland, 2012.

Murawski, M. J. & Atanasov, A., *Messerschmitt Bf 109 Early Versions*, Kagero Publishing, Poland, 2015.

Nicolle, D. & Nordeen, L., *Phoenix over the Nile. A History of Egyptian Air Power 1932-1994*, Smithsonian Institution, USA, 1993.

Norton, B., *Air War on the Edge*, Midland Publishing, Hinckley, England, 2004.

Olrog, M. & Wünderlich, M., '*Messerschmitts für den Tenno*', *Flugzeug Classic*, May 2012, p. 54–59.

Payne, M., *Messerschmitt Bf 109 Into the Battle*, Air Research Publications/Kristall Productions Ltd, Surbiton, UK, 1987.

Price, A., *The Last Year of the Luftwaffe May 1944 to May 1945*, Greenhill Books London, 2001.

Prien, J., Stemmer, G., Rodeike, P., & Bock, W., *Die Jägdfliegerverbände der Deutschen Luftwaffe 1934 bis 1945. Teil I Vorkriegszeit und Einsatz über Polen – 1934 bis 1939* Struwe's buchdruckerei und Verlag, 2002.

Punka, G. *Hungarian Air Force* (Squadron/Signal Publications, Inc., Carrollton, USA, 1994.

Rajlich, J. & Senhal, J., "Tatra Eagles' The Slovak Air Force in Combat, 1942–1945', *Air Enthusiast Issue* 56, Winter 1994.

Ramsey, W. G., *The Battle of Britain: Then and Now, Third Edition,* Great Britain, 1987.

Sárhidai, G., Punka, G., & Kozlik, V., *Hungarian Eagles*, Hikoki Publications, Great Britain, 1996.

Savic, D. & Ciglic, B., *Croatian Aces of World War 2*. Osprey Publishing, Oxford, UK.

Schmoll, P., *Nest of Eagles: Messerschmitt Production and Flight-Testing at Regensburg 1936-1945,* Ian Allan Publishing, Hersham, UK.

Shores, C., Foreman, J., Ehrengardt, C.-J., Weiss, H., & Olsen, B., *Fledgling Eagles*. Grub Street, London UK 1998.

Stapfer, H.-H., '*Emil geht fremd*', *Flugzeug Classic*, August 2015, pp. 32–35.

Stenman, K., 'Finland's Front Line The Bf 109 in Finnish service', *Air Enthusiast*, Issue 50, May–July 1993.

Urbanke, A., 'The Luftwaffe's Last Throw of the Dice', *Aeroplane Monthly*, July 2005 p. 82–85.
Urech, J., *The Aircraft of the Swiss Air Force since 1914*. Verlag Th. Gut, Stäfa ZH, 1975.
van Ishoven, A., *Messerschmitt Bf 109 at War*, Ian Allan Ltd, Great Britain, 1974.
Weal, J. '*Jägdgeschwader Richthofen*: Phoenix Twice Risen', *Wings of Fame*, Vol. 1. Aerospace Publishing Ltd, London, UK, 1995.

Internet

http://www.flensted.eu.com
http://www.ww2.dk
http://www.kurfurst.org
http://www.rafmuseum.org

Index